£10

SCOTTISH THEMES

Frontispiece

SCOTTISH THEMES

Essays in honour of
Professor S. G. E. LYTHE

edited by
JOHN BUTT & J. T. WARD

SCOTTISH ACADEMIC PRESS
1976

Published by
Scottish Academic Press Ltd,
33 Montgomery Street
Edinburgh EH7 5JX

SBN 7073 0125 4

Printed in Great Britain by
R. & R. Clark Ltd, Edinburgh

Contents

Foreword

The history of the University of Strathclyde is a subject which fascinates me a great deal, and it was my first real awareness of the special history of this institution in Glasgow, which came to me in 1937 when I began to meet graduates, that ultimately led to my acceptance of appointment as Principal in 1959. From 1960 to 1975 I have seen very great changes in the nature of this institution which started life in 1796. As many will know, the inspiration which led to the foundation of a new kind of centre of learning in Glasgow in 1796 was based on the ideals of Professor John Anderson, FRS. For many long years after his death some of his most far-sighted ideas were vigorously pursued in Anderson's Institution but they were not ideas which found ready or general acceptance in the higher educational scene in the United Kingdom. Historians looking back on Anderson and his work realise that he was right in many of his arguments and that his opponents were often totally wrong in refusing to recognise this fact. Today we take for granted many of the wise concepts that engaged his thinking two hundred years ago and were expounded in his notable last will and testament.

We realise, for example, that technology is an extremely important integral part of university activity: that the universities must be in the forefront of teaching and research in all of the applied sciences. The passion with which Anderson advocated this met with little response in universities in his own day, but the College founded in his name made great progress. Sometimes it was reduced in scope and scale by actions from outside but it always maintained adequate vitality and energy to pursue its primary goals. In some ways the work of Anderson influenced the birth of the Scottish College of Commerce in 1845, which amalgamated in 1964 with the Royal College of Science and Technology – an amalgamation which took place very shortly before the new University became a fully accredited member of the British university scene.

As has already been implied both Colleges were successful in all their university-level work for very many years before complete recognition came their way. Indeed in the early 1960s one in eight of the technologists graduating from the UK universities and colleges under University Grants Committee surveillance came from the Royal College of Science and Technology. Partly for this reason the College had a world-wide reputation, a reputation which in many ways was more keenly appreciated overseas than at home. The staff of many new universities throughout the world have, in substantial measure, been drawn from among the graduates of the University of Strathclyde and especially from those of the Royal College.

It was in 1961 that Sir Keith Murray (now Lord Murray) as Chairman of the University Grants Committee was able to tell me that his Committee and the Government had decided that the Royal College should become a new university. He indicated there was a number of substantial administrative obstacles in the way and it would take some little time to overcome these in a suitable fashion. By March 1962 he informed me that it would be appropriate for us to proceed with the creation of some new Schools of Study. It had been agreed at an earlier date that the most appropriate new School would be one that would involve the College in social sciences. Five new departments were considered and agreed to be the most appropriate. The records of these five, including Economic History, have fully vindicated the early decision to proceed with work in this new field.

By 1962 interviews for appointment to the foundation Chairs in the new disciplines were being held. One of these first foundation Chairs was offered to Edgar Lythe. The references supplied to the appointing committee revealed the fact that the University of Strathclyde (the name adopted for the University from the date of the granting of the Charter in April 1964) would be very fortunate indeed if Edgar Lythe accepted the Chair; it could be guaranteed that, as a scholar of high repute, he would provide a desirable complementary side to an institution concerned primarily with technological studies and that his outstanding creative talent would be admirably suited to the task of shaping the future of the University in social sciences and particularly in founding a strong department of Economic History. At this time it is clear that Edgar Lythe did indeed find this challenging assignment to be one to which he could bring his deep knowledge and one which provided him, in many ways, with the opportunity that he desired and clearly deserved. The department has built up its reputation through the dedication and inspiration of its teachers and through the publication of many works in learned journals. Books published by the members of staff have been extremely well received, and examination of these books shows that they will fill a special place both in the literature of economic history and of history in general. In the strength of the department we find the best possible tribute to the leadership which it has enjoyed under Edgar Lythe. Perhaps mention should be made here of the volume entitled *An Economic History of Scotland 1100–1939* which has rapidly come to be regarded by many as the authoritative introductory work in its sphere and a truly distinguished study of the social and industrial history of Scotland. At a time of wide discussion of devolution such a major work fills a real gap in the literature pertaining to Scotland. As co-author Edgar Lythe has produced a volume which will meet many needs for a very long time.

As Principal of the University I have naturally been well aware of the success of the department and its attraction to students but it is as a person and not a department Head that I deeply appreciate all that Edgar Lythe has done in his years of service to the University. In very many special tasks he brought the maturity of his judgement to bear and often without any recognition whatsoever of his efforts. More obviously for the last four years (1972 to 1976) he has been Vice-Principal of the University, the third to occupy this office. The duties of the Vice-Principal appear on paper relatively light and in fact the total range of duties required according to the paper definition of the office is not onerous. In actual fact the official remit in no way resembles the functions carried by such a man as Edgar Lythe, a man always prepared to contribute more in practice. To a Vice-Principal such as he has proved to be has fallen the heavy task of solving a large number of the inevitable human problems that arise; in some areas this is evident as for example in the control of disciplinary affairs or as Convenor of the Senate/Student Committee. Yet such service represents only the tip of the iceberg because so much of the real work has to be effectively and quietly pursued. In none of these tasks did the wisdom of Edgar Lythe as Vice-Principal prove inadequate, and his insight proved invaluable in solving many problems. His work contributed greatly to the maintenance of good relationships at all levels, from those of the new young entrant to those of members of Senate and Court.

Often the public overlook the fact that a university such as Strathclyde is a large society of able talented people. In the case of Strathclyde the total of students and employees exceeds 10,000. The ramifications of personal and working relationships in such an institution are many and varied, and anyone seriously engaged in the wise supervision of such an organisation must be possessed of many unusual gifts and talents. Edgar Lythe has demonstrated all the required talents and with true skill and real humanity has helped greatly to set the course of his University along the right lines.

I would venture to guess that in spite of his major influence on the University as such it is in his personal work as a scholar and in his founding rôle and leadership of the large department of History that Edgar Lythe will personally find his deepest satisfaction. To me this has seemed evident on the many occasions when he has had to address students and staff. The pleasure of achievement of the scholar was, in my opinion, very evident on such occasions.

I trust that both the continued growth and development of the discipline of history within the university of Strathclyde and the continued ability of the University to play its full part in the university affairs of the country will provide him with his real reward on the occasion of retirement from his heavy official duties. His contribution to the creation of his University has been a most notable one.

SAMUEL CURRAN

Professor S. G. E. Lythe

This collection of historical essays is intended to mark the retirement, in September 1976, of Professor S. G. E. Lythe as the head of the Department of History in the University of Strathclyde. As a *festschrift* it is perhaps rather unusual as it has been prepared – very secretly – only by some colleagues who are currently working with its unsuspecting recipient. A long line of past colleagues and an immense array of former students who share our feelings of admiration, respect, gratitude and affection for Edgar Lythe simply could not be invited to contribute to this little volume. We did not venture to make an invidious selection of potential contributors from the army of distinguished men and women with whom Professor Lythe has worked during his long academic career. Instead, we invited our present colleagues, who have most cause to be grateful, for Professor Lythe's wise leadership and constant kindness – and to regret the passing of an era in their own lives.

Few other people shared in our furtive preparations over the last three years. Mrs Joan Lythe was let into the secret long ago and very kindly aided us in the preparation of her husband's bibliography. As representatives of the countless host of people who have had the pleasure of enjoying her friendship and generous hospitality, we hope that she will understand that this book is affectionately dedicated to her, as well as to Edgar. How many young students and novice lecturers have benefited from Mrs Lythe's charming welcome, warmhearted kindness and sympathetic advice (invariably crowned by her superb cooking) we cannot estimate; but we know that they – scattered over the world as they now are – would wish to join in our thankful tribute to a gracious and generous lady.

Sir Samuel Curran, the Principal and Vice-Chancellor of the University of Strathclyde, kindly agreed to write our foreword. We are most grateful to him. It is very pleasing to us that a distinguished scientist should pay such a warm tribute to a distinguished historian. And it is highly appropriate that Lord Snow's warnings about the dangers of 'two cultures' should be answered by the attitudes and policies of the leaders of a university which was originally entirely 'scientific', but which has succeeded in bridging the alleged gap between the sciences and the arts. That Urania and Clio can happily walk together at Strathclyde is due to the vision and honest endeavours of men like Sir Samuel and Professor Lythe.

Our third *confidante* was Mrs E. M. Thrippleton. Despite many other duties, she cheerfully and carefully prepared our work for the printers. We greatly appreciate her vital contribution to this volume.

Edgar Lythe was born and brought up in the East Riding of Yorkshire, an area of lovely villages, ancient landed estates, varied farming and highly independent rural characters. His parents were good Yorkshire folk, who deeply cared for the quality of village life in Walkington and assiduously collected its memorials. Cricket, gardening, antiquities and the delights of practical craftsmanship appear to have been Professor Lythe's earliest and long-continuing interests. After a distinguished career as a pupil at the ancient grammar school in the market town of Beverley, he went up to Cambridge, as an exhibitioner of Selwyn College. He read History and Geography, taking a First in the Tripos.

After Cambridge, Professor Lythe worked as an extra-mural lecturer for what was then the university college at Hull. In 1935 he began his outstanding Scottish career by accepting the lectureship in economic history at the Dundee School of Economics, a 'power-house' of Scottish economic thinking which exercised enormous influence from its little building in Bell Street. Edgar and Joan (who had now graduated in Arts at Leeds University) were married on 11 August 1938 and initially lived in Monifieth, later moving to Broughty Ferry, where their house in Brook Street became a notable centre of kind hospitality and eminently sensible counsel.

Wherever he worked and lived, Edgar adapted himself to local circumstances. From Hull he investigated East Yorkshire's agricultural drainage problems; at Dundee he pioneered the study of local history, especially as the honorary editor of the valuable series of pamphlets issued by the Abertay Historical Society, founded in 1947. To his Cambridge MA he added a London University diploma in public administration. And on 15 October 1941 Joan presented him with a daughter, Charlotte, who inherited her parents' intellectual abilities and is now a distinguished lecturer in economics at the University of Dundee and a prominent archaeologist.

The Second World War inevitably interrupted Edgar's academic career. Like most of his generation, he joined the armed forces, serving as an officer in the Royal Air Force. Apart from uproarious reminiscences of early 'square-bashing' at Blackpool, Edgar has modestly refrained from telling us much about his wartime career. We know that, when he was crossing the English Channel, his ship was sunk by enemy action. There have been exciting and dangerous experiences in our Professor's career.

In 1945 Edgar returned to a changing Dundee. He resumed his brilliant teaching at the School of Economics and established his reputation as an extremely popular extra-mural lecturer to a wide variety of audiences. As always, he cared immensely for the quality of his teaching and for the environmental development of his adopted city. In 1955, following a report by the late Lord Tedder, the School of Economics was incorporated within Queen's College, Dundee, a constituent part of the University of St Andrews. Edgar Lythe thereafter set the standard of teaching and research in a little department which had to adapt its commitments from the requirements of the London University BSc (Econ) syllabi to those of the St Andrews School of Arts MA and finally to the Social Science course offered by the embryonic University of Dundee. He was very properly promoted to a senior lectureship in 1959 and became an extremely popular adviser of studies to early generations of Dundee arts and social science students. His second book, *The Economy of Scotland in its European Setting, 1550–1625*, published by Oliver and Boyd in 1960, was warmly welcomed and rapidly became a seminal influence on younger scholars interested in the pre-industrial economy of Scotland and its trade. His departure in 1962 was deeply regretted by both staff and students. Behind the formal dinners, speeches and presentations there lay a deep affection, admiration and respect for the man who shaped the contours of the department.

In 1962 Edgar moved to Glasgow as the first professor of Economic History in the Royal College of Science and Technology, the basis of the University of Strathclyde from 1964. In addition to presiding over the little Department of Economic History, originally composed of five teaching members and now (as the Department of History) consisting of fourteen members, he became the first Dean of the School of Arts and Social Studies within the growing University. For three consecutive terms of office – totalling nine years – he admirably performed pioneering duties in a new and difficult field. At the same time he continued to deliver lectures, the immense popularity of which inevitably arouses colleagues' envy, to care for his companions and students with kindly advice and encouragement and to play a major rôle in the planning of a new University. His appointment as Vice-Principal in 1972 was the culmination of a career devoted to honest and honourable treatment of his fellows. Despite great administrative, teaching and research commitments, Edgar Lythe continued to play his part in the life of the community. Uncountable talks freely given to groups in many areas of Scotland should be remembered. Public service, ranging from advice on the Scottish fishing industry to long involvement in the planning of Scottish education (notably as chairman of the governors of the Hamilton College of Education) must be recalled. Typically, Edgar has taken a major position in the planning of community action in Pollokshields, his adopted area of Glasgow.

As his beneficiaries, we most greatly appreciate Professor Lythe's personal qualities – the integrity and honour with which he has graced our profession, the wise and kindly help and advice which he has given to so many under-graduates and the delightful companionship and generous aid which he has always accorded to his colleagues. It is as grateful and appreciative friends, who have never previously been allowed to express adequately their thanks to Professor and Mrs Lythe, that we now dedicate this little volume to them.

This book consists of a series of essays written by most of Professor Lythe's current colleagues in Strathclyde's History department. It represents (we hope) something of the scope of Edgar's historical interests. Dr Tom Devine, the first Strathclyde graduate to join the History teaching staff, starts the book with an essay on mid-seventeenth-century Scotland, on which he and Professor Lythe are acknowledged experts. Tom McAloon, who joined us after a long career at the Scottish College of Commerce, contributes the second chapter. Baron Duckham, the leading historian of the Scottish coal-mining industry and a prominent transport historian, adds to his reputation in the third chapter.

Dr Gordon Jackson shares Professor Lythe's East Yorkshire background.

Already an established authority on the history of Hull, he writes of the whaling enterprises which once intrigued Edgar. Dr Hamish Fraser has long been involved in 'labour history', as both an editor and author, and represents a society of which Edgar was the first president. His story of the Glasgow spinners synthesises many previously controversial accounts. Miss Barbara Thatcher teaches banking history, but is also a distinguished member of the Episcopal Church of Scotland, upon one of whose activities she contributes her essay. Dr Jim Treble is a social historian who has been heavily involved in the investigation of insurance history. John Hume has for many years specialised in recording and photographing industrial archaeological remains, particularly in Glasgow and Western Scotland, and here examines one aspect of his work. Our own contributions deal with subjects dear to us, within the fields of 'economic' and 'political' history.

Ten people with different interests and beliefs have written this book. What unites the authors is a desire to mark Edgar's retirement and to express our gratitude, affection and respect to him and Joan.

JOHN BUTT

J. T. WARD

Bibliography of the works of Professor
S. G. E. Lythe

'Report on the Furniture Industry in Scotland', in *Light Industries for Scotland* (Scottish Econ Cmt 1938), 21–48.

'Drainage and Reclamation in Holderness' 1760–1880, in *Geography* XXIII (1938), 237–49.

'The Origin and Development of Dundee', in *Scott Geographical Magazine* 54 (1938), 344–57.

'The Economic History of Dundee to 1760' in *Scientific Survey of Dundee*, British Association (1939).

'The Organisation of Drainage and Embankment in Mediaeval Holderness', in *Journal of the Yorks Arch Society* XXXIV (1939), 282–95.

British Economic History since 1760 (Pitman, 1950).

'The Dundee and Newtyle Railway', in *Railway Magazine* (1951), 546–50.

'The Arbroath and Forfar Railway', in *Railway Magazine* (1953), 53–9 and 128–33.

'Scottish Trade with the Baltic 1550–1650', in *Dundee Economic Essays*, ed J. K. Eastham (1955), 63–84.

Life and Labour in Dundee from the Reformation to the Civil War (Abertay Hist Soc, 1958).

'The Union of the Crowns in 1603 and the Debate on Economic Integration', in *Scott Journal Pol Econ*, V (1958), 219–38.

The Economy of Scotland in its European Setting, 1550–1625 (Oliver & Boyd, 1960).

'Shipbuilding at Dundee down to 1914', in *Scott Journal Pol Econ* IX (1962), 219–32.

Gourlays of Dundee (Abertay Hist Soc, 1964).

'The Dundee Whale Fishery', in *Scott Journal Pol Econ* XI (1964), 158–69.

'The Tayside Meal Mobs', in *Scott Hist Review* XLVI (1967), 26–36.

'James Watt and the Strathmore Canal Project', in *Transport History* I (1968), 67–70.

'James Carmichael', in *Three Dundonians* (Abertay Hist Soc, 1968).

'Britain, the Financial Capital of the World', in *Britain Pre-eminent*, ed C. J. Bartlett (Macmillan, 1969), 31–53.

'The Historian's Profession', in *The Study of Economic History*, ed N. B. Harte (Cass, 1971).

[with T. M. Devine] 'The economy of Scotland under James VI', in *Scott Hist Review* L (1971), 91–106.

'The Economy of Scotland under James I and VI', in *The Reign of James VI and I*, ed A. G. R. Smith (Macmillan, 1973), 57–73.

[with J. Butt] *An Economic History of Scotland 1100–1939* (Blackie, 1975).
Various reviews and articles in *Scots Magazine, Times Supplements* and other
     newspapers.

I

The Cromwellian Union and the Scottish Burghs: The Case of Aberdeen and Glasgow, 1652-60

The Parliamentary Union of 1707 was a unique constitutional water-shed in Scottish history. Yet in itself union between England and Scotland was no novelty. Half a century before, the army in the south had effected a conquest of Scotland which had resulted in the so-called 'Cromwellian union' of 1652–60. 'Unity' in this context was a response to English military diktat rather than an expression of Scottish aspirations. Inevitably therefore, the conditions of the new relationship reflected the southern government's desire to bring stability and security to its northern frontier.[1]

Much is already known about this brief period when Scotland was annexed to England. A series of volumes issued by the *Scottish History Society* and a variety of other publications enable the interested student to acquire a fairly clear impression of political and religious life at the time.[2] Unfortunately, however, the economic historian has not been as well served. Recently, the economy of the first quarter and last forty years of the seventeenth century has been described in some detail but the middle decades remain 'an obscure period'.[3] Yet the known and massive gaps in data have not inhibited several writers from judging Scottish economic experience although some of this work is reduced in value by a tendency to *a priori* reasoning and to bold generalisation based on a series of literary sources and diary accounts likely to be biased. This criticism may indeed be most pertinently directed at an important article

[1] The origins of the union have been studied in most detail by Gordon Donaldson, *James V to James VII* (Edinburgh and London, 1965), 343–57. Relevant documents have been printed in C. H. Firth (ed), *Scotland and the Protectorate, 1654–9* (Scottish History Society, 1899), *Scotland and the Commonwealth* (Scottish History Society, 1895) and C. S. Terry (ed), *The Cromwellian Union* (Scottish History Society, 1902). Although union was effective from 1652, a number of obstacles prevented it being formally established by act of parliament until April 1657.

[2] Ibid. For detailed references to publications on the subject see Donaldson, op cit, 418–9.

[3] The phrase is Prof T. C. Smout's. See *Northern Scotland*, I (1973), 235. The works referred to are S. G. E. Lythe, *The Economy of Scotland in its European Setting, 1550–1625* (Edinburgh and London, 1963), and T. C. Smout, *Scottish Trade on the Eve of Union, 1660–1707* (Edinburgh and London, 1963).

written by Theodora Keith, the pioneering historian of Scottish trade, published as long ago as 1908, but whose viewpoint has influenced most writers to the present day.[4]

Keith was concerned to repudiate vigorously any suggestion that Scotland had benefited from the union. She admitted that the end of the civil wars re-established a secure context for commercial activity and that the Scots were allowed to trade freely both in England and her transatlantic colonies for the first time. But, in her opinion, these advantages were illusory and were more than counter-balanced by higher customs duties, heavy taxation by the commonwealth government and commercial legislation designed to suit English but not Scottish interests. Thus, the export of skins, hides and wool, traditional Scottish staples, was banned. Furthermore, in her opinion, the Anglo-Dutch war of 1652–4, a conflict with one of England's greatest rivals but one of Scotland's best customers, confirmed the malaise in overseas trade which had developed in the 1640s. As Keith concluded:

> On the whole, therefore, it does not seem that the country benefited materially during the Interregnum. Poverty was great, manufactures could not be set up. Trade, both inland and foreign decayed, and showed little sign of recovery, and the bankruptcy of the country contributed towards the bankruptcy of the whole government and the downfall of the Protectorate.[5]

This assessment was based partly on the apparently obvious fact that Scotland was exhausted after the civil wars and that the negative legislation of 1652–60 could not possibly have accomplished anything but the prolonging of distress. Miss Keith then supported this assumption by citing evidence from such sources as were available to her at the time. Inevitably the historian of the Convention of Royal Burghs made full use of that body's records. However, while petitions to government from the Convention are informative about its desire to ameliorate the lot of its members and cut tax assessment they are of more limited value, unless used very carefully, concerning the true nature of burghal conditions.

In this short essay a modest attempt will be made to test Keith's arguments against the commercial history of two leading Scottish burghs during the Cromwellian Union. In the 1650s, according to the tax roll of the Convention of Royal Burghs, Aberdeen and Glasgow, were ranked the third and fourth towns respectively in Scotland in terms of wealth and commercial influence. Both served regional economies in the north-east and west-central parts of the country. Each was taxed according to its position in the burghal tax roll by the

---

[4] 'Economic Conditions under the Commonwealth and Protectorate', *Scott Hist Rev*, V (1908), 274–84. Recent writers broadly agree with Keith's assessment. Prof Donaldson concludes that 'economic conditions were such that no section of the community had much opportunity to prosper during the brief period of commonwealth rule' (op cit, 351). To Professor Smout, 'the arrival of the Cromwellian Union after years of anarchy did nothing to restore prosperity: Scotland was too enfeebled to take much advantage of the opportunities it offered' (op cit, 195, citing Keith's article).

[5] Keith, loc cit, 17.

governments of the protectorate.[6] There is no obvious evidence that either was fortunate enough to escape the privation or the effects of the civil wars and their aftermath.

In September, 1644, for instance, Aberdeen had been sacked by the Earl of Montrose's levies after the battle of Justice Mills. A graphic account described how:

> Montrose followis the chaiss in to Aberdeen, his men hewing and
> cutting down all maner of men they could overtak within the
> towne, upone the streitis or in thair housses, and round about the
> towne as oure men wes fleing with brode swerdes but mercy or
> remeid. Thir cruell Irishis, seing a man weill clad, wold first tyr him
> and souf the clothis onspoyllet, syne kill the man. We lost thrie
> piece of cannon with muche armour besydes the plundering of oure
> toune housses, merchand butthis, and all, which wes pitifull to sie
> . . . the Irishis killing, robbing and plundering of this toune at thair
> plesour and nothing hard bot houling, crying weiping, murning
> throw all the streittis.[7]

Three years later, in the autumn of 1647, a severe plague struck the burgh, killing 1,600 persons on one estimate, and temporarily depopulating the town.[8] Over the period 1639–48, the town council calculated that thirty-two merchant vessels had been lost and nearly £164,000 Scots spent on town defence, quarterings and acquisition of weapons.[9] Glasgow fared little better in the era of war before the union although, unlike Aberdeen, it was not plundered by enemy troops.[10] Nevertheless, in 1652, a crisis of even greater magnitude overtook the burgh when a major fire destroyed eighty closes and rendered 1,000 families homeless.[11]

The experience of these two towns during the Cromwellian Union will be considered principally on the basis of data relating to their seaborne commerce. Unfortunately in the case of both Aberdeen and Glasgow, centrally administered customs accounts, the historian's favourite tool for trade studies, are not available for the relevant years. Alternative materials were therefore employed. For Aberdeen the major source was the *Shore Work Accounts*. These were compiled as a result of a decision by James VI in 1596 to grant Aberdeen the privilege of collecting levies on vessels using the town's harbour, the sum accruing to be

[6] Although Glasgow's assessment was temporarily suspended because of the fire in the town in 1651. For histories of the two burghs at this time see W. Kennedy, *Annals of Aberdeen* (1818); T. C. Smout, 'The Glasgow Merchant Community in the seventeenth century', *Scott Hist Rev*, XLVII (1968); 'The Development and Enterprise of Glasgow, 1550–1707', *Scott Journ of Political Economy*, VII (1960).

[7] John Spalding, *Memorialls of the Trubles in Scotland and in England 1624–1645*.

[8] 'Aberdeen Burgess Register, 1631–1700', *The Miscellany of the Third Spalding Club*, II (1906).

[9] Louise B. Taylor (ed), *Aberdeen Council Letters*, III (London, 1952), 68–169 (hereafter cited as *Aberdeen Council Letters*). At this time £1 Scots equalled 1s 8d sterling.

[10] See, for instance, references to taxation and quarterings in J. D. Marwick (ed), *Extracts from the Records of the Burgh of Glasgow, 1630–1662* (Glasgow, 1882) (hereafter cited as *Glasgow Burgh Records*).

[11] Ibid, 229–30.

used for maintenance and extension to the quay. Through good fortune, a record of receipts from this impost, which incorporates details on the volume of commerce and shipping using the port, has survived in an almost continuous series from 1596 to 1810.[12]

Despite their obvious value, the *Accounts* must be treated with caution. It is difficult, for instance, to say anything with much confidence about the precise changes in the *value* of commodity trade over time. Contemporary weights and measures varied both in description and meaning and this renders conversion to uniform measurement well nigh impossible.[13] Moreover, it is apparent that the administrative competence of those charged with the collection of the levy also varied, though perhaps not to such an extent as to invalidate the value of the source altogether. It might be added that since the records relate to a harbour rather than a port as administratively defined, a small proportion of goods could have passed through the town and not been registered in the *Accounts*.[14] This criticism, on the other hand, is less likely to relate to the burgh's foreign commerce.

In order to circumvent these problems, the aim here will simply be to aggregate the annual arrivals and departures of merchant vessels. This exercise can provide a crude index of trading activity and at the same time is less likely to be distorted by some of the flaws in the *Accounts* described above. As Professor Smout has said, from the point of view of the contemporary customs official, 'The coming and going of boats in themselves are easy to see and easy to count'.[15]

The main source of information for Glasgow's trade was the *Register of Ship Entries* at Dumbarton from 1595 to 1658. This is preserved in the Dumbarton burgh archives and lists ships arriving in the Clyde from ports furth of Scotland.[16] In fact, almost all this trade seems to have been on Glasgow's account. Two local historians, Dr Macphail and Mr Roberts, have assessed the value of the *Register* as an indicator of the Clyde's foreign commerce by checking entries in it against three contemporary analyses: a list of ships engaged in the wine trade in April–May 1597, the return of the Collector of Customs in Glasgow for the period November 1626–Novermber 1627 and the report of the English customs commissioner, Thomas Tucker, in 1655. Their conclusions suggest that when the *Register* is supplemented by additional information extracted from the *Dumbarton Common Good Accounts* it offers 'a fairly accurate picture' of seaborne commerce on the Clyde.[17] Some qualifications, however,

[12] These are housed in the Charter Room in Aberdeen Town House and are hereafter referred to as *Aberdeen Accounts*. Those for the period 1596–1670 have recently been edited and published in Louise B. Taylor (ed), *Aberdeen Shore Work Accounts, 1596–1670* (Aberdeen, 1972).

[13] In a review of Miss Taylor's edition, T. C. Smout has shown the massive variety in contemporary measures of apparent uniformity. See *Northern Scotland*, I (1973), 236.

[14] A point made in Robin Craig's review of the *Accounts*, *Economic History Review*, 2nd ser, XXVIII (1975).

[15] *Northern Scotland*, I (1973), 236.

[16] A summary of this material appears in 'Abstract of Ship Entries at Dumbarton', in Fergus Roberts and I. M. M. Macphail (eds), *Dumbarton Common Good Accounts 1614–1660* (Dumbarton, 1972), 260–73 (hereafter cited as *Dumbarton Register*).

[17] Ibid, 262.

must be borne in mind. There is evidence that before about 1620 the level of the timber trade may have been underestimated and the sources only describe the import side of foreign commerce while giving no information concerning the volume of coastal trade carried on in small boats. Because of these gaps, material from the Glasgow burgh records and the burgess register was also employed in this essay. As recent work has shown, changing levels of registration of merchant and craftsmen burgesses can provide an approximate guide to the economic fortunes of a Scottish burghal community.[18]

In April 1654, the Town Council of Aberdeen petititioned government that as a result of war and taxes, '. . . this place is become so miserable that almost there is non in it than can subsist or have any liveing'.[19] The suspicion that this

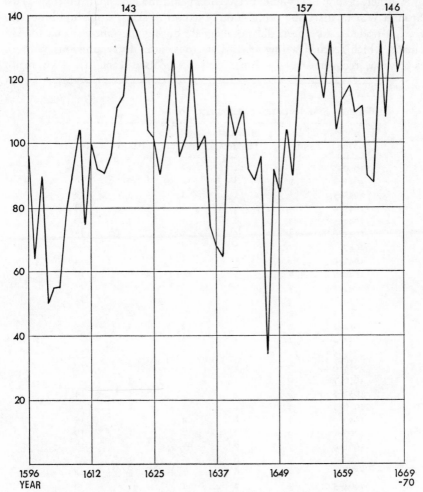

FIG. 1. Total number of entries and departures, 1596–1669 (Aberdeen).

[18] Smout, loc cit (1968); T. M. Devine, 'Glasgow Merchants in Colonial Trade, 1770–1815' (unpublished PhD thesis, University of Strathclyde, 1971), I, 16–7.
[19] *Aberdeen Council Letters*, April 1654, 228.

statement was an example of special pleading is fully borne out by the evidence of trade data. One year before the declaration was made, the total number of entries and departures at the burgh's harbour reached 154, the highest figure for the entire period, 1596 to 1670.[20] Nor was this a fluke year. The depression in trade of the later 1640s seems to have ended in the following decade. As Figure 1 illustrates [p 5], the commerce of Aberdeen had been quite obviously affected by war and pestilence in the earlier period. The plague year, 1647, for example, stands out clearly as one of depression with entries falling to 37. However, this trend was reversed from 1652 and the level of activity suggested in the following eight years was more comparable with the 1620s and 1630s than with the era of the Bishops Wars and English invasions.

Further, despite the conflict between England and Holland from 1652-4, the Spanish War of 1657, and prohibition of export of skins, wools and hides, the foreign trade of Aberdeen did not stagnate during the union. Total foreign entries which reached a low of five in 1652, after three previous years of depression, recovered in the subsequent period (see Table 1). Two major

TABLE 1

'FOREIGN' SHIP ENTRIES AT ABERDEEN, 1640-65

Year	Norway	Holland/ Flanders	France	Baltic	Total
1640-1	7	12	2	9	30
1641-2	9	8	2	7	26
1642-3	5	15	3	5	28
1643-4	4	6	3	—	13
1644-5	3	9	1	3	16
1645-6	4	5	3	1	13
1647	1	2	2	—	5
1647-8	—	3	—	1	4
1648-9	7	5	—	6	18
1649-50	4	6	1	—	11
1650-1	1	7	2	3	13
1651-2	2	5	2	2	11
1652-3	2	—	2	1	5
1653-4	3	3	3	6	15
1654-5	10	13	4	10	37
1655-6	6	8	3	—	17
1656-7	10	6	5	3	24
1657-8	6	4	3	1	14
1658-9	4	11	1	1	17
1659-60	4	2	4	3	13
1660-1	6	10	2	1	19
1661-2	7	9	—	3	19
1662-3	9	6	6	1	22
1663-4	5	6	8	3	22
1664-5	3	2	1	—	6

Source: *Aberdeen Accounts*, 1640-65

[20] *Aberdeen Accounts*. All references in subsequent paragraphs unless otherwise stated are to this source.

sectors of overseas commerce, crucial to the prosperity of Aberdeen, were both particularly active after the malaise of 1647–52 (see Table 1). The renewal of the timber trade from Norway may perhaps indicate revival in the urban economy. Wood at this time was the universal packaging material, especially relevant to the Aberdeen fish trade, as well as being vital in building and construction.[21] Significantly too, commercial relationships with Holland and Flanders seem to have deteriorated during 1652–3, coincident with the Anglo-Dutch War. But, as Table 1 shows, this was only a temporary disruption. The Dutch market was particularly important before the union as a source of demand for salmon and plaiding, the two great exports of Aberdeen. Export figures for the latter correlate with evidence already presented of a generally higher level of business activity in the 1650s than had characterised the previous decade. From 3 fardels of plaiding in 1650–1, total volume rose to 14 in 1652–3, 92 in 1654–5, 92 in 1655–6, fell to 44 in 1657–8 and increased again to 98 in 1659–60. In 1645–6 there was only one reference to plaiding exports and none in 1647–8.[22] While assessment over longer periods is made difficult by changing nomenclature of weights and measures, it would appear on the evidence available, that 1652–60 does compare favourably with the period 1610–30, and with the 1660s.[23]

This well documented revival in commercial fortunes was reflected too in the extension and improvement of the burgh's harbour. When Tucker visited Aberdeen in 1655 he was very favourably impressed by the work being carried out there.[24] Since financial support accrued from the levy on vessels using the port, this construction work can be regarded as both a cause and effect of the town's recovery.

While therefore there is substantial support for the proposition that Aberdeen achieved a return to 'normal' levels of commerce during the union there are fewer indications that free trade permitted the growth of a vigorous new relationship either with England or her colonies. Most entries in the *Accounts* continued to relate to coastal trade with other north-east ports or Dundee and Leith to the south; 'foreign' trade was almost exclusively with traditional customers in Norway, Holland, France and, to a lesser extent, the Baltic. Between 1652–60 only eleven ships either from English ports or owned by English merchants visited Aberdeen. Five of these were freighted, however, by Scottish merchants and only two carried manufactured goods; most shipped salt and lime.[25] Clearly here there is no basis for a recent assertion that 'free trade allowed the import to Scotland of English manufactured goods, more cheaply produced than those of Scotland, and they went a long way to drive Scottish manufactures off the market'.[26] Furthermore, the Aberdeen men

[21] Lythe, op cit, 144–5; Smout, op cit, 154–5.
[22] In the 1640s–60s a fardel measured between 400–700 ells.
[23] *Northern Scotland*, I (1973), 237.
[24] 'Report by Thomas Tucker upon the settlement of the Revenues of Excise and Customs in Scotland A.D. MDCLVI', *Miscellany of the Scottish Burgh Records Society* (1881) (henceforth cited as *Tucker's Report*).
[25] *Aberdeen Accounts*.
[26] Donaldson, op cit, 352.

showed little apparent inclination to move into the English or colonial market. Seventeenth century commercial relationships functioned on a foundation of trust and personal acquaintance developed over generations by merchant families in an epoch of high risk and insecure markets. War and political change, especially if only of short duration, did not seriously disturb these established business networks, and, in addition, paucity of capital resources often inhibited diversification as effectively as 'conservatism'.

The foreign trade pattern of Glasgow, the most rapidly growing burgh in Scotland, differed somewhat from Aberdeen. As the focus of the Clyde region it specialised in the importation of salt and wine from France and the export of salted fish. Yet, its commercial history during the middle decades of the seventeenth century was remarkably similar to that of the northern burgh. Both towns seem to have experienced difficulty in the years 1646–51 and each achieved a higher level of activity thereafter. If anything, perhaps, the data

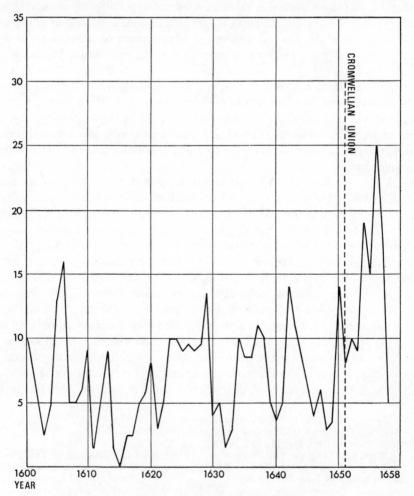

FIG. 2. Ship entries: Dumbarton, 1600–58.

suggest that the rate of recovery was more spectacular on the Clyde than on the Dee. Between 1654 and 1657 entries at Dumbarton of vessels from ports outside Scotland were greater than at any period since 1620.[27] [see Figure 2, p 8]. The average number of entries between 1652 and 1658 (when the *Register of Ship Entries* ends) was 15·3 per annum, compared with 8·3 from 1600–10, 8·6 from 1620–30, 6·3 from 1631–40 and 7·8 from 1641–50.[28]

Alternative measurements of Glasgow's economic condition give a similar impression of sustained recovery. Registration of craftsmen and merchant burgesses show an interesting correlation over time with the level of ship entries in the Clyde.[29] This may indicate that the guilds regulated the number of new burgesses at least partly according to the level of business activity. For

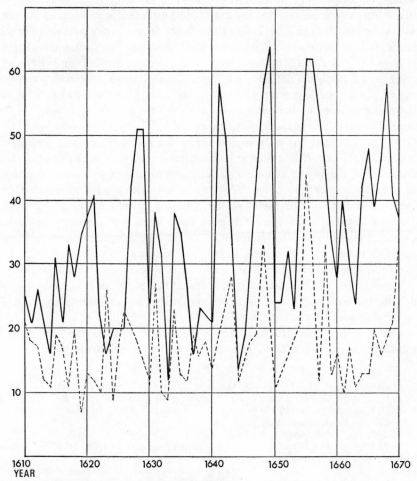

FIG. 3. Merchant and craftsman entries, Glasgow, 1610–70; C=————; M=– – – –.

[27] *Dumbarton Register.*
[28] Ibid.
[29] J. R. Anderson (ed), *The Burgesses and Guild Brethren of Glasgow 1573–1750* (Edinburgh, 1925).

instance, both burgess and ship registers show falls in the early 1620s, early and late 1630s and early 1650s together with substantial gains in the early 1640s and mid 1650s [See Figures 2 and 3]. Just as significantly there was a fairly marked correlation between merchant and craftsmen enrolments over the same period. As Figure 3 reveals, the number of new burgesses registered between 1654–8 was high and can be compared with other years of peak enrolment throughout the century.[30]

In the later 1640s and early 1650s there was considerable emphasis in the Glasgow burgh records on the ill effects of war and taxation on the town's economy.[31] The absence of such complaints thereafter is perhaps in itself eloquent testimony of better times. Yet, in addition, positive indicators of a more prosperous burghal economy emerged. In 1659, the Convention of Royal Burghs pointed out that the coal trade, in which Glasgow had an interest, was doing well.[32] Four years before this a new coal work had been set up in the burgh and the town council had advanced 2,000 Scots merks to encourage it. In the same year £600 Scots were employed to extend the College.[33] Even the great fire of 1652 does not appear to have unduly disturbed the return to normality. £1,000 sterling were paid out by the Commander-in-Chief, Scotland from 'the treasury of the sequestrations' to aid the rebuilding programme.[34] Several Scottish burghs also gave subsidies and in July 1654, by ordinance of the Lord Protector, the town's contribution to the monthly cess was suspended because of the material damage it had sustained as a result of the fire.[35] In the aftermath of the disaster economic activity was stimulated by the development of employment opportunities. Wrights, masons and others were recruited, 'quherever they can get them, in the countrey or ellis quhair'.[36] Certainly Thomas Tucker, who visited Glasgow three years after the fire, made no comment about its ill effects in his praise of the burgh's success:

> This towne . . . handsomely built in forme of a crosse, is one of the
> most considerablest burghs in Scotland, as well for the structure as
> trade of it . . . the situation of this towne in a plentifull land, and
> the mercantile genius of the people are strong signs of her increase
> and groweth.[37]

Her 'increase and growth' during the Comwellian Union was indeed substantial if the Dumbarton registers are any guide. Between 1600–50, the

[30] Ibid.
[31] *Glasgow Burgh Records*, 197, 199, 209, 209.
[32] J. D. Marwick (ed), *Extracts from the Records of the Convention of the Royal Burghs of Scotland, 1615–76* (Edinburgh, 1878), 475.
[33] *Glasgow Burgh Records*, 308, 316.
[34] Ibid, 255, 7 and 17 September 1652.
[35] Ibid, 291, 11 July 1654. This monthly abatement was partly a reflection of the protectorate's policy of appeasing the middle and lower classes with the aim of reconciling them to the union and breaking the influence of the clergy and aristocracy. General Monck asked for tax relief for the burghs in 1654 because 'they are generally the most faithful to us of any people in this Nacion'. The inhabitants of Glasgow, in particular, 'being a good people' he was anxious that they have abatements. See C. H. Firth (ed), *Scotland and the Protectorate, 1654–9* (Scottish History Society, 1899), 162.
[36] *Glasgow Burgh Records*, 3 July 1652.
[37] *Tucker's Report*, 26.

major proportion of Glasgow's foreign trade was handled by foreign-owned vessels freighted by Glasgow merchants. From 1651, however, this pattern was apparently altered with, as Table 2 demonstrates, a considerable expansion in the number of Glasgow-owned ships. At the same time, this development was paralleled by an apparent fall in the number of Dutch-owned vessels. From a total of 48 such entries between 1642 and 1650, there was a drop to only 2 in the period 1651–8. One is tempted to link all this with the effects of the Anglo-Dutch war of 1652–4 but there remains the strong possibility that a continued Dutch presence was concealed by false registration papers, forged because of the opposition of the protectorate government to the involvement of foreign vessels in the British carrying trade.[38]

During the period of union there was an extension, albeit on a limited scale, of English shipping activity on the Clyde. Over the half century, 1600–50, only twelve entries related to English-owned vessels. Between 1652–8 eight English ships were registered. Yet this figure still only amounted to just over 8 per cent of total entries throughout the union. Six of the eight vessels carried salt and/or wine from France, and were clearly being employed as carriers in the Biscay trade rather than as pioneers in a new Anglo-Scottish trading development up the west coast.[39]

As in the case of Aberdeen, there is no evidence that the Glasgow men took advantage of the access given by government to trade freely in the English colonies. Tobacco does appear in the *Register of Ship Entries* but on only one occasion was it listed between 1652–8 when a cargo was imported by a vessel from Rotterdam. Five years before union, in 1648, the *Antelope* of Glasgow shipped 20,000 lb of tobacco from the French island of Martinique. In this sector, however, financial weakness inhibited steady expansion; long voyages to

---

TABLE 2

SHIP ENTRIES AT DUMBARTON, 1595–1658

Date	Total entries	No of entries Glasgow owned
1595–1600	70	14
1601–10	43	36
1611–20	39	6
1621–30	77	21
1631–40	64	11
1641–50	75	2
1651–8	104	43

Source: Fergus Roberts and I. M. M. Macphail (eds), *Dumbarton Common Good Accounts, 1614–1660* (Dumbarton, 1972), 264

---

[38] *Dumbarton Register.*
[39] See also P. McGrath, *Merchants and Merchandise in Seventeenth Century Bristol* (Bristol Record Society, 1955), 278–81.

distant lands on an annual basis would still have called for greater resources than those of the typical Scottish merchant of the time.

It seems plain that the Cromwellian Union was not disastrous for the two leading burghs considered in this study. While few new exciting developments took place, both towns seem to have fairly quickly re-established the level of commercial operations which prevailed before the civil wars. It would be dangerous, on the other hand, to assert that their experience was typical of other burghs, or, indeed, of Scotland as a whole. The 'Scottish economy' in the seventeenth century was in essence the aggregate of a series of local and regional economies which often displayed independent characteristics. It would seem, for example, on the basis of the available evidence, that Dundee, the second largest burgh in the land, continued a decline, which had begun before 1652, but which was probably exacerbated by the plundering of General Monck's army in 1651.[40] For three consecutive years thereafter not a single Dundee ship moved into the Baltic.[41]

TABLE 3

TOTAL NO OF VESSELS, WITH SCOTTISH DOMICILE PASSING EASTWARDS TO BALTIC, 1635–57

Year	No of vessels
1635	93
1637	69
1638	47
1639	27
1640	43
1641	53
1642	59
1643	47
1644	21
1645	35
1647	17
1648	17
1649	20
1650	11
1651	5
1652	11
1653	—
1654	9
1656	9
1657	12

Source: N. E. Bang (ed), *Tabeller over Skibsfart og Varetransport gennem Øresund, 1497–1660* (Copenhagen, 1906 and 1922)

---

[40] *Tucker's Report*, 26; Smout, op cit, 140; S. G. E. Lythe, *Life and Labour in Dundee from the Reformation to the Civil War* (Dundee, 1958), 27–30.

[41] N. Bang (ed), *Tabeller over Skibsfart og Varetransport gennem Øresund, 1497–1660* (Copenhagen, 1906 and 1922) (henceforth cited as *Sound Toll Registers*).

Indeed, Scottish commerce to the Baltic as a whole apparently did not experience the resilience characteristic elsewhere and while the *Sound Toll Registers*, the major historical source for Baltic trade, are open to criticism and possibly understate the extent of Scottish shipping activity, there is no doubting the general downward trend which they reveal (see Table 3).[42] It is true that the general level of commercial activity in the Baltic did falter as a result of the Dutch War. Nevertheless, the Scottish share fell disproportionately from 3·7 per cent of total ships, 1630–9, to 2·3 per cent in 1640–9 and 0·7 per cent, 1650–7.[43] This may reflect the fact that those burghs which specialised in Baltic trade, notably the south-east congerie of Leith, Dundee, St Andrews and Anstruther, had a markedly worse experience at this time than Aberdeen and Glasgow (see Table 4). Most of them had suffered heavily in the troubles of the 1640s. As Professor Lythe has remarked, 'Dysart's experience was probably typical: it was, so its representative said, "an antient and flourishing burgh royall . . . till the year of God 1644 and 1645 it came to decay by the intestine and unnatural war against Montrose, where the most pairt of the skippers and

TABLE 4

DISTRIBUTION OF SCOTTISH SHIPS ENTERING THE BALTIC, DISTINGUISHED BY HOME PORT, 1565–1655

Year	Total	Aberdeen	St Andrews	Anstruther	Dundee	Leith	Montrose	Others
1565	18	3	0	0	5	7	1	2
1575	87	3	12	4	22	21	3	22 (1)
1585	29	3	6	4	3	7	0	6
1595	72	6	7	10	15	20	2	12 (2)
1605	51	2	3	2	11	9	4	20 (3)
1615	53	2	4	11	13	12	2	9 (4)
1625	73	1	6	10	15	14	9	18 (5)
1635	74	6	5	10	6	8	4	35 (6)
1645	40	3	2	5	1	3	1	25 (7)
1655	30	5	3	0	5	5	4	8 (8)

1. Notably Dysart (7), Kinghorn, Kirkcaldy, St Monance and Pittenweem (3 each).
2. Notably Craill (3), Dysart and Kinghorn (3 each).
3. Notably Burntisland (4), Kirkcaldy (3), Pittenweem, Craill and Ayr (2 each).
4. Notably Burntisland (3), Kirkcaldy (3).
5. Notably Kirkcaldy (4), Craill (3), Bo'ness and Queensferry (2 each).
6. Notably Pittenweem (7), Burntisland (5), Bo'ness and Queensferry (4 each), Kirkcaldy (3).
7. Notably Pittenweem (4), Queensferry (4), Glasgow (3), Burntisland and Kirkcaldy (2 each).
8. Notably Burntisland (3).

Source: S. G. E. Lythe, 'Scottish Trade with the Baltic, 1550–1650', in J. K. Eastham (ed), *Economic Essays in Commemoration of the Dundee School of Economics* (Dundee, 1955), 69 after the *Sound Toll Registers*.

[42] For the weaknesses of the *Sound Toll Registers* see J. Dow, 'A comparative note on the Sound Toll Registers, Stockholm Customs Accounts and Dundee Shipping Lists, 1613–22', *Scandinavian Econ Hist Rev*, XII (1964), 79; T. M. Devine and S. G. E. Lythe, 'The economy of Scotland under James VI: a Revision Article', *Scottish Historical Review*, L (1971), 101.
[43] *Sound Toll Registers*.

traffiquers were killed and destroyed" '.[44] Because it was the political and administrative heart of Scotland, this region was always likely to be particularly affected in a period of civil war.

Nevertheless, if the Aberdeen and Glasgow data do reflect conditions in their respective hinterlands, it can be tentatively concluded that the north-east and west-central areas were more fortunate. It is not easy to explain why this should be. The nature of economic activity at the time may have helped. An agricultural economy with a limited commercial sector functioning mainly on the exchange of food and raw materials is less vulnerable to the adverse long-term effects of war than the sophisticated industrial states of modern times. In the Scottish economy of the seventeenth century the crucial determinant of business activity was not war but the yield of the harvest, although occasionally one obviously affected the other. The limited evidence for the north-east and Clyde regions suggests very high grain prices in the period 1648–52 but thereafter a

TABLE 5

SCOTTISH GRAIN IMPORTS FROM THE BALTIC, 1635–57

Year	Rye (Lasts)	Wheat (Lasts)	Barley (Lasts)	Oats (Lasts)	Flour (Lasts)
1635	54	6	0	0	29
1636	1,382	28	158	37	0
1637	146	6	73	0	2
1638	77	15	70	0	0
1639	4	0	0	0	0
1640	304	48	0	0	0
1641	324	103	23	0	0
1642	489	10	36	16	5
1643	772	115	12	49	2
1644	81	6	0	0	0
1645	94	0	0	0	65
1646	0	0	0	0	0
1647	80	0	0	0	0
1648	15	0	0	0	0
1649	172	0	126	60	2
1650	14	0	0	0	0
1651	0	0	0	0	0
1652	0	0	0	0	0
1653	0	0	0	0	0
1654	0	0	0	0	0
1655	0	3	0	0	0
1656	0	0	0	0	0
1657	0	0	0	0	0

Source: N. E. Bang (ed), *Tabeller over Skibsfart Og Varetransport gennem Øresund, 1497–1660* (Copenhagen, 1906 and 1922)

[44] S. G. E. Lythe, 'Scottish Trade with the Baltic 1550–1650' in J. K. Eastham (ed). *Economic Essays in Commemoration of the Dundee School of Economics, 1931–1955* (Dundee, 1955), 70.

drastic fall in most years until the Restoration. For instance, the average annual fiars prices for 'ferme bear' in Aberdeenshire was £7 15s 0d per boll from 1648–52 and £4 6s 8d from 1654–8 which was as low as any point in the century. The same trend was displayed in prices for small oats and malting barley.[45] While fiars returns are not extant for the Glasgow area, other data also indicate a drop in grain prices as a consequence of better harvest conditions. In March 1654 the Town Council drew attention to the fact that 'victuall is become so cheipe'.[46] Significantly too, burghal price control of food products, which occurred regularly in the 1640s, seems to have been abandoned from 1651.[47] Moreover, there is no trace of grain imports from Ireland or elsewhere in the *Register of Ship Entries* such as tended to be common during years of food shortage. It may be suggested, therefore, that harvests in these parts of Scotland were adequate during these years.[48] The country's 'emergency granary' in the south Baltic was hardly utilised between 1652–7 whereas recourse to it had been frequent throughout the later 1630s and 1640s (see Table 5). As Professor Lythe has argued, high grain prices often meant the diversion of scarce currency to the buying of food overseas, a consequent fall in demand for other goods and the sapping of business initiative.[49] Therefore, it could be that stabilisation of domestic food supply at least created the opportunity and the context for commercial recovery. It may well be too that the deleterious impact of war on the merchant marine of *some* burghs has been exaggerated. In a 'Compt of losses be sea sustainst be the inhabitants of Aberdeen', it was reported that 32 vessels had been lost between 1639–48. Although these losses were sustained during war, however, not all were the result of war. For a start, twelve of the ships belonged to other ports and were merely freighted by Aberdeen merchants. Goods, if lost as a result of pirate or privateer action, could be ransomed. Furthermore, on the calculation of the Town Council itself, only eight vessels disappeared because of the action of pirates or enemy ships. Thus, the merchants of Aberdeen lost, on average, less than one vessel per annum as a result of hostilities to 1648.[50] Even during the Anglo-Dutch war of 1652–4, the Lords of the Admiralty of Zeland gave convoy to Scots vessels as far as Newcastle and also issued safe conducts 'by which they passed freely home to Scotland, without any hinderance of men of warre or private freebooters that had letters of retortion from the States Generall'.[51] During the Spanish War of 1659 Scottish merchants continued to venture abroad

> but under the covert and pretext of being Dutch, in whose ports
> they enter theyr shippes and sayle with Dutch passes and mariners

[45] 'Fiars Prices in Aberdeenshire' in *Miscellany of the Third Spalding Club* II (1906). For the value of fiars prices as a crude indicator of market trends see Rosalind Mitchison, 'The Movement of Scottish Corn Prices in the Seventeenth and Eighteenth Centuries', *Economic Hist Rev*, 2nd ser, XVIII (1965).

[46] *Glasgow Burgh Records*, 283, 4 March 1654.

[47] Ibid.

[48] East Lothian apparently had a different experience. See Mitchison, loc cit, 281.

[49] Lythe, op cit, 28.

[50] *Aberdeen Council Letters*, 124.

[51] Elinor J. Courthope (ed), *The Journal of Thomas Cuningham of Campvere, 1640–1654* (Scottish History Society, 1928), 245–6.

> or els bring home theyr goods in Dutch bottomes, which are made
> over by bill of sale, and so become the shipps of the natives when
> they arrive there but once unladen, they depart, and are then
> Dutch bottomes again.[52]

The fact that maritime hostilities increased risk and diverted commerce for short periods from accustomed routes is beyond doubt. Equally, however, their longer term effects should be kept firmly in perspective.

[52] *Tucker's Report*, 30.

T. M. DEVINE

2

A Minor Scottish Merchant in General Trade: the case of Edward Burd 1728–39

The account books of Edward Burd junior show that he was in business in Edinburgh between 1728 and 1739.[1] The earliest other evidence that we have of him is contained in a diary which he kept while acting as a super-cargo on a trading voyage from Leith to Newfoundland and thence to Barcelona, returning to Leith in 1727.[2] This shows that by 1728, he had been already trained as a merchant since it incorporates many accounts prepared by him relating to his transactions on the voyage. Indeed it may have served as a finishing school for his commercial training and thus gave him the practical responsibility for his future career.[3] If this was its aim, it served him well. His diary shows that he carried a cargo of miscellaneous merchandise from Scotland, part of which he sold in Newfoundland, there purchasing cod, which he sold in Barcelona, and from there bringing a small amount of wine and other sundry items back to Leith. The documents relative to these transactions were meticulously kept and leave one with a very favourable impression about the training of an early eighteenth century Scottish merchant.

The diary also disclosed that he had been trained in a wider sense for his future responsibilities. For example, it shows that he dressed well in an age when dress betokened both class and authority. In Barcelona in 1727, he recorded that he had bought two suits, two wigs, handkerchiefs, lace, mixed silk stockings, and a silver snuff box. In Bordeaux, in that same year, he bought another suit, and a 'ribbon for my cane'. It is clear that in a sartorial sense he was anxious to maintain his personal and professional standing.

In the same way, his literary ambitions were far from being ordinary. His diary records that he possessed two sets of books, the first of which he was keen enough to carry on a hazardous voyage across the Atlantic. Their titles

---

[1] Scottish Record Office [SRO], MP 26–9, Waste Book and Journal 1728–34; accounts, letters and other papers 1720–40 of Edward Burd, wine merchant, Leith.

[2] SRO, RH 9/14, *Edinburgh and Leith Papers* – Journal of a Voyage Leith–Newfoundland–Barcelona, etc. by Edward Burd younger, merchant, Edinburgh, 1726–7.

[3] E. Trocmé, *Le Commerce rochelais de la fin du XVe siècle du XVIIe, etc.* (Paris, 1952), 18–19, outlines the responsibilities of supercargoes; R. Davis, *The Rise of the English Shipping Industry* (1962), 170 *et seq* has a comprehensive discussion of their duties.

are worth quoting in full:

> Idea rationaria or the Perfect Accomptant, Wingates Arithmetick, The Compleat Compting House, Hatton's Arithmetick, Ane Introduction to the first Principles of the Mathematicks by W. Alingham, a Treatise on Perspective written originally in ffrench, the Mariners New Calendar, the 4th Volume of the Spectator, The Laws of Poetry explained, Aristotles Art of Poetry Translated from the Original, Miscellanies of Prose and Verse by Dr. Swift, Drydens Miscellanies Vol. 1st. The Odes, Satyres & Epistels of Horace done into English by Mr. Creech, The Turkish Spy Vol. 7th the Art of English Poetry by Edward Bysh Gent, Vol. 1st. Vulgus Brittanicus or the British Hudibras, Shakespeares Comedies, Histories & Tragedies, Scarron Novels, The Campaign a Poem, ane Essay on Criticism, Love & Empire, a play—The Compleat Horseman or perfect ffarier, Boyers royal ffrench Dictionary abridged, La Guerre d'Italie, ou memoires de Comte de . . . Boyers ffrench grammar, Mr. Scots ffrench grammar, Gordons Geographical Grammar, the Civil Wars in Scotland under the Conduct of James Marquiss of Montrose by Willm. Adams—Enchiridion, Seasonable Advice a pamphlet, Seneca's Morals, 3 peaper books, a slate, the Holy Bible.

These books are a rare mixture of the practical and the aesthetic, to which he added several French titles, purchased in Bordeaux in 1727. This would seem to show that he aspired to an even wider culture than the average merchant of that time, although it is clear from the correspondence between him and his business associates that they had interests similar to his. Their letters range over a wide spectrum of economic, commercial, agricultural, political, strategic, social, and sociological topics. In these, one sees what a Scottish merchant of the time thought important to observe and comment upon, suggesting the many-sided facets of a class, who were well educated in the widest sense. Burd's diary and his other correspondence leave the reader in no doubt that he possessed these qualities, as well as an impressive cosmopolitanism. One is made aware of these attributes when one considers his religious attitudes, which are less partisan than one would expect from the scion of a family that had defended the Presbyterian settlement of 1688.[4] This moderation may be seen in many of his letters, of which the following quotation contained in his diary is typical. He is commenting upon English commercial factors in Barcelona:

> There are 3 English houses kept here Viz that kept by Windas and Girnan the first the English, and the other the Dutch Consull. That kept by Gregory ffrench and one kept by Harris, all of them very good men. The 2 Consulls have more than half the bufiness in the place, most of the ships from England and Holland being consigned to them. Mr Ffrench has the greatest part of his from Ireland and some from Scotland. They that consign to him have their goods better secured in his hands than with any of the others; in case of a sudden rupture with Spain: he being a denizen of Barcelona, and of

[4] *Register of the Privy Council* [RPC], Vol XIV, 145–147.

the popish religion. What business Mr Harris has is from Bristol &
a small matter from London.

There is little religious prejudice displayed in this excerpt in which he is pre-
occupied with business affairs. Instead there is an urbanity and a freedom from
the deep religious and political fanaticism which characterised the preceding
century.

When one examines Burd's family background, one can see how many of
these and other characteristics can be attributed to his antecedents. For example,
one finds Burd's grandfather taking part in a naval action in 1666 off Barbados
in support of the current establishment,[5] and his father leading an expedition
to reduce the Bass Rock in 1694, then held by supporters of the Jacobite cause.[6]
We also find him concerned in an incident to expel the Episcopalian minister
from Cranston Kirk in 1689,[7] whereas in 1685 he had been on the king's side
during the Monmouth rebellion.[8] It is obvious from these instances that
political and religious vacillation was part of a more fundamental purpose as
far as the Burds were concerned. Indeed one could suggest from a study of some
other of their attributes that they were more concerned with the maintenance of
a class structure that served them well.

In this role, we see them as members of the lesser gentry. Burd's grandfather
commanded a merchant ship of 180 tons, carrying seventy men and twenty
guns.[9] The size of his ship suggests that he was a man of means, as does his
marriage to Magdalen Howieson,[10] the daughter of a landed family, a status
which he confirmed by buying the lands of Ford in 1679,[11] previously having
been made a burgess and guild brother of Edinburgh in 1670.[12]

Burd's father had a similar career, first as the captain of a merchant ship,[13]
then as a captain in the Scottish navy. He married Elizabeth Hunter, a Bo'ness
merchant's daughter in 1698[14] and in the following year he became a burgess and
guild brother of Edinburgh.[15] A similar award was made to him by Glasgow
Town Council in 1704,[16] and he thus became a leading citizen of the two main
trading communities of Scotland. Subsequently, he became the laird of Ford on
his father's death in 1702.

Research on Burd's mother revealed that her family background closely
resembled that of her husband. Her father was a shipowner and merchant in

[5] Genealogical Account of the family of Burd [GA] held in the manuscript section of the
National Library of Scotland.
[6] Ibid.
[7] RPC, Vol XIV, 145–7.
[8] RPC, Vol XII, xxii.
[9] GA.
[10] Ibid.
[11] Ibid.
[12] SRS, C. B. B. Watson (ed), *Roll of Edinburgh Burgesses and Guild Brethren 1406–1700*
(Edinburgh, 1929), 87.
[13] RPC, Vol XIV, 620.
[14] GA.
[15] *Roll of Edinburgh Burgesses.*
[16] SRS, J. R. Anderson (ed), *The Burgesses and Guild Brethren of Glasgow 1573–1750*
(1925).

Edinburgh, and eventually he too became a landowner.[17] Her relations had careers similar to the Burds. One of her nephews, John Stirling, became Provost of Glasgow,[18] and he and Edward Burd, junior jointly inherited land bequeathed to them by the Hunter family at Bothkennar and Blairmuckhill.[19] Thus Burd's maternal relations comprised a close network of kin and family connections who were engaged in foreign trade, seafaring, merchanting, and landowning, a diversity that does not suggest the class divisions in Scottish society that one might expect from a study of their occupations. Furthermore, there was a professional leavening, members of the family being found in the law and the ministry. Others had careers in commerce in London, in the navy, and there was a selection of young men who spent their lives in commercial pursuits abroad.[20] In these they represented a family norm in Scotland for people of this background as other studies for this and other areas of Scotland make clear.[21]

Burd epitomises how well suited this social framework was to the contemporary economic situation in Scotland. It had important attributes which served him and his associates well. In the first instance it made him the centre of a network of acquaintances who supplied him with valuable mercantile information,[22] interspersed with small talk which showed their close connections. However, the latter feature was the shadow rather than the substance of their relationship, which was solidly grounded in the objectives of commercial life. In this sphere, he and his friends can be observed trading with France in the traditional way, aided by a factor who was a boyhood acquaintance, and who was himself part of a firm based on Edinburgh, run by his father and two brothers. Trade with the West Indies was maintained by two of Burd's immigrant friends who handled his transatlantic cargoes, and offered him information on what to export. There were many dealings with Edinburgh associates in London, mostly on the subject of finance and its supply; we can also see him acting as a factor for a group of Glasgow merchants to export agricultural products for the North Atlantic trade, the connection in this case being his cousin, Robert Stirling, who was one of the group.

These undertakings for a merchant of Burd's significance are impressive. They conjure up the picture of a major entrepreneur drawing upon large resources of stock and capital to maintain his business. It was certainly not like this. Burd was a very minor trader, indeed – as his account books show – he had few tangible resources. What he had was his status in the community, and the prospect of a landed inheritance in the future. It was clearly on the basis of

[17] Crichton Parish Register, 23 April 1705.

[18] R. Renwick (ed), Extracts from the Records of the Burgh of Glasgow, 1718–1738 (Glasgow, 1889), 306.

[19] Various entries in the Index to the General Register of Sasines 1700–20 show that the maternal side of Burd's family were landowners.

[20] Burd papers, passim; also GA.

[21] SRO, Inventory of the Bught papers, especially Section 6, which contains references to various letters of Bailie Gilbert Gordon, Merchant in Inverness; W. Mackay (ed), Letter Book of Bailie John Steuart of Inverness 1715–22 (Edinburgh, 1915), Scottish History Society, Second Series, Vol 9; T. M. Devine, The Tobacco Lords (Edinburgh, 1975), 4–5.

[22] Burd papers, passim.

the last two assets that he was able to start a business and maintain it in the commercial capital of Scotland with circulating capital of £5 4s 4¼d,[23] and some goods that he had purchased during his Newfoundland voyage. In these respects he represented the type of Scottish merchant of whom it has been said, 'there are few trades which cannot be carried on with a smaller stock in Scotland than in England'. His associates were no different in these national characteristics of an economy that had to be managed if economic progress was to take place in a way that would maintain the pool of enterprise represented by men such as Burd. Otherwise, the decisive moment on the way to further progress might have been checked. How this was done is the subject of this study of the credit structure of the period which was a crucial component of such advance.

The Credit Structure

Significant changes had taken place in the organisation of domestic credit in the period between the Union and 1728 when Burd set up his business in Edinburgh. An analysis of the position at the former date[24] shows the effect that periodic currency crises had on the Scottish economy, 'accelerating economic retrogression or stagnation if not actually causing them'. The same enquiry shows that the manner of settling obligations was by internal bills between the wealthy and on long credit and cash settlement among the poor.

> Bills of credit can never serve the uses of money – because no man
> can be compelled to believe anything to be good but what he thinks
> is so, and if people whether from reason or fancy shall not think
> bills as good as money, they cannot be forced on them.

It goes on to say on the subject of a liquidity crisis in 1704 caused by the outbreak of the war with France:

> The relationship, in fact, between the volume of credit currency
> and its specie equivalent depends both on the stability of confidence
> and the familiarity with the use of credit instruments. When the
> first collapsed, the second was not so fully developed that it could
> support the economy. Silver was indeed "a substitute for confidence"
> and the whole system of transmuting credit by bill was ultimately
> dependent on the specie equivalent of these bills.

The Burd papers show that by 1727, if not earlier, the situation so analysed had materially changed as far as domestic bills were concerned. In the first place, there is a great deal of evidence to suggest that there was less resistance to the use of bills, and that, among a wide spectrum of small merchants, retailers and petty tradesmen, they had become the main lubricant of their commercial activities; and for this economic group this development was crucial in a country chronically short of cash.[25]

For over a century bills had been used extensively in international trade,

---

[23] An analysis of the Waste Book shows this.
[24] T. C. Smout, *Scottish Trade on the Eve of the Union* (1963), 124 ff.
[25] H. Hamilton, *An Economic History of Scotland in the Eighteenth Century* (Oxford, 1963), 311.

but now they were involved in a wide range of domestic transactions. One could expect that this would happen as the lower levels of society became more familiar with them. There was another reason. Originally, bills had been promissory notes which normally had to be redeemed at 40 days sight, although this period varied according to circumstances. By 1727, there is a great deal of evidence to show that these bills circulated for far longer periods, a phenomenon that Adam Smith commented upon later in the century.[26] At least part of the reason for this practice was the payment of interest on any excess period. Burd paid 5 per cent for this service, the same rate as was paid on heritable bonds at the time. The consequences of this development are seen in the following humorous illustration from the Burd papers:

> . . . and also to inform you that this two nights I have not gott
> one owres rest for you by my wife for she has sworn that if you do
> not pay the interest the day or the morrow that she will give John
> Carmichael and you a charge of horning before Wednesday four o'
> clock . . .

This suggests that the redemption of the bill was not so important as the payment of interest. It was thus an impetus to keep bills in circulation, at least among acquaintances especially when the person was a good risk. Even if not, the first drawer of the bill was made liable for the payment of the bill.[27] It is suggested that this is why so many of Burd's own bills were outstanding for long periods of time.[28] In his case the effect of this is clear. What was initially a short-term credit device could now be used to serve long-term ends and thus add to the stock of circulating capital. Furthermore, it probably helped to develop two other attributes, the frequency with which bills were used, also the very small sums involved in some transactions. This and the other features are apparent from Burd's Waste Book.

Of the eighteen items recorded in the period 1 January to 20 February 1728, ten at least were settled by bills. Most of these were for very small sums which do not conjure up the financial sophistication associated with the term bills of exchange, as they were used by Burd in international trade. For example, the bill of 27 January was discharged by a barter arrangement comprising a pair of boots, two pairs of shoes, one pair of slippers, and a cash payment of 1/2d. On 31 January six pairs of silk stockings were paid for by a bill that the purchaser had received from another merchant. On 6 February, Burd significantly records, 'Sold to Mrs. Small for ready money a silk handkerchief – 3/6'. Of further interest is the evidence of merchants discounting bills on 31 January and 16 February. There is also an item showing a lawyer moving funds from one merchant to another by transferable bills.

From these instances, and many others in Burd's account books and statements, one can suggest that by 1728 domestic bills had become an auxiliary currency, and argue too that they had acquired a flexibility, which was a significant development from the time when they had been an elementary IOU

---

[26] Ibid, 317, quoting Adam Smith.
[27] infra p 23 for discussion of a legal action.
[28] The final statement of his affairs shows this.

for financing single deals. Now they possessed a degree of negotiability among business associates. Thus, they had taken on one of the main characteristics of an official currency. Again, this was a new feature and suggested a vitality and a sophistication in the economy that would not be apparent from a study of specie and its circulation.

The same tendency is apparent when one considers how the state helped in an institutional sense to diversify the credit arrangements of the country. For example, the Scottish customs allowed merchants to pay their customs duties by instalments. The entry in the Waste Book for 23 May 1732 shows two merchants acting as sureties for Burd. Payment was spread out over a period of eight months in four instalments. Merchants gave their customers similar concessions. A bill owed by Burd to an Edinburgh merchant for £289 3s 6d was paid in three instalments over the period of a year. And even the Kirk played its part as a letter of 1 March 1737 in the papers shows the Kirk Session of Cranston asking Burd to pay a debt, '. . . also pay your bill to the Session, they have present use for their money'.[29]

What the Kirk hallowed, the law enforced by recognising the most diverse credit facilities. A legal action raised by a merchant named Jamieson in 1736 illustrates this:

> I James Jameson Shipbuilder in Leith whereas Gilbert Burkell
> Shipmaster in Queensferry by his bill of date the eight day of
> August one thousand seven hundred and thirtyfive years drawn by
> him upon and accepted by Edward Burd junior merchant in Leith
> ordered him to pay . . . on his order at his house six months after
> the date the sum of twenty four pounds sterling for value received
> and was thereafter by me endorsed to George Keir and Halyburton
> merchants for value received of them (notwithstanding of my said
> endorsation) duly protested in my name against the said Edward
> Burd.

As may be seen this legal action concerns an original bill of exchange which had supported four transactions before becoming the subject of litigation. Other instances in the correspondence show that although recourse was often made to the law about failure to pay debts, such action seems in the main to have been taken against a defendant after a great deal of preliminary pressure and haggling for payment. However, when legal action was taken, it was effective. A letter to Burd from Henry Monteith, Bo'ness, dated 7 May, 1736 shows this: '. . . I received yours and there is at present a greater necessity of taking back your Bill than giving it away if you alow Diligence to be done on that Bill you will Certainly ruin me. . . .'

This practice of course would vary according to the temperament of individual merchants, some indulging in litigation more readily than others. However, a letter dated 25 November 1733 to Burd from his father suggests that certain conventions regarding the pressures which could fairly be brought on a debtor were becoming recognised, '. . . am surprised Mr. Hutchesone

---

[29] Burd had also raised money from the Kirk Session on a heritable bond. This transaction is referred to in his accounts.

should be so pressing there being onlie 14 daies past since term and the most rigid durer will alowe 3 weeks or a month'.

A consideration of conventions of this kind, simple as they are, allow one to put the whole question of bills of exchange being used in the domestic economy of Scotland in the early eighteenth century in perspective. Without a doubt, they were a development of earlier forms of credit. However, when one considers the difficulties associated with their use against a background in which the total money supply was probably smaller than the bills in circulation, it required a fairly disciplined society, aware of the necessity for goodwill between creditor and debtor, to make their continued use effective. If such qualities had been missing, the whole system might have periodically collapsed in an avalanche of lawsuits, above all at times when the economy was at the mercy of such natural hazards as bad harvests.[30] When such events occurred, it must have taken a great deal of constraint to refrain from going to law. Society therefore must have exerted some form of control on litigious individuals to maintain credit in the long-term interests of the economy. It did so by developing minor conventions, by using the institutional framework of kirk and government to extend credit, and by employing the law to uphold a plethora of transactions which in the last analysis depended a great deal upon trust among individuals.

These characteristics of the domestic credit structure can also be observed playing a part in the financial arrangements for foreign trade. There again, contemporaries might complain about the lack of specie, but this was offset by the diversity of credit made available to the merchant. We know, for example, that Burd started to import wine for the first time by selling some of his inheritance. However, later he kept his business going by raising money on heritable bonds;[31] this helps to explain why the universal practice of the period was for merchants to consider their personal and business assets to be part of their estate, confirmed by the book-keeping conventions of the period.[32]

He was also given credit by his factor in Bordeaux, Walter Pringle. The factor was able to do this through the medium of his father and two brothers who lived in Edinburgh and who looked after his interests there. As one would expect, many of the letters between Burd and Pringle dealt with the subject of finance, and in these one may observe the same kind of conventions that characterised the domestic bill of exchange. For example, in March 1732 Pringle writes to Burd as follows: 'You need never be uneasy about your bills in my father's hands', suggesting that Burd would have his credit extended if necessary. The same flexibility is seen even when Burd has difficulty in paying at a later date in 1736.

> ... All that you have to do is to talk with my Brothers Robert and
> John on the subject, and if they consent to our further dealings,
> they have only to write me a line and you may depend on my
> continual regard for your Interest.

[30] Smout, op cit, 125–7.
[31] These are referred to in his final statement of debts.
[32] A. C. Littlejohn and B. S. Yamey (eds), *Studies in the History of Accounting* (1956), 264.

At this time, Burd was beset with difficulties. Therefore, what Pringle required was his standing with the Edinburgh merchant community to be endorsed by his brothers. Another letter of 7 February 1736 shows that the factor was also aware of the general conditions that affected the provision of credit.

> ... You know how irregular your payments have been since the
> first of our dealings [1731] which was not only most inconvenient to
> my father, but also drew amongst with it a very great and unavoid-
> able expense on me. ... You know that the payments in our
> country are generally indifferent, and as my small fortune cannot
> alow me to be much in advance, without being attended by great
> loss and inconvenience ...

Apart from the special pleading about his impoverishment, Pringle here makes it clear that he also understands Burd's difficulties, and that it is in this context that his pleas for payment are being made. On reading the other correspondence on the same subject that passed between them, one is impressed by the remark-able forbearance that existed in their relationship. However, one can see that this was being strained by difficulties of a structural nature, which was restricting Scottish enterprise even in traditional markets. One can imagine too how these would be magnified without the use of bills of exchange if currency for one reason or another was in short supply. Trading, it might be thought, would inevitably be badly handicapped.

However, this was not so. In the very many items of the Burd correspond-ence, in the account books, in the Newfoundland journal, which deal with diverse foreign markets, such as the main centres of the Mediterranean, Bordeaux, Jamaica, Newfoundland, the use of specie for settlement was never mentioned. Every financial allusion, whether implicit or explicit, has bills of exchange as a central feature. Furthermore, with insignificant exceptions all of the bills referred to were those raised on the London money market.

In some respects, there is nothing remarkable about this at a time when this market dominated European finance along with Amsterdam. Indeed, English capital was made available to Scottish foreign enterprise in earlier periods.[33] The difference here is one of degree. As we have discussed, Burd was not a spectacular entrepreneur, few of his associates were, and yet bills of exchange or other credit devices originating in London were so prevalent a part of their trading pattern that one could say with some conviction that without them enterprise at this level would have been impossible at that time. Consider, for example, that Burd used English bills for his Bordeaux trade, and that even Pringle who supplied Burd with credit, was himself connected with the London bill market, as the following letter shows:

> Since mine of 11 October I have not any from you. I am extremely
> surprised to hear by last post from Mr. C. Flower [London broker]
> that you had not retired his draught on you and that his friend had
> advised you that in case you did not do it soon, he would return it
> to London: he adds that he did not doubt that my last bill on you
> would meet the same fate. Add to all this that I am advised that

[33] Smout, op cit, 122–3.

you still owe two hundred pounds of my former bills on you.

I cannot forbear expressing my astonishment at your way of acting, a small advance for a time to oblige you I should not much regard but such as this I cannot at all brook, and further I have reason to complain of you heavily for desiring me to draw on you payable in London, when you have not taken any manner of Care of my bills which both exposes yourself and me.

London 31 1/8
Amsterdam 55 5/16
Hamburg 27 3/8

There are many other letters written in similar vein about other trading areas such as those between Burd and a merchant Hardie on the subject of West Indian trade. However, the best composite illustration of the omnipresence of English capital is contained in the documents relating to the Newfoundland voyage, where it is shown as providing sustenance for a venture that was speculative and rudimentary.

Here was a voyage that was organised on traditional Scottish lines. In this respect, had it not been to Newfoundland, it could have been directed by Scottish merchants of two centuries before. Burd acted as a supercargo. The ship, *Christine* of Leith was a travelling market. 'You are to take the boat and go from place to place and make sale of the Bread'. This bread, 101½ cwt of it was provided by six Edinburgh merchants, who sponsored the voyage. A small additional cargo was carried for others, the captain's wife, the captain, another Edinburgh baillie, Burd himself. Here, the similarity with the past ended. Cod had to be purchased on the authority of a bill of credit provided by a London broker. Furthermore, there is evidence from Burd's observations in the Journal that other credit from England could readily be obtained.[34] Also, we find Burd obtaining cod from various English shippers on bills to be redeemed in London, as well as using English organisation for factoring, insurance, and protection throughout the trip from Newfoundland to Barcelona, and then to Bordeaux and Leith.[35]

The importance of this development is outlined by Sperling:[36]

> Without such facilities as the London money market the rapid
> expansion of trade and investment in the nineteenth century would
> have been impossible . . . [and] was no less so for the expansion
> which came in the late seventeenth and early eighteenth centuries
> and thus the method of financing trade in that early period is a
> matter of considerable importance in our understanding of economic
> development in the century before the Industrial Revolution.

This observation of Sperling is not specifically related to Scotland. Therefore

---

[34] Journal entry: '. . . therefor any body that have a mind to purchaſs a Cargoe here, would doe well to get their Credit upon *Exeter*, because this saves trouble to those they buy their fish from, in having their money remitted to them from London to Bristoll.'

[35] Journal, passim.

[36] J. Sperling, 'The International Payments Mechanism in the Seventeenth and Eighteenth Centuries', *Ec Hist Rev*, 2nd Series, Vol XIV, 1961–2, 446.

the importance of the Burd papers is that they demonstrate conclusively that what was true for other areas was also true there. English credit was being made available to the smallest type of Scottish merchant. This indicates that the relationship between Scotland and England was continuing to develop in significant ways, which must be an important factor in explaining the further expansion of Scotland's colonial trade, and her industry late in the eighteenth century. One must say, however, that at the beginning of this period Scotland had human and organisational assets, which she utilised well. Compared with her great neighbours, England and Holland, she had scanty economic resources, but she had more nebulous ones that were going to be of real significance when the time came.

T. McALOON

3

English Influences in the Scottish Coal Industry 1700–1815

Though the history of the Scottish coal industry in the century which the late Henry Hamilton made peculiarly his own is now tolerably well known,[1] there remain several areas of interest where further research and speculation might prove fruitful. One such sphere is the extent and significance of English influences in Scottish coal mining between, very roughly, the Act of Union and the year of Waterloo. Economic historians have long recognised the importance of foreign contacts to Scottish growth and have frequently stressed the importance of access to wider markets gained from closer integration with England.[2] Not unnaturally, perhaps, Scotland's entry into the common market of the Old Colonial System has been most remarked upon; and though it has been taken for granted that the easier advance of English ideas into Scotland after 1707 was often stimulating, the process has lacked extensive documentation.

In the economic sphere, at least, many eighteenth-century Scotsmen conceded that assimilation of English practices was a likelier spur than a threat to Scottish culture.[3] Indeed emotional nationalism is conspicuous largely by its absence from most contemporary discussion of comparative technologies – a situation which doubtless rested on Scotland's wider European contacts from Renaissance times.[4] Possibly Alexander Wedderburn spoke for more of his

[1] See for instance Henry Hamilton, *An Economic History of Scotland in the Eighteenth Century* (Oxford, 1963), 185–9, 205–12; Baron F. Duckham, *A History of the Scottish Coal Industry 1700–1815* (Newton Abbot, 1970). A list of relevant monographs and articles appears in my bibliography in the reprinted edition (1971) of R. L. Galloway, *Annals of Coal Mining and Coal Trade*, Vol I (1898).

[2] H. Hamilton, *The Industrial Revolution in Scotland* (Oxford, 1932), 3–4; Andrew M. Carstairs, 'Some Economic Aspects of the Union of Parliaments', *Scottish Journal of Political Economy*, II, 1 (1955); R. H. Campbell, *Scotland Since 1707: the Rise of an Industrial Society* (Oxford, 1965), 38–42; G. S. Pryde (ed), *The Treaty of Union of Scotland and England, 1707* (1950).

[3] 'Sir John Clerk's Observations on the present circumstances of Scotland, 1730', ed T. C. Smout, *Miscellany* of the Scottish History Society, Vol X (Edinburgh, 1964), 175–212; N. T. Phillipson, 'Scottish Public Opinion and the Union in the Age of the Association', in N. T. Phillipson and Rosalind Mitchison (eds), *Essays in Scottish History in the Eighteenth Century* (Edinburgh, 1970), 143.

[4] See S. G. E. Lythe, *The Economy of Scotland in its European Setting 1550–1625* (Edinburgh and London, 1960); T. M. Devine and S. G. E. Lythe, 'The economy of Scotland under James VI: a Revision Article', *The Scottish Historical Review*, L, 2, No 150, October 1971.

fellow countrymen than even he supposed when he wrote in 1756:

> If our Agriculture and Manufactures were improved and carried on
> to the height they could bear, we might be near as easy and
> convenient in our circumstance, as even the People of our Sister
> Kingdom England . . . if we are far behind [he urged] we ought to
> follow further.[5]

And as Dr Phillipson has recently noted, Wedderburn liked to picture Scotland as being still in 'a state of early youth, guided and supported by the more mature strength of her kindred country'.[6] It is a commonplace that Scotland made great strides in the development of her mineral resources during the eighteenth century. It will be suggested here that a significant feature of this industrial evolution, in so far as it concerned coal, was an ultimate dependence on English experience. An attempt to demonstrate this proposition must necessarily lead us into some of the byeways as well as the highways of the interrelationships in technology, capital and entrepreneurial inputs. At the risk of an all-to-obvious pun, it may be pleaded that a subject as down to earth as coal extraction must not neglect to start at grass roots.

Before the Union, English involvement in the Scottish coal industry would appear to have been minimal and assuredly less than the seventeenth-century interest in Scottish lead noted by Professor Smout.[7] Nef's comments on the Scottish experience do not suggest other than that North Britain's coal industry, in practice perhaps more than in theory, had to be largely self-sufficient in both capital investment and technical skills during the sixteenth and seventeenth centuries.[8] Nor can it be doubted that even by 1707 Scottish coal mining technology was on almost all counts more backward than that existing in England's great northern coalfield of Durham and Northumberland. The fact that it has become almost fashionable to point out that one of the most advanced collieries in the whole of Britain in the early seventeenth century was at Culross merely proves the rule by its clearly unique status in Scotland.[9] Indeed, in the preamble of the lease by which Sir George Bruce of Carnock acquired the mining rights there in 1575, especial mention was made of Bruce's exceptional attributes and he was specifically commended:[10]

> for his great knowledge and skill in machinery like *no other man has*
> *in these days*; and for his being the likeliest person to re-establish
> again the Colliery of Culross, which has long been in desuetude . . .

[5] Quoted by Phillipson, loc cit, 143.

[6] Ibid.

[7] T. C. Smout, 'Lead-mining in Scotland, 1650–1850', in P. L. Payne (ed), *Studies in Scottish Business History* (1967), 103–35. See also idem, 'The Lead Mines at Wanlockhead', *Transactions of the Dumfriesshire and Galloway Natural History Society*, XXXIX, 1962. The English connection finds mention, too, in W. S. Harvey, 'Lead Mining in 1768: Old Records of a Scottish Mining Company', *Industrial Archaeology*, VII, 3, 1970.

[8] J. U. Nef, *The Rise of the British Coal Industry* (1932), passim. This is of course not to deny the influence of some outside ideas, particularly from Germany; see my *Scottish Coal Industry*, 71–2, and Lythe, *Economy of Scotland*, 48.

[9] A. I. Bowman, 'Culross Colliery: a Sixteenth-Century Mine', *Industrial Archaeology*, VIII, 4, 1970.

[10] Quoted in 9th Earl of Dundonald, *Description of the Estate, particularly of the Mineral and Coal Property . . . at Culross* (Edinburgh, 1793). The full text is given on pp 9–11. My italics.

Certainly Bruce spared no pains in developing the mines. He sank a moat pit on the foreshore of the Forth and installed an Egyptian wheel powered by horses to drain the workings from another shaft. A. I. Bowman, has argued that the date of this innovation cannot have been later than 1590 and reminds us that Bruce's employment of such a wheel is still the earliest certainly known to us within the context of British coal mining.[11] Its source was quite conceivably a plate in Agricola's *De Re Metallica* which had appeared in 1556.

Culross quickly became an object of national pride, a source of wonder to princes and even, somewhat improbably, an inspiration to poets. James VI is believed to have visited the mine in 1617 while the 'water poet', John Taylor, penned one of the more enthusiatic effusions of his *Pennyless Pilgrimage* about a year later. Nef, too, has assured us that 'no such ambitious industrial undertaking had hitherto been thought of in Scotland'[12] – a remark which perhaps suggests a curiously intimate knowledge of the economic dreams of the day. No reliable details of the exact scale of investment involved have come down to us, but despite Bruce's central rôle it remains not improbable that at least some English expertise may have underpinned the enterprise. The roughly contemporary Burgh records of Dunfermline mention the presence of English workmen (in less than flattering terms, let it be admitted),[13] while one of the mine's features praised by Taylor, namely the underground headings 'artificially cut like an arch or vault' have proved to be more common at this period than once was thought.[14] However Bruce's example assuredly bred some progeny. It is clear, for instance, that Egyptian wheels had by the 1690s become a reasonably common mode of draining those Scottish collieries which could not be worked by simple levels or adits.

Yet it is well to remember that the Egyptian wheel drained pits by the primitive method of chain and buckets. For the introduction of genuine mine pumps Scotland had undoubtedly to turn to outside assistance. Windmills, introduced at first very slowly from England and Holland from the fifteenth century onwards were occasionally pressed into colliery service to operate pumps. Sinclair had urged the windmill's theoretical superiority over horsepower for just this problem of mine drainage in 1672,[15] but actual recorded instances of such use are usually eighteenth-century.[16] Scottish skills were scarce and in 1708 John Young, a native of Montrose, was sent to Holland at public expense to learn from Dutch prototypes.[17] But whether Holland or England injected further technical knowledge is somewhat academic. The windmill never won a very common distribution in Scotland (two recent writers conclude

---

[11] Bowman, 'Culross Colliery', loc cit.

[12] Nef, *Coal Industry*, I, 43.

[13] A. Shearer (ed), *Extracts from the Burgh Records of Dunfermline* (Dunfermline, 1951), 126.

[14] Similar arch-shaped vaulting has been discovered, for instance, in mediaeval mine workings accidentally broken into at Chopwell Colliery, County Durham. See A. R. Griffin *Coalmining* (1971), 6.

[15] George Sinclair, *Hydrostaticks* (Edinburgh, 1672); I have used the second edition: *Natural philosophy Improven by New Experiments* (1683), 298. Sinclair mentions his having seen effective windmills in Holland specifically.

[16] Duckham, *Coal Industry*, 77–8.

[17] Robert Bald, *A General View of the Coal Trade of Scotland* (Edinburgh, 1808), 7–8.

that only about 100 were erected for all purposes whatsoever between the sixteenth and nineteenth centuries)[18] and coalmasters in particular commented unfavourably on its reliability.[19]

Yet by the early eighteenth century water undoubtedly represented the most serious single obstacle in all but the most under-developed coalfields. As mines of necessity probed deeper, so the need for efficient pumping became acute. Though entrepreneurs in the less heavily exploited areas continued the time-honoured ploy of extensive rather than intensive operations,[20] the method was wasteful, was often thwarted by transport problems and was by definition no longer applicable in the more advanced fields. It must be conceded that the provision of adequate drainage is so central to the evolution of mining and occupies so large a part of its investment strategy that one cannot escape some consideration here of its progress in Scotland. Moreover it is one area in the development of the Scottish coal industry where English influence is only too evident.

The 6th Earl of Mar was the first Scots coalowner to invite an English engineer of real stature to Scotland. Faced with the imminent ruin of his mining enterprises at Alloa by flooding, the earl dispatched his colliery manager to Newcastle in 1709 to procure drawings of the best means of drainage available. In the following year he offered George Sorocold a fee of £50 to inspect his mines.[21] Sorocold, a considerable figure in the history of hydraulic engineering, was responsible among many other projects for the water power at Thomas Lombe's famous silk mill near Derby, for various schemes of river navigation and for the early water supply of several towns.[22] He advised replacement of the earl's bucket and chain drainage by a beam pumping engine driven by a waterwheel. According to Robert Bald, writing just under a century later, the advice could not be immediately taken – not, as one might suspect from a lack of liquid capital, but because 'still there could be found no person in Scotland to put his plans in execution'.[23] Since Bald's father was manager of the Alloa Collieries from 1774 – a position to which Robert eventually succeeded – and since presumably both had access to the records, the explanation for inaction may well be no exaggeration. Yet that this engine or a similar one *was* built later is certain; for when William Brown, the famous Tyneside mining viewer, visited the Erskines' mines at Alloa in 1774, he found a waterwheel of

[18] Ian L. Donnachie and Norma Stewart, 'Scottish Windmills: an Outline and Inventory', *Proceedings of the Society of Antiquaries of Scotland*, XCVIII, sessions 1964–6, 276–99.

[19] Sir John Clerk II of Penicuik complained about a frequent 'Want of Wind, which one wou'd not readily suspect in a Country like Scotland', 'Dissertation' [on coal mining], Clerk of Penicuik MSS, S[cottish] R[ecord] O[ffice] GD 18/1069 (1740); see also Baron F. Duckham, 'Some Eighteenth-Century Scottish Coal Mining Methods: the "Dissertation" of Sir John Clerk', *Industrial Archaeology*, V (1968).

[20] Extensive mining normally implied shallow workings at the outcrop (the so-called 'in-gaun e'en') and the sinking of small bell pits which were abandoned as soon as drainage or other difficulties were encountered.

[21] Bald, *Coal Trade of Scotland*, 10.

[22] F. Williamson, 'George Sorocold of Derby. A Pioneer of Water Supply', *Derby Archaeological Society Journal*, LVII (new series, X, 1936).

[23] Bald, *Coal Trade of Scotland*, 11. See also T. C. Smout, 'The Erskines of Mar and the Development of Alloa, 1689–1825', *Scottish Studies*, VII (1963).

exceptionally sophisticated design being employed not merely for drainage, but to wind coal.[24]

A number of beam or 'bob' engines powered by waterwheels can be accounted for in both the Scottish coal and lead industries, and in most cases English influences appear strong. In 1738 or 1739, for example, the 10th Earl of Rothes had one installed at Strathore, Fife. This engine was fitted with twin beams and its builder was Stephen Row (or Rowe), almost certainly an Englishman. Surviving records of the Rothes MSS shows that its crank and pump barrels were imported from south of the border.[25] Yet another such engine built to an English design was that erected for the 6th Earl of Leven in 1785 or 1786. The Leeds Engineer J. Green provided the initial survey and plans, though their execution in modified form was the work of Henry Renwick.[26] Incidentally, we ought not to underestimate the ingenuity of much water-powered machinery; and it perhaps helps us to maintain a correct perspective if we recall that many of the best engineering minds of the century – such as Smeaton's – gave considerable thought to its improvement or that for the provision of rotary motion it found increasingly wide industrial employment outside mining. Despite its ancient lineage water power was still a developing technology both theoretically and practically until the age of James Watt.

Yet however significant the rôle of water power in facilitating deeper coal winnings and however obliging the Scottish weather in providing generally ample sources of water, the insistent pressures of an expanding market soon demanded mining operations beyond the capacity of even the improved water engines to sustain. The first successful application of steam to mine pumping occurred in 1712 at the Coneygree Colliery, Tipton, near Dudley.[27] Before the end of the decade the Newcomen engine had also reached Scotland. Inevitably all the early engines erected north of the Tweed represented an introduction of what was until beyond mid-century basically the spearhead of English mechanical technology. Until the founding of Carron Ironworks there was no possibility of local supply, however thoroughly Scotsmen had understood the engine's principles. Scotland was thus functionally incapable of providing her

[24] Statistical Account of Scotland, VII (1793), 616; Bald, Coal Trade of Scotland, 89. Brown was so impressed by this engine (which possessed double sets of buckets, divided vertically, and could be instantly reversed) that he built one in the Tyne coalfield. It is tempting to think the basic design was originally Sorocold's.

[25] Rothes MSS (Kirkcaldy Museum), estimate and papers (some undated of c 1738). Row(e) was introduced to Strathore by Lord Elphinstone, who had viewed the mines for the earl. It is just possible that he was connected with the Row family, mentioned as waggon-makers, etc, at 'Fellon' [Felling?] Colliery by E. Hughes, North Country Life in the Eighteenth Century: vol I: the north east 1700–1750 (1952), 155 n. Row also reported on the coalfield at Campbeltown in 1743 (information from Mr J. Howdle).

[26] Leven and Melville MSS, SRO GD26/V/352, documents dated 1785, including a plan of 6 May 1785.

[27] J. S. Allen, 'The 1712 and other engines of the Earls of Dudley', Transactions of the Newcomen Society, XXXVII (1964–5). There has been a fair amount of controversy about the site of Newcomen's first engine. See the summary in L. T. C. Rolt, Thomas Newcomen: the Prehistory of the Steam Engine (Dawlish, 1963), 61–5 and the bibliography, 143–5; J. S. Allen, 'The Introduction of the Newcomen Engine from 1700–1733', Transactions of the Newcomen Society, XLII (1969–70).

own steam power for a good fifty years after its appearance in England, and until the 1760s dependence in this respect on engineering capacity south of the Tweed was consequently absolute.

Exact dating of the advance of steam technology in Scotland remains a little difficult, but primacy for erecting a Newcomen engine still probably belongs to the York Buildings Company who built one in c 1719 at Tranent Colliery, East Lothian – mines acquired from the forfeited estates of the 5th Earl of Winton after the 1715 Rising.[28] This engine we can now number as the eighteenth or nineteenth set up in Britain, and it was quickly joined by other Scottish examples at Saltcoats in Ayrshire, Elphinstone, Stirlingshire, and, apparently, at Dryden near Edinburgh – all, moreover, in the period c 1719–20.[29] By the time the Savery patent – under which the early Newcomen engines were built – had expired in 1733 at least eighty-three such engines had been erected of which only seven or eight were in Scotland. At least eight had been sent abroad. A number of 'possible' engines has recently been tabulated by Mr J. S. Allen of the Newcomen Society which could bring the total to 106 by the end of the patent, but the Scottish sub-total would remain unaffected.[30] The very latest research indicates a much larger number of Newcomen engines having been produced by 1800 than most scholars have suspected and indeed they may have been as many as 1,700.[31] By this date only about eighty Scottish mining examples are yet known – fewer for instance than existed in the Durham – Northumberland coalfield alone in 1769, the date of John Smeaton's famous survey there.[32]

Despite Scotland's less than impressive record in the introduction of steam power to her coalfields, there is no doubt that Scots coalmasters welcomed the Newcomen engine in principle and were not deterred by any possible local resentment against innovation or the associated immigration of skilled crafts-men. They recognised that the transmission of technical knowledge rested on their willingness to admit, with respect to England, that 'contact with another state of civilisation' was vital. A few coal proprietors made journeys south and we are fortunate in having the journals kept by the Midlothian coalowner Sir John Clerk II of Penicuik of his pilgrimages to both Newcastle and White-

---

[28] D. Murray, *The York Buildings Company* (Glasgow, 1883), 65. J. L. Carvel, *One Hundred Years in Coal: the History of the Alloa Coal Company* (Edinburgh, 1944), 13, suggests that a very early Newcomen engine was built at Alloa, but I have not seen reliable confirmation of this.

[29] Baron F. Duckham, 'Early Application of Steam Power at Scottish Collieries: a Note and Query', *Industrial Archaeology*, VI (1969); idem, *Coal Industry*, 81–2; J. H. G. Lebon, 'The Development of the Ayrshire Coalfield', *Scottish Geographical Magazine*, XLIX (1933).

[30] I am indebted to Mr Allen for allowing me to see his typescript of addenda to his paper of 1969–70 cited in note 27.

[31] Professor J. R. Harris in his 'Employment of Steam Power in the Eighteenth Century', *History*, LII (1967) demonstrated the inadequacy of all previous estimates, though his own figures, particularly for Scotland, have proved to be too low. Dr J. A. Robey of the Newcomen Society probably now possesses the fullest list.

[32] My own estimates, like those of Professor Harris, now seem rather conservative but I doubt whether further research will uncover a total of more than about a hundred Scottish colliery steam engines by 1800. See my *Coal Industry*, 81–7.

haven.[33] In 1724 he visited the collieries of Richard Ridley to scrutinise at first hand both mining methods and the local steam engines. As he recorded,[34]

> In order to understand my coal affairs I thought fit to take a Trip to Newcastle for there I understood that the perfection of coal [working] was to be learned both in relation to the Machines necessary above Ground & the easiest ways of working below Ground.

The journal leaves no doubt that Clerk learnt much from his visit, and some of the ideas he noted were later incorporated in his own collieries at Loanhead, Midlothian – as the family muniments bear witness. It is worth mentioning that Clerk took with him his son James, later destined to assume management of the family coal concerns. Since Sir John himself, James, and a younger son, John Clerk of Eldin, all became respected coalmasters, amateur mineral surveyors and mining 'engineers' often consulted by their fellow coalowners, it is clear that notions culled from English practice might be widely diffused. In fact overt reference to Newcastle methods occurs in at least one of the surviving opinions written by Sir John Clerk on the mines of one of his neighbours.[35] Clerk also composed a 'dissertation' on what he considered the best mining technology of his day and although apparently never published, it was read among his circle of acquaintances.[36] In it he shows familiarity with the proceedings of the Royal Society and with that early and delightfully quaint treatise of Tyneside mining, *The Compleat Collier* (Newcastle, 1708). He also demonstrates awareness of Belgian technology, a fact which tends to confirm that Scots continued to be receptive to new ideas, whatever their source, and were no way mesmerised by English example alone. Clerk's journey to Whitehaven in 1739 likewise put him in touch with West Cumberland mining practice.[37] He was unimpressed personally with the coalowning Sir James Lowther ('. . . in the midst of great riches [he] lives but in a poor way. He is an indolent old man and knows nothing of coalworks')[38] but he admired his mines, together with their waggon-ways and steam power under the efficient direction of the great Carlisle Spedding.

At both Newcastle and Whitehaven Clerk expatiated on the virtues of

[33] There are now many printed references to Sir John Clerk. Those immediately relevant are noted in the references to Baron F. Duckham, 'Life and Labour in a Scottish Colliery, 1698–1755', *Scottish Historical Review*, XLVII (1968), but see especially J. M. Gray (ed), *Memoirs of the Life of Sir John Clerk. . .*, Scottish Historical Society, Vol XIII (Edinburgh, 1892). The journals of the trips to Newcastle and Whitehaven have now been published (the former selectively): F. Atkinson, 'Some Northumberland Collieries in 1724', *Transactions of the Archaeological & Antiquarian Society of Durham & Northumberland*, XI (1965) and W. A. J. Prevost (ed), 'A trip to Whitehaven to visit the coalworks there in 1739 by Sir John Clerk', *Transactions of the Cumberland & Westmorland Antiquarian and Archaeological Society*, new series, LXV (1965).

[34] Clerk of Penicuik MSS, SRO GD18/2106, 'Journey to England in Aprile 1724'.

[35] Ibid, SRO GD18/1074, 'Observations on the Coal Works of Ormistone', 15 April 1743. Here he commends the economy of Newcastle methods of haulage and winding and states that his own 'coaliers, as in England, go all down, by the Rop[e]s & buckets which bring up the coal'.

[36] See the reference to my article on the 'dissertation' in note 19.

[37] Ibid, GD 18/2106, 'Journey to Whitehaven in 1739'.

[38] Ibid.

steam pumping and confided to his earlier journal that the Newcomen engine was 'one of the finest inventions ever discovered'. Yet steam was not introduced into the Loanhead mines during the lifetimes of either Sir John II or James, whilst, as has been hinted, the spread of the engine, despite enthusiasm was slow in Scotland. In 1769, when Smeaton calculated that some 100 engines had been built in Durham and Northumberland, Scotland had apparently no more than fourteen or fifteen.[39] The dilemma, as Clerk himself recognised, was the problematic nature of investment in steam power, given the Scottish economic context. Until the age of coke-burning ironworks and a more buoyant demand from other industrial and domestic consumers, the sinking of between £1,000 and £1,500 in a Newcomen engine and its equipment was a decision hard to justify except at the very largest mines.[40] Many Scots coalmasters were small producers with no considerable reserves of capital and few, even on the Forth, had developed a sizeable export trade. Doubtless they would have pleaded with Adam Smith that the degree of specialisation or technical sophistication possible was determined by the extent of the market.

One could also of course argue that the close involvement of petty lairds with mining[41] – and the estate colliery was still the typical unit of production for well into the eighteenth century – was one of the factors restraining a wider market-consciousness in the Scottish coal industry. As Devine and Lythe have recently pointed out, with reference to an earlier period it is true, much 'coal and salt production . . . could legitimately be viewed simply as extensions of landed estate exploitation';[42] and while typically a desire for greater cash sales was usual, there were lairds with an evident distaste for really large-scale output and a fear of the disruptions of industrialisation.[43] Before the 1760s, too, steam meant sending south of the border for help. Whilst there is testimony that most coalmasters welcomed English ideas, a native frugality did not always relish the expense of their importation.

English investment in mining ventures north of the Tweed was one theoretical solution. In practice, however, the influx of English capital into Scottish coal was hardly likely to be considerable so long as profitable outlets for such investment remained open in the local coalfields. And yet, following the Act of Union, some awakening of English intervention in northern mining was, as Professor Smout has shown, evident in silver and lead. The facts that Forth and Ayrshire coal had often ready access to tidal water and that Scottish seasale was innocent of so powerful an organisation as the Vend at Newcastle,[44]

[39] This is my own estimate.

[40] The cost of several Scottish engines is known and this range seems a fair average. By contrast a water wheel with beam-operated pumps cost only about £250, Duckham, *Coal Industry*, especially chapter 3.

[41] The background to the rôle of landowners in the Scottish coal industry in this period is supplied by T. C. Smout, 'Scottish landowners and economic growth', *Scottish Journal of Political Economy*, IX (1964) and my *Coal Industry*, 141–69.

[42] Devine and Lythe, 'Economy of Scotland under James VI', loc cit.

[43] Duckham, *Coal Industry*, 168–9.

[44] I do not wish to suggest there were no attempts to organise among, say, the Forth producers. In fact references in several family muniments, but particularly in the Cadell of Grange MSS [N]ational [L]ibrary of [S]cotland, Acc 5381, show regular meetings of the chief coalmasters were held. This was also true of the Glasgow area.

or was free from the domination of two or three large families as in West
Cumberland, were enough to attract *some* investment. The possibility of extending Scotland's share of the Irish coal market (in the case of Ayrshire) or of
contributing to the rich London trade from the Forth were the stimuli to English
investment. Moreover the capital cost of opening a new seasale mine in Scotland
was generally believed to be less onerous than its counterpart in England.

The York Buildings Company, which at one time or another had a finger
in almost every available economic pie – and which like the busy cook usually
succeeded in burning them all comprehensively – invested some £3,500 in
colliery facilities at Tranent on the former Winton estates.[45] Such financial input
was high by the standards of the day in Scottish coal mining. But despite their
enlarging the harbour at Port Seaton (Cockenzie) and building what still
seems to be the first authenticated waggonway in Scotland to it from the mines,
the Company proved unable to net £500 profit per annum from their coal and
salt complex. The works eventually passed, first by lease and then by sale, into
the hands of John Cadell of Cockenzie, brother of William Cadell, founder of
Carron.[46] We shall have occasion to mention the family again.

In Ayrshire the earliest appearance of substantial English capital in mining
occurred at Saltcoats, where the temporary eclipse of the Cuninghame family
after the death of Robert in 1717 left a void in local coal exploitation never
properly filled until the flamboyant Robert Reid Cuninghame began operations
in 1774.[47] After unsuccessful local efforts to continue the mines had failed two
successive English consortia ran them: the first from c 1712 to 1728, employing
a Newcastle engineer to oversee the technical operations; the second with at
least some capital from as far afield as Falmouth until 1731.[48] Neither fared
materially better than the local lessees had done and, like the York Buildings
Company, their retiral from coal winning was somewhat ignominious. Most
English exertions in Scottish mineral affairs in this period remained directed
towards lead exploitation where the industry was, as a large-scale venture,
younger than coal and where the hope of a lucky strike in prospecting offered
more seductive attractions for the optimistic than did the seemingly more stable
coal industry. No English investment in Scottish coal during the first half of
the eighteenth century was at once long-term and important. Thus much of the
penetration of Tyneside or West Cumberland mining technology came rather
through personal contact than through English capital, though there must have
been some spill-over from English involvement in lead, if only because a

[45] Murray, *York Buildings Company*, 22, 65–6.
[46] Ibid, 65–6; H. M. Cadell, *The Story of the Forth* (Glasgow, 1913), 175; idem, *The
Rocks of West Lothian: an Account of the Geological History of the West Lothian District* (Edinburgh and London, 1925), 325–6; Cadell of Grange MSS, NLS, Acc 5381, bound Vol 1.
[47] *Statistical Account of Scotland*, VII (1793), 9–10; N. M. Scott, 'Documents relating to
Coal Mining in the Saltcoats District in the First Quarter of the Eighteenth Century.'
Scottish Historical Review, XIX, 1922; Baron F. Duckham, 'Mining Technology at a West
of Scotland Colliery 1770–1800: a Case Study', *Industrial Archaeology*, X, 1, February
1973.
[48] Duckham, *Coal Industry*, 171; Anon, *Stevenston Past and Present* (Saltcoats, 1902), 31;
George Robertson, *A Genealogical Account of the Principal Families in Ayrshire*, Vol I (1823).

number of Scottish landowners who participated in lead mining were also coalowners.[49]

With the founding of Carron Ironworks in 1759–60, however, a new phase begins, catching increasing momentum from the establishment of further ironworks from the 1780s. Carron's history has been well analysed by Professor Campbell.[50] Let us, however, remind ourselves that of the three original founding partners (William Cadell Senior, John Roebuck and Samuel Garbett) the latter two were Englishmen. Moreover they had connections with South Yorkshire and the Midlands and, as far as they were necessarily interested in coal, they represented a mining tradition different from that of the North East and North West of England which had hitherto not unnaturally been the chief sources of English influence at work.

Carron decisively broke the 'cake of custom' in Scottish coalmining as it did in ironmaking. Unlike the earlier incursions of the Furness ironmasters who sought to establish a charcoal iron industry in the West Highlands,[51] Carron had an immediate impact on the local coal industry. Even before the first furnace was blown in, the partners, worried about both the quantity and quality of their coal supplies, had taken direct action to inject greater dynamism into the local situation. By investing in iron, the partnership had also committed itself to investment in coal. One of the company's first employees was a 'burner of coal' to test the standard of the available resources. He came, significantly from England.[52]

The company's early history is replete with agreements with neighbouring lairds for coal supplies or, even more typically, with the partnership itself taking up mining leases so that operations could be prosecuted with greater vigour – as at Kinnaird, Quarrole, Brightons, Westerton, Reddingmuir, Shieldhall and Carronhall.[53] As early as 1761 a count of the Carron labour force showed 246 out of a total of 615 engaged in mining. But the scale of fuel needs, together with what was seen as a possibly fruitful business opportunity, meant that the partners themselves quickly became independent coalmasters in their own right. In each of the major coal companies so established, English capital played a part: namely in the Bo'ness Colliery leased by John Roebuck from the dukes of Hamilton; and in the Grange Coal Company owned ultimately by the Cadells.

Since outline histories of these concerns already exist,[54] it is more relevant

---

[49] The earls of Hopetoun spring to mind, but there were also in any minimum count the dukes of Buccleuch, at least one Earl of Cassillis, Sir John Erskine of Alva and various lesser lairds.

[50] R. H. Campbell, *Carron Company* (Edinburgh, 1961). An earlier reference is H. Hamilton, 'The Founding of Carron Ironworks', *Scottish Historical Review*, XXV, 1928.

[51] See Alfred Fell, *The Early Iron Industry of Furness and District* (Ulverston, 1908).

[52] Campbell, *Carron Company*, 33.

[53] J. M. Reid, *Traveller Extraordinary; the Life of James Bruce of Kinnaird* (1968), 32, 286–7, 300–1; Campbell, *Carron Company*, 49.

[54] Cadell, *Rocks of West Lothian*, 326–39; T. J. Salmon, *Borrowstounness and District, being Historical Sketches of Kinneil, Carriden, and Bo'ness* (Edinburgh and London, 1913), passim; Duckham, *Coal Industry*, 174–9; Cadell of Grange MSS, NLS, Acc 5381, bound Vol 1.

here to try to estimate the significance of the English involvement in them. Briefly, on financial criteria alone, neither Roebuck at Bo'ness nor the Cadells' English partners at Grange (the Beaumonts) were very successful. Roebuck died insolvent in 1794 while the activities of John Beaumont junior at Grange were unfortunate, to say the least. The Grange lease had been taken up in 1770 by William and John Cadell (sons of the co-founder of Carron) in equal partner- ship with Beaumont, but the Cadells had soon assigned the tack to Beaumont, aided by his younger brother Charles.[55] The sederunt book and other sources confirm that John Beaumont soon developed a 'triffling [sic] manner of con- ducting his undertaking'[56] and he proved quite unable to produce a minimum of 200 tons of saleable great coal a week – a commitment he had made to the Cadells in 1775. By 1778 Beaumont owed the Cadells some £15,700 in royalty arrears, lease penalties and other debts and two years later John and William took operations back into their own hands entirely.[57] But English contact at these collieries, as well as at some of the mines leased by Carron, has a wider importance than is to be discovered merely by inspecting balance sheets. John Beaumont, for all his personal failings (and he does not seem to have allowed business to interfere over much with pleasure) was directly connected with Tyneside mining practice, where his father, John Beaumont senior, worked mines at Newbiggin and Brunton. Beaumont senior was made of sterner stuff than his son, and his advice on both technical matters and accountancy pro- cedures was sought on several occasions by William Cadell.[58] At a more general level, one English technological influence was the improvement of both surface and underground transportation through the spread of the waggon- way.

As early as 1754 the then lessees of the Duke of Hamilton's minerals on the Kinneil estates had employed the Tynesider, William Brown, to supervise the installation of what was probably the first underground railway in Scotland – at Bo'ness Colliery.[59] This was extended by Roebuck and the innovation was applied to some of Carron's mines near Falkirk. Surface lines were introduced on several mining sites, mostly following in construction the traditions of the English Midlands. As is well known, Carron Company imported skilled work- men from Coalbrookdale and both this fact and the example of the earlier line at Tranent (well known to the Cadells) determined the form of these early horse railways. By the late 1760s ,when a waggonway on the north bank of the Forth from the Alloa collieries of the Erskines had been opened, several Shrop-

[55] Cadell of Grange MSS, NLS, Acc 5381, bound Vol 2. Charles Beaumont was later the author of *A Treatise on the Coal Trade* (1789).

[56] Ibid, bound Vol 2, sederunt book minute of 16 January 1778. Already in July 1776 Beaumont's management and mining strategy were being questioned and it is clear from the records that he allowed his personal affairs to interfere greatly with his business responsi- bilities.

[57] Ibid, bound Vol 2, sederunt book minutes of 16 January, 25 May, 26 June, etc, 1778; 'General Meeting' 30 October 1780.

[58] Ibid, Box 14/3, correspondence between William Cadell jnr and John Beaumont senr, dated 7 December 1771 to 27 August 1772. Beaumont senr appears to have visited and viewed the Grange pits in 1772.

[59] I have seen no earlier example in my perusal of Scottish mining plans.

shire-type railways contributed to the transport infrastructure of the Forth coal industry, the longest being a line of some three miles.[60]

Many other Scottish colliery lines quite independent of the Carron syndrome were also underpinned by English inspiration or engineering expertise. The arrival of the Newcastle pattern of waggonway, with its more generous gauge, was almost certainly in the baggage train, so to speak, of John Dixon who came to Govan from Sunderland around mid century. Dixon is credited with the construction of a wooden railway on Newcastle principles between Knights-wood and Yoker shortly after 1750. In the mid 1770s his more famous son William, eventually to become owner of Govan Colliery and founder of a dynasty of coal and iron, built a further line from the Govan pits to the Clyde at Springfield.[61] Two similar Newcastle-type waggonways were laid to bring coal to Ayr harbour at roughtly the same date.[62] West Cumberland influences seem probable here. Back in the east, the Fordell Waggonway, built about 1770 to link Sir John Henderson's mines with the harbour of St Davids, also possessed direct Tyneside ancestry,[63] while the nearby line from Halbeath Colliery to Inverkeithing, opened about ten years later, had William Brown as consultant engineer and a man spelling his name of Thompson the English way as builder. When the Earl of Elgin was persuaded to introduce waggon-ways to his great Charlestown complex of coal and limestone, it was to Tyneside (in the shape of the engineers William Brown and Ralph Carr) that he turned for advice. And when the Pitfirrane mines – in which the Beaumonts and Cadells were for a time involved – were linked to Limekilns in 1777, the railway builder was yet another Newcastle man, George Johnson.[64] Finally, in review-ing English influences behind the evolution of early Scottish colliery railways, one might note that the grandest project of all, the Kilmarnock to Troon Railway was laid by yet another Englishman, the famous William Jessup. This line, opened progressively in 1811–12 was built almost entirely with the capital of the 3rd and 4th dukes of Portland to convey their coal to the Irish market via their new harbour facilities at Troon.[65]

[60] M. J. T. Lewis, *Early Wooden Railways* (1970), 133–4, 255; *Statistical Account*, VIII (1793), 617–8; *New Statistical Account*, VIII, 30–1; The painting of Alloa dry dock by David Allan shows the Alloa waggonway in the background. A reproduction appears in T. Crouther Gordon, *David Allan of Alloa 1744–96, The Scottish Hogarth* (Alva, 1951), opp p 4. Allan's father, incidentally was the Erskine's shore grieve at Alloa and had formerly worked in the colliery counting house!

[61] Lewis, *Early Wooden Railways*, 133. The rise of William Dixon is discussed in my *Coal Industry*, 181–4.

[62] *Statistical Account*, II (1791), 270.

[63] Some fascinating details about this waggonway are preserved in the Henderson of Fordell MSS, SRO, GD172/835/2; /836; /841/1–3; /950–1. B. Baxter, *Stone Blocks and Iron Rails* (Newton Abbot, 1966), 231, suggests an earlier date (c 1752) for the Fordell railway. Lewis, *Early Wooden Railways*, 134, seems to imply that the earlier 'branch' was a road, if I read him correctly.

[64] Lewis, *Early Wooden Railways*, 134–5.

[65] J. Priestley, *Historical Account of the Navigable Rivers, Canals and Railways Throughout Great Britain* (large edn 1831), 398–9; Anon, 'The Duke of Portland's Railway', *Locomotive Magazine*, April 1906; *New Statistical Account*, V, 537–8, 554. It ought to be added that a pioneer work on these Scottish lines was G. Dott, *Early Scottish Colliery Waggonways* (reprinted from *Colliery Engineering*, 1947).

A quite different development in Scots coalmining whose beginnings can again be traced directly to English intervention stemmed from the introduction of workmen from south of the border. This practice, as we have noted, had early precedents, though the scale had been small. The first and second Clerk baronets, for instance, had imported English skilled labour and Sir John Clerk I was deeply impressed by the advice he received from a neighbouring coal-master, William Biggar. 'Most of the Sinkers or mynders in my works are Newcastle men wch I bring from thence, finding them incomparable befor ours both for work, honnestie & Civilitie. I know no way [he told Clerk] so fitt for you to provyde y-self as sending to Newcastle'.[66] But until the age of Carron it remained usual to introduce English workers only for specially difficult feats of sinking or to act as colliery officials – the Clerks employing both a Tynesider and a Yorkshireman as mine officers at one time.

With the arrival of coke-burning ironworks and an increasing demand from other sectors, the long-standing problem of labour shortage in Scottish mines was severely exacerbated.[67] Several of the newer mining partnerships which grew up in the latter half of the eighteenth century, and especially the iron companies themselves, had to evolve a more open attitude to labour recruitment and thus to the institution of collier serfdom – which they typically came to feel was a barrier to fresh supplies of workmen entering the industry. William Cadell had no qualms in 1771 in begging John Beaumont senior of Denton, Newcastle, to engage on annual bond '6 .. 8 ... or 10 steady workmen' and dispatch them to Grange.[68] Efforts to employ both free and unfree labour alongside each other were uncommon before 1760 though not unknown. Carron Company, however, spread its net of labour enticement wide, reaching out both to the Highlands and England. Interestingly, it was through some of their English miners, imported from Shropshire by Garbett and Roebuck, that the important extractive method known as longwall working came to Scotland. A document produced in a Court of Session process in 1777 could already enthuse about 'the whole breast of coal [being] heaved down and carried off, nothing being left except the rubbish', and claim (with some exaggeration) that longwall extraction had become 'pretty generally adopted'.[69]

Not surprisingly the independent mining enterprises established by Carron's first partners also employed longwall working where conditions warranted, a fact possessing ample testimony in both surviving business records and a number of contemporary mining plans. The technique was undoubtedly an innovation which made fairly spectacular progress in Scotland. Well before the end of the century it was practised in parts of Stirlingshire, West Lothian,

---

[66] Clerk of Penicuik MSS, SRO GD18/1016, William Biggar of Woolmet to Sir John Clerk I, 15 May 1703.

[67] The literature on labour supply and serfdom is now quite large. See the references in Baron F. Duckham, 'Serfdom in Eighteenth Century Scotland', *History*, LIV (1969) and in my *Coal Industry*.

[68] Cadell of Grange MSS, NLS, Acc 5381, Box 16, bundle 3, William Cadell to John Beaumont senr, 23 December 1771.

[69] Signet Library, Edinburgh: Court of Session Papers, 595; 1 (Beaumont *v* Carron Company), 1777.

Lanarkshire, Clackmannanshire and Fife; and the 9th Earl of Dundonald ardently commended it to his fellow coalmasters in his booklet of 1793.[70] Longwall working, besides its obvious economic value of leaving virtually no coal behind (in contrast to traditional 'stoop and room'), placed the thinner seams within the realm of practical mining and also encouraged a greater division of labour in the mine.[71] Along with the earlier waggonways, it represented the influence of the English Midlands and it was, as it happened, a technique which could not have been learnt from Tyneside where variants of bord and pillar working persisted.

The employment of English labour at Scottish pits was never quantitively very considerable and certainly never approached the proportion of immigrant workers common in the lead industry. It was, too, by no means an unmixed blessing. The inducements extended to English workmen to try to persuade them to settle in an alien environment, their freedom from life bondage and their different speech and habits were none of them calculated to inspire harmonious labour relations. There were pressures enough in the later eighteenth century making for a rapid deterioration in the relationships between coalmaster and collier in Scotland without adding the natural resentment against favoured immigrant labour. Carron Company, at the spearhead of economic change and social transformation in the coalfields of East Stirlingshire and West Lothian experienced intense bouts of labour turbulence, some of which was surely connected with the potentially explosive mixture of English and Scots workers in a context where the latter enjoyed fewer privileges.[72] The mines at Kinneil were likewise plagued by jealousies between the two national groups in 1760.[73] But it would be false to suggest that it was the normally modest infusion of English labour which really precipitated the strikes and riots. The very presence of English miners was itself but a consequence of the severe labour shortage and the now rotting framework of the traditional system of adscription. It was the coming of larger-scale industrialisation, symbolised by Carron and the other new ironworks from the 1780s, which threw the customary pattern of labour relations into a paroxysm from which it could not recover.[74]

It seems clear, too, that English management was not always equal to the complex business of handling Scottish mine labour. John Grieve, eventual partner of the Cadells at Grange, reacted bitterly to the suggestion made by William Cadell in 1773 that English underground management would improve the colliery:[75]

> We have had sufficient experience of the incapacity of the generality
> of that set of Newcastlemen called Viewers. Such are perfectly
> incapable of governing Scots colliers. . . . Were we to seek a better

[70] Dundonald, *Culross*, 55.
[71] This was noted by Robert Bald, *Edinburgh Encyclopaedia* (1830 edn), XIV, 353.
[72] Campbell, *Carron Company*, 44.
[73] Hamilton MSS, Hamilton Burgh Library, Journal of John Burrell, 11 February, 14 June, 22, 23 September, 10 November, 23 December 1760.
[74] Duckham, 'Serfdom in Eighteenth-Century Scotland', loc cit.
[75] Cadell of Grange MSS, NLS, Acc 5381, Box 15/1, John Grieve to William Cadell jnr, 11 December 1773.

[undermanager] the rational lookout would be among the oversmen
bred in the Country.

Giving technical advice was one matter; assuming responsibility for the day-to-
day operations of a mine was another, especially during the troubled era before
the first emancipation Act of 1775.

The last two decades of the century witnessed the establishment of several
additional ironworks, from the foundation of Clyde in 1786 to the laboured
birth pangs of the Leven (Balgonie) works in 1801–3. All these new companies,
like Carron a generation previously, experienced difficulties in securing adequate supplies of coking coal and were compelled to integrate vertically back-
wards into coal extraction.[76] Some of the companies moreover had English
connections – which ensured that English influences continued to be brought to
bear on northern mining. Glenbuck Ironworks, Ayrshire, was largely a spill-
over from West Cumberland with successive partnerships based on Workington and subsequently Whitehaven interests. Certainly some English management, too, was employed.[77] English capital and entrepreneurial initiative, this
time mainly from Tyneside and London, underlay the founding of the Leven
Ironworks and its later reconstruction.[78] Even at Wilsontown Ironworks a
proportion of both capital and expertise came effectively from outside Scotland,[79] while several important contacts with Coalbrookdale seem to have
influenced the firm's mining operations as well as their ironmaking.

At the bigger collieries remaining outwith the sphere of the iron companies,
too, English mining consultants continued to be invited north when the more
serious entrepreneurial decisions were pending. The great John Buddle viewed
Sheriffhall Colliery in 1805,[80] while when the Marquis of Stafford determined to
revitalise the ancient coalfield of Brora in 1812–13, it was not a Scottish engineer he called upon, but John Farey of Derbyshire.[81] And if the marquis's own
Midland connections might explain his choice, they would not account for the
4th Duke of Buccleuch commissioning the same engineer to advise him 'very
comprehensively' on his coal interests at Dalkeith in 1816.[82] Evidently some
coalmasters still accepted England's primacy, though doubtless regretting, with
Dundonald, that Scotland remained somewhat lacking in that professional
corps of mine viewers who 'be regularly bread [sic] to the business like at
Newcastle'.[83] And this surely suggests one of the central reasons for the continuing penetration of English influences into Scottish mining; the fact that,

[76] The essential reference for all these companies is John Butt, 'The Scottish Iron and
Steel Industry before the Hot-Blast', *Journal of the West of Scotland Iron and Steel Institute*,
LXXIII, No 6 (1965–6). See also J. R. Hume and J. Butt, 'Muirkirk 1786–1802: the creation
of a Scottish industrial community', *Scottish Historical Review*, XLV, 2 (1966).

[77] SRO, Unextracted Process: Skene, 5/35/38, agreement of 26 December 1807.

[78] Butt, 'Scottish Iron Industry', loc cit.

[79] I. L. Donnachie and J. Butt, 'The Wilsons of Wilsontown Ironworks (1779–1813);
A Study in Entrepreneurial Failure', *Explorations in Entrepreneurial History*, 2nd series, IV,
2 (1967).

[80] Buccleuch MSS, SRO GD224/455/1, 'State of Management of Sherriffhall [sic]
Colliery', year ending 26 October 1805.

[81] Duckham, *Coal Industry*, 22.

[82] Buccleuch MSS, SRO GD224/525, John Farey to Duke of Buccleuch, 21 May 1818.

[83] Dundonald, *Culross*, 56.

given the ultimately stultifying history of much Scottish coal exploitation through the unit of the smaller landed estate, there simply had not evolved enough management and engineering skills to go round during the decades of more rapid expansion after 1760.[84]

The point has come to round up the reasons for English influences in Scottish coal mining – which were mainly technological – assuming the form and chronology they did. While it is true that the Union itself made contacts both easier and more likely between the English and Scottish coalfields, it was probably a predisposing rather than decisive factor. Though there was an unmistakable excitement in some English quarters after 1707 at the prospect of mineral exploitation in Scotland it applied chiefly to lead and, hopefully, to silver. We have anyhow noted that well before formal union English skills might be sought by Scots coalmasters. Possibly for some lairds closer acquaintance with English manners helped to stimulate that spirit of social and economic emulation which was often so characteristic of their attitudes to their southern neighbour in the eighteenth century. And where this was allied to a need to increase cash incomes (especially where the flesh-pots of London beckoned) it would be no great step to develop an increased willingness to import English ideas and techniques.[85] The gradual self-destruction of a distinctively Scottish gentry has frequently been deplored, but perhaps it was in practice the price that had to be paid for the remarkable receptivity of this class to new influences, at least some of which were beneficial to Scotland. It was of course a process which pre-dated the Union in its origins.

In many respects the Newcomen engine was emblematic of the degree of technological superiority possessed by England; and Scotland's inability to produce the engine at all before 1760 or in any quantity before about 1770 meant that increasing communications with English coalfields became irresistible. (Of course it could justly be claimed that whatever Scots learnt about steam from England, it was a debt they were more than to repay in the person of James Watt.) We have seen that contacts originally governed by the diffusion of steam technology overflowed into that other vital adjunct of mine operation: the waggonway, where Midland or Tyneside skills were long needed north of the Tweed. In the significant sphere of extractive techniques it has been argued that the establishment of coke-burning ironworks – where English capital and entrepreneurial initiative often played a more than marginal rôle – brought improvement in its wake. Again, until Scotland's coal industry experienced a critical growth rate and could throw up large enough business units than was the norm before 1760, there was little chance of there evolving sufficient skills in either management or colliery engineering. Indeed, the rise of the professional Scots coal viewer cannot be discovered until the late eighteenth or early nineteenth century. Even by 1815 the number of native viewers of a

[84] Baron F. Duckham, 'The Emergence of the Professional Manager in the Scottish Coal Industry, 1760–1815', *Business History Review*, XLIII, 1 (1969).

[85] There are many references to the receptiveness of the Scottish gentry to outside influences, for example, in Phillipson and Mitchison, *Essays in Scottish History*. See espec, 3, 142–3, 235–6.

stature approaching that of Robert Bald was still too low for self-sufficiency. Dundonald had hardly exaggerated in 1793 when he had wrily lamented that, with respect to directing a Scottish mine, it was still considered 'a sufficient recommendation for that most important office, to have been a *Carpenter*, *Blacksmith*, Gentleman's *Gardener*, or a Clerk to a Counting House'.[86] Until time alone could increase the supply of suitable men, recourse to England smacked of inevitability. Or perhaps Scots have always known when it was wise to temper nationalism by cosmopolitanism. Dr Johnson's quip that the fairest prospect before a Scotsman was the highway to England may be unjust, but we may fairly picture our 'lad o'pairts' on road for England meeting a trickle of mining talent coming in the opposite direction.

Yet if many of the influences at work may be viewed chiefly as the importation of enterprise and technical resourcefulness, it remains true that some Englishmen chose to come to Scotland and operate within a context of a more backward coal industry at a time when, according to Ramsay, 'English ministers did not know much more of Scotland than they did of Tartary'.[87] Assuredly we still know too little of the motivation behind individual ventures. It seems however that 'pull' rather than 'push' factors were at work, notably optimistic expectations that mineral concessions would be cheaper in Scotland (by no means always true) and a patronising belief that under 'frontier' conditions little more than a modicum of drive was needed to expand a market not fully appreciated by native producers.[88] In practice English entrepreneurs more than once miscalculated the extent of labour costs in Scottish mining and underestimated the difficulty of developing effective seasale mines or over-valued the quality of coals. As Smout remarked, with English involvement in Scottish lead in mind: 'dubious mineral concerns were fatally attractive to the eighteenth century instincts for gambling and amateur science'.[89] Yet despite the heavier English investment in lead extraction and processing it could still be argued that English influences in the Scottish coal industry were of more strategic importance in the long run if only because coal was ultimately more important than lead and more central to the process of industrialisation.

Scotland's industrial revolution as a case distinguishable from, though interrelated to, that of England is at last winning more attention from economic historians. From Hamilton onwards the features of Scotland's experience have been described and the analysis refined.[90] Many writers have now commented on the probable impact of the union of 1707 on Scottish culture and economy (or economies, if we think of the Highlands). English scholars, when they have looked to Scotland at all, have tended to stress the contribution of individual

---

[86] Dundonald, *Culross*, 56.

[87] Quoted in H. G. Graham, *The Social Life of Scotland in the Eighteenth Century* (1899), I, 3.

[88] In fact business records (eg the Cadell MSS) show the larger enterprises making every effort to exploit the market. The Cadells for a time employed an agent (Charles Beaumont) in London.

[89] Smout, 'Lead-mining in Scotland', loc cit, 103.

[90] I am thinking of the work of R. H. Campbell, T. C. Smout, John Butt, Rosalind Mitchison and W. H. Marwick among others.

Scots to England's development, whether as entrepreneurs or civil engineers, or have made flattering references to the supposed relevance of Scottish popular education. Writers on Scottish growth in the eighteenth century, on the other hand, have rightly urged the rôle of wider market opportunities in helping to unbind the Scottish Prometheus. Professor Campbell has emphasised the importance of the Union in this latter respect and suggested that 'when after the 1780's the Scottish economy was resting on a basis laid by achievements apparently its own, it was in reality resting on a foundation established through Union with England'.[91]

The fact that the Scottish coal industry was able to win few sales outlets of consequence in England after the Union in no way invalidates this thesis generally. The case of mining might, however, possibly persuade us that it is worth examining the rôle of English influences, especially in the realm of techniques in a little more depth. To do so would carry no imputation about the primacy of market factors. Most scholars have of course recognised the importance of new ideas entering Scotland from south of the border during the eighteenth century, but have we not sometimes taken the matter (and its process) as read? It is possible that efforts to chart English influences in Scotland over wider economic fields than mere coal mining would be worthwhile – and one thinks perhaps of cotton spinning and glass manufacture as obvious examples. Such studies might paradoxically help us to highlight, as Campbell seems to imply,[92] the uniquely Scottish experience of economic growth. Certainly in coal mining English penetration did little to lessen the essential 'Scottishness' of the industry's history. But it does help to explain it.[93]

[91] Campbell, *Scotland Since 1707*, 42. There is an excellent and penetrating comment on the economic meaning of the Union in pp 1–9.

[92] Campbell, 'The industrial revolution: a revision article', *Scottish Historical Review*, XLVI (1967).

[93] This chapter is a much-shortened version of a paper originally read to the Conference of Scottish Economic Historians held in the University of Aberdeen, March 1974.

BARON F. DUCKHAM

4

Government Bounties and the Establishment of the Scottish Whaling Trade, 1750–1800

I

There was a time in the nineteenth century when Scottish vessels played a major rôle in Britain's Arctic whaling trade, when two or three Scottish ports made most of the running and one of them – Dundee – was indisputably the centre of the trade.[1] It had not always been so. For almost two centuries Scotland took little part in whaling, and it was not until 1750 that any serious attempt was made to establish a permanent interest in the trade. The object of this essay is to explore the success of this attempt and, in particular, to consider the effects of government assistance in the creation and sustenance of a trade in valued raw materials.[2] But first, in order to understand the obstacles to whaling which necessitated – and almost negated – government assistance, it is necessary to consider Scotland's earlier unsuccessful flirtation with whaling.

Arctic whaling was initiated by the English towards the close of the sixteenth century as a by-product of their search for the North East Passage. The Northern waters entered by explorers such as Willoughby and Chancellor abounded with whales, the oil value of which was known through the small-scale traditional fishery for migratory whales off the coast of the Bay of Biscay, but there was no way in which the northern whales could be caught from sailing ships. The breakthrough came with the discovery of Spitsbergen, which provided the shore bases essential for a Basque-type fishery in the Arctic. With a buoyant market among soap-makers, there was ample scope for a rapid growth of whaling, but from the beginning it was bedevilled by the monopolies beloved of princes and merchants alike.

The more damaging form of state-supported monopoly, mercantilism, endeavoured to secure maximum economic advantage for one country at the

---

[1] S. G. E. Lythe, 'The Dundee Whale Fishery', *Scottish Journal of Political Economy*, XI, 158–69.
[2] This study of whaling was part of a wider study of Scottish trade and shipping generously supported by the Houblon-Norman Fund of the Bank of England, to which I am greatly indebted.

expense of others, and in following this apparently desirable end the British strove harder to exclude the Dutch (who followed them to the Arctic, using British pilots) than they did to catch whales.[3] Whalers sailed in battle-fleets until their extraordinary profits were swallowed up in extraordinary costs. A tacit agreement then gave the Dutch the north of Spitsbergen, while the British, by right of discovery, kept their original 'best' bays in the south – which soon proved to be the worst. Within a couple of decades the Dutch had forged ahead in straight competition.[4] Whereas the British appear never to have adequately learned the techniques of the fishery from the Basque specialists they employed, the Dutch soon mastered it and passed on their hard won skills to their children. Moreover, the British had a limited market, whereas the Dutch, through their vast international trade, had access to wide-ranging markets from which the British were largely excluded. Furthermore, in their mercantile marine the Dutch possessed a fund of experience in the herring fishery and a plentiful and cheap supply of ships, capital and labour which the British could not yet rival.[5] Long before the Civil War, the Dutch had moved into a position of undoubted superiority which left little room for the British. It was soon cheaper and easier to import oil and whalebone from Holland than it was to search for it amid the hazards of the Arctic, and any attempt to re-establish British whaling was faced with the uphill task of learning a trade in order to compete with a successful trade carried on with economy by experts.

Quite apart from difficulties springing from Dutch competition, British whaling was hamstrung by internal strife. It was not, properly speaking, 'British' whaling at all, but the monopoly of the Muscovy Company, which repulsed interlopers from both England and Scotland with as much vigour as it showed towards the Dutch.[6] It was therefore in the midst of both external and internal wrangling that Scottish whaling began. In no legal fashion could an independent whaling trade be established outside London; yet Scots alleged that the Muscovy Company would not (or could not) supply Scotland with oil which they were themselves debarred from obtaining direct from the Arctic. In fact the position of Leith merchants was little different from that of Hull merchants, but they had an element of nationalism on their side, and while James I had no desire to upset the Muscovy Company, James VI endeavoured to placate his Scottish friends, and, after a false start by the shortlived Scottish Greenland Company,[7] gave a patent to Nathaniel Udwart, a leading Scottish

---

[3] Thomas Edge, *A briefe discoverie of the Northerne Seas*, printed in S. Purchas, *Hakluytus Posthumus, or Purchas His Pilgrimes* (Hakluyt Society, Glasgow, 1906), Vol XIII, p 16. The best brief account of the trade is probably still to be found in the first two chapters of William Scoresby, *An Account of the Arctic Regions*, Vol II (Edinburgh, 1810). See also J. T. Jenkins, *A History of the Whale Fisheries* (1921), and the early chapters of my forthcoming *History of the Whaling Trade*.

[4] W. M. Conway, *Early Dutch and English Voyages to Spitsbergen in the Seventeenth Century* (Hakluyt Society, London, 1894), passim.

[5] V. Barbour, *Capitalism in Amsterdam in the Seventeenth Century* (Baltimore, 1950), 21, 23–4, 28. Some of the early ships employed by the Muscovy Company had had to be hired in Holland; ibid, 33.

[6] Edge, op cit, 16.

[7] *Calendars of State Papers* [*CSP*] (*Domestic*), James I, Vol CXXII, No 77, July 1622; S. G. E. Lythe, *The Economy of Scotland, 1550–1625* (1960), 60–1.

monopolist, to supply Scotland and his own soapworks in Leith with oil.[8]

Udwart had the patent, but had neither the expertise nor the ships and capital to supply Scotland with oil. Expertise he acquired in the shape of ex-Muscovy Company men; the ships and some of the capital were provided by his friends among the merchants not of Leith but of Yarmouth. Immediately the Muscovy Company disputed a Scottish patent employing English resources, and expensive legal battles before the Privy Council, and constant friction in Spitsbergen, did nothing to encourage perseverance on either side. In 1629 Udwart complained to the Scottish Privy Council that he had lost £4,000 sterling in sending out ships that year, 'hoping that we, who are his majesty's subjects, should not have been debarred that liberty which other nations do promiscuously enjoy without controlment'.[9] While the Scottish Privy Council supported him, and spoke of the 'liberties' of Scotland, little could be done, and matters came to a head in 1634 with a 'battle' in Spitsbergen between the two companies which sent both sides scurrying to their respective Privy Councils.[10] A compromise giving the Scottish company the right to fit out one-sixth of a specified total British tonnage (and giving similar rights to other interlopers in England) came too late to save the trade. While the British had done their best to limit involvement, the Dutch had done everything to attract capital and shipping 'promiscuously' into the trade. Their competition was over-whelming in the politically and economically troubled decades around the middle of the century, and British whaling disappeared in a fog of despair. Futile attempts to revive it after the Restoration – the last in Scotland being in Leith, in the early 1680s[11] – only served to emphasise the end of an unattractive episode in British trading history.

Scotland's initial involvement with whaling was, therefore, an unmitigated disaster. While another small nation across the North Sea built up a fleet numbering almost 200 ships by the 1680s, Scotland could muster only two, and then only for a short time. The average Dutch catch was around 600,000 barrels when the Scottish catch in 1682 was 25![12] This different order of magnitude goes a long way towards explaining why Scotsmen were reluctant to adventure in the Arctic for several generations, and why there was nobody capable of directing or participating successfully in the whaling trade. The failure to establish a foothold at the beginning, and to master the basic skills thereafter, was a handicap of immense proportions when other factors were beginning to move in favour of further adventures. It was particularly unfortunate, for instance, that major geographical and technical changes took place in Arctic whaling after the British withdrew from it, so that they had no significant experience in the open-sea fishing along the Greenland ice which had replaced the bay-fishing in Spitsbergen.

The situation for the English was no better, but the supply of capital available for adventures of almost any kind was much greater in the early eighteenth

---

[8] CSP, Charles I, Vol XXXII, No 52.
[9] Register of the Privy Council of Scotland, 2nd series, Vol I, 1625–7 (Edinburgh, 1899), 356.
[10] CSP, Charles I, Vol CCLXXV, No 30, and CCLXXXII, No 37.
[11] Scottish Record Office [SRO], Papers of Sir John Clerk of Penicuik, GD 18/2568.
[12] Ibid, Accounts for the Year 1682; Scoresby, Vol ii, 156.

century, and whaling was revived in the 1720s when the wealthy South Sea Company spent a decade and invested a quarter of a million pounds, simply proving that – for whatever reasons – the English were still incompetent whalers. Nevertheless, the forced withdrawal from the trade of one of the richest corporations in Britain had one good result insofar as politicians were at last forced to take an interest in whaling. Oil was rapidly becoming a vital raw material. Its original use in soap had ended with the decline of bay-fishing,[13] but it found an expanding market in the textile industry, was a superb lubricant, and was the only cheap material suitable for the lighting of streets and public buildings before the discovery of coal gas. Moreover, the flexible plates of 'whalebone' (baleen) through which the Greenland right-whale filtered its plankton food were in great demand among the fashion-conscious for petticoat hoops and stay 'bones', and a whale's bone at this time was as valuable as its blubber. Nevertheless, as the South Sea Company discovered, it was impossible to make profits, while novices learned the trade and the Dutch held the market, without some form of government assistance.[14]

The time was propitious. Walpole's mercantilist government was eager to achieve national self-sufficiency and especially to reduce the trade deficit with Holland. In a century of recurring war, it also craved the strategic advantage of a large naval reserve to be obtained by augmenting the number of ships and seamen during peacetime. An attempt was made to kill two birds with one stone in 1733 when a bounty was offered to the whaling trade. Any vessel over 200 tons which was properly equipped, which had the specified number of seamen and apprentices, which registered its purpose at the local Custom House, and which spent a specific period in the Arctic (to be proved by the 'logs' which whalers were compelled to keep), was entitled to a bounty of twenty shillings per ton (at measured capacity) whether or not she was successful in the fishery.

The bounty came too late for the South Sea Company, and was too small to encourage many imitators. There is conflicting evidence over both the amount of bounty paid and the number of ships involved, but the most generous source gives an average of only four ships fitted out in England between 1733 and 1749 and none at all from Scotland.[15] They were generally unsuccessful, with average catches of only 13·5 tuns of oil,[16] and not until the middle of the century was there any growth of interest in the trade, when the government advanced the bounty to forty shillings per ton. Other factors added their encouragement, chief of which was probably an increase in the international price of oil, which in the British market was represented by an advance from around £15 a tun in the early 1740s to almost £30 in the early 1750s.[17] Every-

[13] In bay-fishing, oil was produced from blubber in Spitsbergen and was relatively pure; in ice-fishing the blubber was brought home for boiling and was contaminated by putrefaction (and unsuitable for soap).

[14] British Museum, Add. MS 25,505, Minutes of the Court of Directors of the South Sea Company, Vol 12, 27 October 1732.

[15] Public Record Office [PRO], Board of Trade Papers relating to the Southern Whale Fishery, 'State of the Greenland Trade', BT 6/93/113.

[16] PRO, BT 6/230, folio 92.

[17] Scoresby, op cit, II 409.

where the demand for oil was growing, and wars and rumours of wars in America and on the Continent, which threatened deliveries to the British market, made a native-caught supply of oil appear both desirable and potentially profitable.

II

The effects of the new bounty were quite dramatic. On the one hand the trade grew faster than ever appeared possible before, and on the other hand it was no longer tied to London. Even ports without extensive hinterlands could dispose of their produce via the coastal trade, so that all that was required was an adequate shipowning base on which the whaling trade could be established. The east coast Scottish ports, despite their paucity of trade, were therefore ideally situated for whaling. They were nearer to the fishing grounds than were the English ports, and they were sufficiently far from London to have their own local market in the Forth-Clyde region where the Scottish Industrial Revolution was to take place. They also had the advantage of cheaper costs and a ready supply of labour trained in the inshore fisheries. Equally important, perhaps, was the fact that most of the ports that came into the trade enjoyed neither the prosperity nor the wide-ranging trades of the English ports or, indeed, of the west of Scotland, with the result that they were more eager to take part in this new venture which did not demand established hinterlands and which was, moreover, heavily subsidised by the state. Within three years there were a dozen whalers operating from Scottish ports, and a successful trade would appear to have been established. It remains to be seen, however, how much economic reality lay behind the façade of 'success'.

The port of Leith was first off the mark in 1749 with the Edinburgh Whale Fishery Company, consisting of six local merchants, a master-mariner and a writer, whose vessel, the 333 ton *Tryall*, was ready for the 1750 season.[18] It shared the fate of many pioneering whalers, but the complete failure of its fishing could not dampen a general enthusiasm. Six vessels were fitted out in 1751: the *Tryall* and the *Edinburgh* from Leith, the *Peggy* and *Glasgow Fisher* from Glasgow, and the *Argyle* and *Campbeltown* from Campbeltown, an important centre of fishing and shipowning on the Clyde. Ships did not, however, remain for long on the west coast. Those of Campbeltown were soon sold to the Edinburgh Whale Fishery Company, and the Glasgow ships were transferred to Bo'ness, thus eliminating the dangerous voyage round the northwest coast of Scotland to Spitsbergen, where the Greenland fishery usually commenced. The west coast ports were in any case subjected to the growing attractions of the transatlantic trades which no doubt served to divert attention from whaling where success soon belied expectations and profits were erratic.

Thus, while Glasgow's prosperous merchants eschewed whaling, it was fervently embraced in east coast ports with few great merchants and fewer great ships. Dunbar entered the trade in 1752 following the establishment of the East Lothian and Merse Whale Fishing Company in September 1751, when

---

[18] Details of whalers and their catches are taken from the bounty certificates preserved in the Scottish Record Office, series E 508.

twenty-three persons subscribed £6,000 sterling in the hope 'that the carrying on the whale fishery from the harbour of Dunbar may be of eminent advantage to the trade of this part of the country'.[19] This was the sort of enterprise and initiative that won empires or lost fortunes, for Dunbar was, by most standards, no port at all. Her decent ships were few and her foreign trade minimal. Indeed, in the early 1760s the three whalers she then operated accounted for almost her entire foreign trade in terms of ship tonnage entering, which averaged only 1,411 tons per annum in 1760–64.[20] In 1752 another place of slight importance entered the trade when Dundee Whale Fishing Company fitted out the *Dundee*, to be joined in 1757 by the *Grandtully*, two ships which in the early 1760s were almost equal to the tonnage leaving the port and roughly a quarter of the tonnage entering. The Aberdeen Whale Fishery Company also entered the trade in 1753, with hopes similar to those of Dunbar and with a whaler purchased from Whitby and renamed *City of Aberdeen*. So great was the enthusiasm along the coast that even such unlikely places as Anstruther and Kirkcaldy were infected for a time in the late 1750s, when there were fifteen or sixteen vessels operating from Scottish ports.

It could therefore be argued that whaling was not a 'natural' progression in the evolution of Scottish trade. The chief trend was towards transatlantic trade which could quite adequately have supplied all the oil that Scotland needed; and the absence of normal economic incentives for the whaling trade is surely illustrated by the fact that total imports from all sources in the years 1733–49 averaged only twenty-nine tuns per annum.[21] Nor did Scotland consume all the oil imported by her new whalers; a quarter of it was re-exported in the years 1753–9 and a third in 1760–69.[22] In some respects this was a hopeful sign, but on the whole it was extremely dangerous for an infant industry to have to search for foreign markets in competition with the Dutch – and the English.

With such a restricted market it seems fair to regard bounty-initiated Scottish, whaling as a more doubtful prospect than its English counterpart, but there was no shortage of entrepreneurs prepared to gamble on success or of smaller men prepared to back them. There were the inevitable gentry seeking speculative investments, men such as Sir Archibald Grant of Monymusk and Sir William Johnston in the Aberdeen company,[23] Sir Michael Stewart of Blackhall in Glasgow[24] and David Kinlock of Gilmerton in Dunbar.[25] Most of the leaders, however, were merchants of greater or lesser degree, such as Robert Finlay, Walter Maxwell and James Watt (of Greenock) who founded the trade in Glasgow, Charles, Robert and James Fall who led the Dunbar company, Andrew and John Cowan who managed the Glasgow ships when they were transferred to Bo'ness,[26] and John Haliburton who appears to have been the man

---

[19] Contract of Copartnery, copy in SRO E508/51/8/11.
[20] SRO, RH 2/4/552, copying PRO T36/13/7: An Account of the Tonnage of Vessels entering and clearing out at Scottish Ports, 1759–84.
[21] PRO, BT 6/93/117.
[22] Ibid.
[23] SRO, E 508/51/8/6.
[24] E 508/51/8/9.
[25] E 508/51/8/11.
[26] E 508/54/8/8.

behind the Dundee company.[27] Supporting them were surgeons, master mariners, customs officers, ministers, a town clerk (Dunbar) and a wigmaker. By and large the subscribers were not the great men of the tobacco and sugar trades, or even the more prosperous men of the continental trades (except in Leith and Bo'ness). They were more commonly smaller people who could support the trade and survive in it largely because of the type of company organisation permitted under Scots law but prohibited under English law. The typical English whaler was owned in shares by people who had no legal or institutional relationship; they were not, in law, a whaler-owning company, but a number of distinct individuals who together owned sixty-four shares in a specific ship. The typical Scottish company, by contrast, was a legally formulated copartnery existing for the specific purpose of engaging in whaling and buying sufficient ships to do it adequately. The difference is important. In Scotland people interested in whaling could buy shares in the local whaling company; in England they bought shares in individual ships. In England expansion therefore took the form of competition between owners which brought too many novice ships into the trade and threatened ruin for everyone; in Scotland expansion took place within existing companies (except in Leith where it took place within two companies, the Edinburgh Whale Fishery Company and the Edinburgh New Whale Fishery Company), and this acted as a brake on over-expansion and may, in the long run, have produced a healthier though relatively smaller trade. It certainly provided a more stable trade.

Entrepreneurs of various sorts were thus attracted into whaling as an adventure spiced with good prices and bounty, and within a short time the trade was an important component of Scotland's total trade so far as *tonnage* was concerned. The sixteen whalers in the mid-1750s had an aggregate tonnage of 4,964, which represented between 6 and 8 per cent of the entire overseas trade. It has been seen that in places such as Dunbar and Dundee whaling was the dominant trade, but even in the major port of Leith whalers were no less than 16 per cent of tonnage entering the port in the late 1750s, while over a quarter of the tonnage leaving the port was accounted for by whalers on their way to the fishery.[28] Indeed, compared with the size of the places from which they operated, it is quite remarkable how well the Scottish whalers compared with the English ones at least up to 1773 (Table 1).

TABLE 1

SCOTTISH WHALERS AS A PERCENTAGE OF ENGLISH WHALERS, 1750–79[29]

1750–4	28·9	1765–9	22·9
1755–9	28·1	1770–4	17·0
1760–4	38·5	1775–9	7·9

[27] E 508/54/8/3–4.
[28] SRO, RH 2/4/552. Ships without cargo were not normally counted by the Customs, but whalers always were.
[29] PRO, BT 6/93/98 for English whalers, BT 6/93/126 for Scottish.

For ten years the number of whalers remained steady at 14–16 vessels and then, in 1763, dropped by a third to another steady plateau until 1776–8. The first major upset came – as in so many trades – with the American Revolutionary War, when the trade plunged to a mere three vessels in 1779, and was carried on by Dunbar and Dundee alone until 1783, when only Dunbar persevered (Table 2).

To some extent the decline was the result of difficulties both economic and practical. War usually resulted in stagnation in some branches of the economy which was likely to affect whaling as much as any other trade, though any great increase in the demand for cloth for uniforms might be a stimulus since whale oil was used in its manufacture. Of greater practical significance was the vulnerability of shipping on the east coast during war, and whalers – slow and heavy – were more vulnerable than most. Occasionally whalers were lost to the enemy and did not share the good fortune of the *Raith* of Leith, captured off Shetland in 1794 and recaptured and brought home by her three remaining crew members.[30] If most ships remained safe, it was because most retired from whaling, or because they took expensive precautions with armaments and convoys. A convoy past Shetland, where French and Dutch privateers awaited the whalers, was advantageous, but even this had drawbacks, as the Dunbar whalers found in 1781, when the expected convoy arrived too late for the legal commencement of the fishing (10 April) and four vessels had their bounties placed in jeopardy![31]

Equally important in the decline of war-time whaling was the attraction of alternative employment. With a heavy demand for government transports, owners raced to secure their £1 per ton per month for carrying troops or supplies. A Board of Trade internal memorandum of c 1786 noted that whereas the costs of outfit and wages rose and danger (and therefore insurance) increased, 'the number of transports necessary for the transportation and supply of the army and navy in America, afforded the owners of the vessels usually employed in the Greenland Fishery an opportunity of employing them in the service of the Government, at a certain and very considerable advantage, more than equal to the uncertainty of a fishing voyage, if unsuccessful, even aided

TABLE 2

SCOTTISH WHALING VOYAGES, 1750–84[32]
(5-yearly averages)

1750–4	9·2	1770–4	9·2
1755–9	15·4	1775–9	6·2
1760–4	12·4	1780–4	4·8
1765–9	8·8		

[30] SRO, E 508/95/8/7.

[31] SRO, CE 1/17, Minutes of the Scottish Board of Customs, 12 April 1781.

[32] Ibid. There is a discrepancy between different sources for Scottish whalers in 1782. BT 6/93/126 has 5; Scoresby, 119 (quoting D. Macpherson, *Annals of Commerce* (1805), IV, 180) has 6. However the bounty returns (BT 6/93/119) allow for only 4, and this figure has been used here.

with the Bounty, and perhaps equal to the advantages of a successful voyage'.[33] Those owners who continued fishing in the hope of better returns from reduced activity were faced with severe problems of manning. Since one object of the bounty was to secure a 'nursery of seamen', it was only natural that the whalers that were not taken into govenment service should expect a severe tax on their men when the navy required them; and it was little help to know that the specialists were exempt from the Press if the rest of the crew were not. Crews were heavily pressed in 1755, for instance, and again in 1757 and 1758, though on these occasions the number of whalers was not seriously affected. The press gangs often took whaler crews because they were easy to get at and were supposed to be good seamen, and then left the whaler owners to mop up straggling (and possibly poorer) seamen whom the press gangs could not catch without difficulty. On the other hand, it was not uncommon for whaler crews to desert *en masse* before they reached the blockading press sloops awaiting them.[34] Far more serious, however, was the prolonged pressing in the late 1770s, which was both 'hot' and indiscriminate. In 1779, for instance, the *North Star* of Dunbar lost not only its sailors but also two harpooners, four steersmen and four line-managers, while the *Blessed Endeavour* lost two harpooners (including the mate) five steersmen, all six line-managers and six apprentices.[35]

To blame the difficulties of whaling on war conditions seems plausible enough at first sight but does little to explain the long term downward trend which was merely punctuated by war. It is significant, for instance, that Scottish whalers did not follow the same pattern as English ones (which also suffered in wartime), with the result that the former were 39 per cent of the latter in 1760–64 but only 8 per cent by 1775–79 (Table 1). Clearly there must be other factors of an economic nature involved. Yet if the decline was caused by foreign competition or by falling prices on the international market, one would expect the English trade to be more affected than the Scottish, since England imported huge quantities of American oil while Scotland imported hardly any. A more plausible answer would seem to lie in the size of the Scottish market, though even this does not explain why Dunbar, for instance, could not ship oil coastwise to London as did Poole in Dorset, or indeed, Nantucket in Rhode Island. A more radical approach would be to turn to such matters as profitability and endeavour to establish whether whaling in this early period was anything more than a costly failure supported merely by the bounty – a trade that was dying but would not lie down. Unfortunately no records of the individual whaling companies have been found, but because whaling was a subsidised trade HM Customs kept extensive records, and these were supplemented by investigations by the Board of Trade in the 1780s.

The first and most obvious point to make is that Scottish whaling had a disastrous record for most of the eighteenth century. It is *not* the case that regular voyages and a steady trade indicate success either in terms of whales caught or

[33] PRO, BT 6/93/115.
[34] Such desertions were noted in detail on the bounty papers, since a whaler only received a bounty if its crew was mustered by the Customs officers when she left and returned.
[35] SRO, E 508/77/8/1–2.

of oil and bone produced. The first ship, *Tryall* of Leith, caught no whales at all on its first two expeditions and only two on its third. Of the other pioneering ships, *Peggy* of Glasgow and *Campbeltown* and *Argyle* of Campbeltown also had clean maiden voyages. Indeed, between 1750 and 1760 no fewer than 34 of 127 vessels returned clean. If we add also those vessels bringing home fewer than three whales, the figure soars to a staggering 97 (Table 3). The significance of these figures lies in the general assertion by owners, accepted by the Board of Trade and repeated by Jenkinson in Parliament, that at least three whales (providing 30 tuns of oil and 30 cwt of bone) were necessary for a subsidised vessel to make a saving voyage.[36] Even on the simplest sort of reckoning almost three-quarters of all Scottish whaling voyages in the first decade ended in loss.

It is not possible to gauge the earning capacity of whalers over time with complete accuracy because the early bounty certificates recorded cargoes in casks of blubber, whereas income came from tuns of refined oil. Generally speaking, one tun of oil could be extracted from 3·3–3·5 casks of blubber in the 1750s and 1760s, so that all-told the first ten years of Scottish whaling (ignoring 1750 with its nil return) produced a sworn catch of 7,784 casks of blubber which would produce something of the order of 2,400 tuns of oil from 127 expeditions, that is approximately 19 tuns per expedition.[37] Although the price of oil varied from time to time, one might, for the sake of argument, take £29 – the very high figure given by Scoresby for 1754[38] – as a constant, and reckon the total earnings from oil at £550 per expedition. This is certainly too high, but still serves to throw doubt on any arguments in favour of *universally* high returns on whaling. To the earnings from oil must be added those from whalebone which again at Scoresby's figure brings the average earnings per voyage to approximately £1,000. This sounds very considerable, but in fact represents £3·3 per ton (excluding bounty) for·the average ship of 299 tons and this, as has been seen, is only half what a transport could earn in six months. When at a later date owners estimated the costs of whaling, the initial outfit was put at £12 per ton, and subsequent outfits at a little under £5.[39] The average 299-

TABLE 3

PERCENTAGE OF WHALERS WITH SPECIFIED CATCHES, 1750–60[40]

No of whales caught	0	1	2	3	4	5+
No of whalers	34	34	19	11	10	19
Percentage of total whalers	26·8	26·8	15·0	8·7	7·9	15·0

[36] PRO, BT 5/3, Minutes of the Board of Trade, 21 March 1786; speech by Jenkinson, 12 April 1786, Hansard, *Parliamentary History* (1816), vol XXV, col 1,377. The supporting evidence handed in by merchants is BT 6/93/93–5.

[37] This estimate appears reasonable; the total oil imported into Scotland in 1751–60 was 2,603 tuns, in which an allowance must be made for oil imported from other sources, which was 44 tuns per annum on average in 1745–9. (There were more than 127 expeditions, but 10 bounty certificates are missing from the collection, chiefly for 1756.)

[38] Scoresby, II, 409, 417.

[39] PRO, BT 6/93/94.

[40] E 508, passim.

TABLE 4

The Performance of Edinburgh Whale Fishery Company, 1750–60
(number of whales (w) and casks of blubber (c))

	tons	1750		1751		1752		1753		1754		1755		1756		1757		1758		1759		1760		Total	
		w	c	w	c	w	c	w	c	w	c	w	c	w	c	w	c	w	c	w	c	w	c	w	c
Tryall	333	0	0	0	0	2	43	4	118	0	0	0	0	3	43	0	0	0	0	0	0	0	9	9	203
Royal Endeavour	331	—		—		9	207	3	83	10	239	5	218	4	83	1	26	1	60	0	0	2	57	35	973
Edinburgh	285	—		—		6	195	3	60	1	58	2	76	3	95	0	0	0	0	1	14	0	16	16	498
Campbeltown	305	—		—		—		7½	207	1	39	6	134	2	36	1	34	3	140	1	57	2	57	23½	704
TOTAL		0	0	0	0	17	444	17½	468	12	336	13	428	12	257	2	60	4	200	2	71	4	114	83½	2,378
Tonnage employed		333		333		949		1,254		1,254		1,254		1,254		1,254		1,254		1,254		1,254		11,647	
Casks per ton		0		0		0·5		0·4		0·3		0·3		0·2		0		0·2		0·1		0·1		0·2	

tonner was thus costing something of the order of £1,400 to put to sea to earn her £1,000, and it would make little difference if she were an old ship because refitting would be more costly, and in any case the food and wages alone would amount to £700.

Fortunately for some owners, averages hide profits as well as losses, and it is necessary to pursue the careers of ships and companies to discover how far they might be above or below average over time. The first ship, *Tryall*, was an obvious disaster, with eight clean voyages in eleven years and a total catch of only nine whales, but if one looks at the performance of all four Edinburgh Whale Fishery Company ships the result is far from encouraging (Table 4). Thus, between 1750 and 1760 the Company employed 11,647 tons of shipping to catch 2,378 casks of blubber, i.e. 720 tuns of oil and 36 tons of bone which, at £29 and £500 respectively, would produce an absolute maximum of £38,898, representing a return of £3·3 per ton, exactly the same as the average for all Scottish whalers. Some companies did better than this. The East Lothian and Merse company managed to catch 2·9 whales per voyage with only two clean voyages, leaving earnings for nine years at £5 per ton. Most people, however, seem to have done worse, with Dundee vessels returning only £2·8 per ton and Aberdeen vessels a mere £0·8 per ton. No shipowner would have regarded this as adequate earnings for a merchantmen, let alone for a vessel for which expenses were so high. Only the £2 per ton bounty made the average operation viable.

One reason for these consistently poor results must surely be that the Scots did not easily learn the trade. Just as the Dutch had learned from the Basques, so the Scots now employed Dutch specialists, and ships that tried to economise by relying on Scots usually paid dear for their false economy. Some companies employed more Dutchmen than others, and though their presence did not guarantee success, no vessel did really well without them in the 1750s and 1760s. Of the 29 vessels that sailed without Dutchmen in the 1750s, 10 came home clean and only 8 had more than 2 whales (Table 5). It seems fairly conclusive that when more than four foreigners were employed the average number of whales rose dramatically, though five men did as well as ten on average. Although ships with nine foreigners managed to catch the highest average of whales, the largest aggregate number – 62 – was accounted for by the twenty vessels carrying seven foreigners.

Another facet of inexperience was to be found not in the shallops but on the quarter deck. Forty captains took whalers to the Arctic in the 1750s, but

TABLE 5

AVERAGE CATCHES OF VESSELS WITH SPECIFIED NUMBER OF FOREIGN CREWMEN, 1750–60[41]

No of foreigners	0	1	2	3	4	5	6	7	8	9	10+
Average No of whales	1·5	1·7	0·6	1·5	1·6	3·8	2·0	3·1	3·7	7·5	3·1

[41] The number of foreign crew members had to be entered in the bounty certificate.

only twenty of them ever caught more than two whales and only eleven of them on more than one occasion. Five men between them captained vessels which caught eighty-nine whales, or 34 per cent of the total catch. This *may* be coincidence, but more likely we are witnessing the emergence of expertise among captains and mates that was to be important at a later date.

No matter how skilled the captain and crew, they could not hope to prosper if too many foreign or British whalers were active in a restricted area or if the weather was bad. Even within Scotland the price obtained for oil and bone was not determined solely by the performance of Scottish whalers. Imports from cheap sources, especially the colonies, were variable; and it was soon apparent that the quantity of oil and bone obtained from Greenland was not entirely determined by the number of whalers active there (Table 6). Many variables made life difficult for whaling men, not least the constant importation of foreign produce into London, which in the 1760s forced the British price for oil and bone down to £16 10s and £340 respectively in 1769.[42] Such a massive reduction since the 1750s, coupled with the poor performance noted above, was more than enough to drive ships out of the trade, war or no war.

The price of oil and bone might have been a greater inducement to owners if in the long run they could be sure of getting it, but they were not. Uncertainty was always present in whaling, and things got no better in the 1760s and 1770s. Between 1766 and 1775, for instance, Scotland sent nine whalers to the fishery (except when ten went in 1773) with a regularity that would be suspicious were the bounty certificates not available to prove the veracity of Customs clerks. Their aggregate catches ranged from 355 tuns of oil in 1774 to five tuns in 1767, and average earnings (excluding bounty) from £1,420 in 1774 to £23 in 1767 (Table 7). Despite the relatively good years 1769, 1772 and 1774, the average income per ship per annum was no more than £645, representing only fractionally over £2 per ship-ton, which was rather less than in the previous decade. Once more the question must arise: to what extend did the average mask the emergence of individual ships making regular good catches?

TABLE 6

AVERAGE NUMBER OF WHALERS, AND IMPORTS AND EXPORTS OF WHALE OIL, 1765–84[43]

	Whalers	Imports		Exports
		Greenland Oil (tuns)	Total Oil (tuns)	Total
1765–9	8·8	131	251	74
1770–4	9·2	208	326	37
1775–9	6·2	159	343	28
1780–4	4·8	174	302	78

[42] Greenland prices, 1766–85, are recorded in BT 6/93/94; general prices, 1769–87, in BT 6/93/137.

[43] PRO, BT 6/93/117, Account of oil imported and exported, 1700–85; BT 6/93/124, Account of oil imported into Scotland, 1765–84.

During four years for which exact catch details are available the incidence of clean expeditions would seem to be fairly evenly spread, though some ships obviously did somewhat better than others (Table 8).

The continuing survival of the whaling trade, with its over-all poor performance, cannot be explained in terms of normal economic forces. Whaling did not respond noticeably to market forces such as prices, or, indeed, to its own poor record. There seems to be good justification for the common claim that whaling was a gamble, and it was, moreover, a gamble financed by the government.[44] The bounty had been intended to support the trade during the initial stages of apprenticeship, but whaling never reached the stage where it could stand alone, with the result that bounties remained a massive part of total income. Scottish whalers in the 1750s earned £125,000 at the very most and received bounties amounting to £82,000; in the years 1766–75 they earned £58,890 and received bounties of £56,302. The bounty was absolutely vital to cover costs and keep the trade going, and when owners claimed they could make a profit (of 11 per cent) on 30 tuns of oil and 30 cwt of bone, they were in fact including on their credit side a bounty which was three times as great as the 'surplus' by which they calculated profit.[45] Below-average vessels invariably made a loss, even with the bounty.

Whatever the theoretical value of Scottish-caught oil, the bounty was a most valuable contribution to the economy of the east coast ports. During the

TABLE 7

ESTIMATED EARNINGS OF SCOTTISH WHALERS, 1766–75[46]

		Oil			Bone		Total	Average
	tuns	val	yield	tons	val	yield	earnings	per ship
1766	86	£22	£1,892	4·3	£400	£1,720	£3,612	£401
1767	5	19½	98	0·3	450	113	211	23
1768	33	19½	644	1·7	400	660	1,304	145
1769	319	16½	5,264	16·0	340	5,423	10,687	1,187
1770	213	18½	3,941	10·7	340	3,621	7,562	840
1771	38	21	798	1·9	350	665	1,463	163
1772	284	17	4,828	14·2	340	4,828	9,656	1,073
1773	149	23	3,427	7·5	320	2,384	5,811	581
1774	355	21	7,455	17·8	300	5,325	12,780	1,420
1775	146	24	3,504	7·3	315	2,300	5,804	645

[44] According to William Wilberforce, who came from a major whaling port, 'the sending out of ships to Greenland, was rather to be regarded as a species of gambling than any sort of regular trade: the risk was great, and the gain sometimes proportionably lucrative; but it was almost entirely a matter of chance'. Hansard, *Parliamentary History*, Vol XXV, column 1,379, 12 April 1786.

[45] BT 6/93/95.

[46] Volume of oil from BT 6/93/124, prices from 6/93/94. The quantity of bone, which was not recorded, is calculated on the standard eighteenth century ratio of 1 cwt of bone to 1 tun of oil. While there were variations owing to size of whale, accidents, and bad management, the ratio is generally fairly accurate; if anything it is likely to be on the generous side, which would merely reinforce the argument put forward in this paper. *NB. Slight discrepancies in the bone column, and in other tables, are the result of rounding figures after calculation.*

TABLE 8

Catches and Earnings of Scottish Whalers, 1766, 1768, 1770 and 1773 [47]

(Oil to nearest tun; bone to nearest cwt)

Name of ship	tons	1766			1768			1770			1773			Average earnings	Average per ton
		oil	bone	£	oil	bone	£	oil	bone	£	oil	bone	£		
Blessed Endeavour	316	0	0	0	0	0	0	28	34	1,083	18	17	668	£438	£1·4
Campbeltown	305	23	25	985	0	0	0	44	46	1,592	9	9	340	729	2·4
Diana	219		—			—			—		0	0	0	0	0
Dundee	352	15	15	630	0	0	0	14	16	531	0	0	0	290	0·8
Leith	333	12	13	514	31	27	1,135	0	0	0	8	7	294	486	1·5
North Star	295	14	16	622	0	0	0	9	17	447	1	0	29	275	0·9
Oswald	284	12	11	478	0	0	0	0	0	0	9	9	344	206	0·7
Peggy	238	12	11	478	2	1	79	0	0	0	12	12	454	252	1·1
Princess of Wales	344	0	0	0	0	0	0	65	49	2,031	33	30	1,249	820	2·4
Royal Bounty	331	0	0	0	0	0	0	54	57	1,960	59	57	2,269	1,057	3·2
Average earnings				412			135			849			565		
Average per ton				1·32			0·43			2·73			1·87		

[47] The Scottish Customs officers did not enter accurate details in the bounty certificates in the early days, insofar as they entered blubber instead of oil, and left the bone out altogether. Periodically they sent the accurate details to London, though not often enough to please the statistical branch! Details for 1766 and 1768 are in PRO T 36/13/4 and for 1770 and 1773 are in T 36/13/5.

years when whaling hardly made ends meet (c 1750–80) the state paid out no less than £185,955 to Scottish whaling firms, and during the half century 1750–99 bounties amounted to £301,746 (Table 9). One can hardly exaggerate the impact of sums of this order on the relatively poor communities of Dunbar, Dundee and Aberdeen. An almost endless array of people benefited directly or indirectly from whaling, which required almost as much labour ashore as it did at sea. Victuallers, coopers, ropers, sailmakers, shipwrights, boat-builders, smiths and many other tradesmen made the ships ready for sea, while blubber-boilers, whalebone cutters, stay-makers and brush-makers processed the materials brought home, and more depended on them for their raw material. At least for the ports, if not for the consumers, there were advantages in subsi-dised whaling; and while it is doubtful if many men grew rich on whaling before 1780 there were countless smaller men who drew modest sums and helped to increase its multiplier effects.

The bounty had, then, created and maintained a modest fleet of ships with their valued reserve of seamen, but it could not create an effective, competitive trade because it could not ensure economic success. Indeed, there was a tendency for the bounty to be self-defeating. If too many ships were encouraged there would be a decline either in average catches or in prices, and in both cases owners would be forced to rely on the bounty for their profit. In other words, the bounty could not for long maintain a larger fleet than was justified by market conditions, and may even have been an unsettling influence insofar as it cushioned those influences. Certainly the infusion of bounty money did not result in self-sustaining growth in whaling, and its effects on capital accumula-tion were therefore both erratic and less substantial than might have been found in a shore-based industry with a stock of continuously productive fixed capital.

Not unnaturally there were many people outside the trade who thought that the rest of the community would be better off without it. Adam Smith, sometime Commissioner of Customs for Scotland, was their most able spokes-man. 'The effect of bounties,' he wrote, 'like that of all the other expedients of the mercantile system, can only be to force the trade of a country into a channel

TABLE 9

WHALING BOUNTIES, 1750–99 (FIVE-YEARLY AVERAGES)[48]

| | Whalers | | Bounties | | Whalers | | Bounties |
	No	tons	£		No	tons	£
1750–4	9·2	2,875	5,751	1775–9	6·2	1,965	3,049
1755–9	15·4	4,688	9,009	1780–4	4·8	1,396	2,518
1760–4	12·4	3,794	7,386	1785–9	25·0	7,314	12,062
1765–9	8·8	2,750	5,500	1790–4	17·6	4,787	6,830
1770–4	9·2	2,837	5,673	1795–9	9·4	2,440	2,571

[48] The number and tonnage of whalers is taken from BT 6/93/126 (1750–86) and BT 6/230, fol 76 (1781–1800); the bounties for 1750–85 are from BT 6/93/119, and those for 1785–1800 are calculated from the tonnage returns. The bounty returns in BT 6/230, fol 92, unfortunately only list Great Britain, and the Scottish returns in the series Customs 17 do not begin until 1796.

much less advantageous than that in which it would naturally run of its own accord'.[49] Nevertheless, it might be of value to the community if capital flowed into whaling in order to bring down the price;[50] but bounties did not do this, since a duty was placed on Dutch whale products to stop them undermining British prices and so defeating the strategic objects of the bounty. Any price fall that occurred resulted not from the bounty but from the flood of cheap American oil which, by good mercantilist principles, was admitted to Britain. Whaling was thus supported by the state and under-cut by the colonies!

By 1786, when the whole question of whaling bounties was investigated by the Board of Trade, there were those (including William Pitt)[51] who denied its strategic value, those who regarded it as a healthy and wealthy trade, and those who thought the bounty played no part in the fluctuations in the trade. The Commissioners of Customs, following Adam Smith, argued that the bounty had been introduced to suckle the trade and that half a century was an inordinate time for weaning. It was, they wrote, 'an expense of such magnitude, that we submit the Public ought to be relieved from it, and the trade left to stand upon its own Bottom – That it may well do so, there is no reason to doubt, from the successful voyages these ships now almost constantly make . . .'[52] Had the trade suddenly become prosperous? The Commissioners' view appears to be supported by the number of vessels entering the trade, and so far as Scotland was concerned Scoresby later asserted that in 1785 'the trade began again to flourish'.[53] There were four whalers fitted out in 1783, thirteen in 1785 and thirty-one in 1787, a figure equal to a third of the Dutch fleet which had hitherto played the major part in the trade. The bounty was of slight importance compared with changes on the supply side as the Dutch trade declined rapidly, and as American oil was excluded from the British market following independence. Prices during the war had already reached a point which encouraged investors in the post war period, and, as if to make over-investment easier, there were many vessels going cheap as the transatlantic trade passed through a period of confusion.

In such circumstances an expansion of the whaling fleet in both England and Scotland was only to be expected, and, given continued exclusion of foreign oil and bone, there was good reason for supposing that the British trade might increase its profitability if only it could improve its catches. There was, however, a lengthy transitional period during which the optimism of the Commissioners of Customs was hardly warranted. An analysis of the Scottish trade in the late 1780s shows no great improvement on past performance (Table 10). The year of greatest activity, 1788, was also a year of minimum returns which soon drove ships out of the trade again. They had not been additions to the naval reserve attracted by the bounty, but speculations – which failed. Even with the bounty, total income per vessel fell more often than not below the £4·86 per ton thought necessary to show any profit at all, and Scottish whalers were no

[49] Adam Smith, *The Wealth of Nations* (Everyman ed 1910), Vol II, 7.
[50] Ibid, 18.
[51] Speech in bounty debate, 12 April 1786, *Parliamentary Hist*, xxv, col 1,382.
[52] Report of the Board of Customs, BT 6/93/132 and BT 5/3, 352.
[53] Scoresby, II, 117.

TABLE 10

PRODUCE AND EARNINGS OF SCOTTISH WHALERS, 1785–90[54]

| | Whalers | | | Total | | | | Average | | | | | Earnings per ton | |
	No	tons	bounties	Oil tuns	Oil £	Bone cwt	Bone £	Oil £	Bone £	Total £	Bounty £	Income £	without bounty £	with bounty £
1785	13	3,846	£7,730	262	5,764	438	5,366	443	413	856	595	1,451	2·88	4·90
1786	23	7,197	14,394	896	16,128	836	9,405	701	409	1,110	626	1,736	3·55	5·55
1787	31	9,057	13,568	929	16,722	1,219	12,190	539	393	933	438	1,370	3·19	4·69
1788	31	8,905	13,226	794	13,498	1,173	7,625	435	246	681	427	1,108	2·37	3·86
1789	27	7,548	11,375	885	15,930	1,190	7,735	590	286	876	421	1,297	3·14	4·64
1790	23	6,297	8,486	536	11,792	517	4,395	513	191	704	396	1,073	2·57	3·92

[54] Calculated from Comparative State of the Greenland Fishery, BT 6/94/59 and 92.

different from the English ones which, it was reported to the Board of Trade, were losing money heavily in the late 1780s.[55] At this stage of whaling the bounty still made the profit for the less fortunate ships and for the trade as a whole, despite the optimism of those who viewed the activity rather than the profitability in the trade.

Real prosperity came, then, not with the great expansion of the 1780s but with the contraction that followed. Even with an enlarged number of whalers, and with the total disappearance of Dutch specialists, average catches in the 1780s had been greater than ever before, with oil passing the desirable 30 tuns in 1786, 1787 and 1789. Given the collapse of the Dutch trade, and the decline in numbers active in the British, those whalers which persevered into the 1790s entered a 'golden age' when vessels were generally 'well-fished' and catches were phenomenally high. At the same time an improving market (rather than shortage) drove the price of oil up to £31 per tun in 1795 and £40 by 1801.[56] Costs were naturally higher during the French wars, but owners were able to economise by using more 'Greenmen' and apprentices, though they were not allowed to employ the even cheaper Shetlanders until 1806. More important, perhaps, was the beginning of a decline in the size of whalers. Larger ships did not perform better than smaller ones though their costs were proportionally greater, and most of the newer vessels were consequently small. The average size of whalers declined as a result from 277 tons in 1785–9 to 260 tons in 1795–9, and vessels such as the 169 ton *Robert* of Peterhead and the 176 ton *Rodney* of Dundee were to be found among the more successful whalers at the turn of the century, when only one vessel could be described as poorly-fished (Table 11).

Unfortunately the Customs Ledgers do not record oil and bone separately for Scotland in the 1790s, but the general trend indicated by Table 11 is easily confirmed from tables of imports at individual ports in 1790–2 and 1799–1802, which show an average of 451 tuns in the former years and 637 tuns in the latter.[57] Since the average number of ships had declined from 20·6 to 10·8, the average catch rose from 21·8 to 82·4 tuns within a decade, with an average of 110 tuns in the best year, 1799, and with no figure lower than 70 tuns.

It was against such a background of growth in catch and earnings that the bounty was gradually reduced. The political power of the whalermen in the English ports was such that they could prolong its life into the 1780s, but the attack on it by the Customs Commissioners was decisive though at the time it was probably based on misconceptions. However, the crucial blow to the old bounty was the realisation in the Board of Trade that an easier and cheaper source of oil was to be found in the Southern Whale Fishery which had previously been dominated by the Americans and which, by the early nineteenth century, was providing more oil to the British market than came from Greenland. If the reduction of the bounty to thirty shillings in 1787, twenty-five

[55] Memorial of Merchants in the Greenland Trade, BT 6/94, fol 87–91.
[56] Prices for 1786–1801 are in BT 6/230, fol 95.
[57] *Accounts presented to the House of Commons of the quantities of . . . articles Imported into Scotland . . . in the three years ending 5 Jan 1793 and four years ending 5 Jan 1803* (1803).

TABLE 11

CATCHES AND ESTIMATED INCOME OF SCOTTISH WHALERS, 1795 AND 1801[58]

		1795						1801					
		Oil tun	Bone cwt	Value £	Bounty £	Total Income £	Income p. ton £	Oil tun	Bone cwt	Value £	Bounty £	Total Income £	Income p. ton £
Aberdeen	Hercules	78	109	3,329	310	3,639	14·7	72	62	3,072	248	3,320	13·4
	Latona	79	121	3,470	295	3,765	16·0	39	39	1,677	236	1,913	8·1
	Robert	46	114	2,380	211	2,591	15·3	47	41	1,993	169	2,162	12·8
	Jane							60	64	2,618	278	2,896	10·4
Dunbar	Blessed Endeavour	74	63	2,814	374	3,188	10·9	73	124	3,323	377	3,700	9·8
	East Lothian	59	69	2,416	471	2,887	7·7	18	32	814	314	1,128	3·6
	North Star							68	47	2,873	312	3,185	10·2
Dundee	Estridge							46	29	1,924	176	2,100	11·9
	Rodney	60	66	2,421	220	2,641	15·0						
	Tay	52	54	2,071	363	2,434	8·4						
Leith	Raith	82	80	3,222	369	3,591	12·2	139	150	6,028	295	6,323	21·4
	Royal Bounty	91	90	3,586	353	3,939	14·0	117	154	5,181	282	5,463	19·4
Montrose	Eliza Swan	75	99	3,167	303	3,469	14·3	121	141	5,288	242	5,530	22·9

[58] Details of catches from returns in PRO T 36/13/8–9 (SRO RH 2/4/553–4); prices from BT 6/230, fol 95.

shillings in 1793 and twenty shillings in 1796 was actually to blame for the decline in the number of vessels engaged in the fishery, then it would appear that a reduction in the bounty was essential to bring about a truly commercial industry; but it is more likely that by the mid-1790s the bounty had ceased to have any but the slightest influence in the trade.

It is difficult to escape the conclusion that the whaling bounty did not achieve its purpose. It did not create a flourishing competitive trade which could stand on its own feet in the face of Dutch or American whaling. It certainly maintained a small fleet of ships in the eastern ports, and in so doing made a useful contribution to economic development in that region, but it did nothing to help the trade towards a position of economic viability, let alone sustained growth. The bounty may even have hindered the development of a sound trade by over-encouraging it and making it too easy for gamblers to push in when prices were rising, to the detriment of those who had previously suffered and were waiting to recoup their losses, though this was less of a problem in Scotland, with its well organised whaling companies, than it was in England.

Whaling declined after the initial enthusiasm because the bounty could not make up for the poor performance of the novices who engaged in the trade, and because both the Dutch and Americans could produce oil at a price which was unremunerative in Britain. When at last the industry showed signs of vitality, with physical success in the 1780s and financial success in the 1790s, it was not because of the bounty but because changes on both the supply and the demand side had transformed the opportunities for whaling. In other words, the Industrial Revolution was forcing up demand at the very moment that Dutch and American supplies were withheld from the British market. Nevertheless, it would be wrong to dismiss the bounty as being of no account. It kept the bulk of the industry going for thirty troubled years, and in providing a modicum of income to the ports, and jobs for the captains and crews, it helped very slowly to build up that corpus of experience in the whaling grounds which the Scots did not have in 1750. If entrepreneurs and captains were able to grasp the opportunities offered to them in the 1780s and 1790s, and eventually build an important Scottish industry in the nineteenth century, it was largely because the government had financed their apprenticeship. State-assisted whaling was not in itself a success, but it provided the roots from which success might spring.

G. JACKSON

5

Capital and Enterprise in the Scottish Iron Industry, 1780–1840

Although the Scottish iron industry has a pedigree going back at least to mediaeval times, its most substantial development began in the late eighteenth century with the formation of Carron Company in 1759. However, much of this firm's output was consumed south of the Border, an indication that the domestic market was basically agricultural, demanding goods made from foreign bar iron rather than cast-iron products.[1] Markets for tools and nails in the plantation colonies added weight to this propensity to import particularly Swedish bar iron,[2] and it was not until the 1780s that further capacity was added to the Scottish pig-iron industry. The pace of industrialisation in Britain stimulated relatively rapid growth up to about 1805, and this first phase of Scottish expansion then gave way to a period of stagnation which lasted for about twenty years. From 1825 up to 1840 a second phase of domestic development proceeded, much more significant in its general economic effects than its precursor. A statistical skeleton of this progress in terms of numbers of blast furnaces, capacity and output is given in Table 1.

TABLE 1

The Scottish Iron Industry: Blast Furnaces, Capacity and Output 1780–1840

Year	Blast furnaces	Capacity	Output
1780	4	4,000	4,000
1796	21	20,000	16,086
1806	29	32,000	23,240
1828	25	45,000	37,500
1830	27	48,000	39,500
1836	34	110,000	110,000
1840	70	245,000	241,000

Sources: J. Butt, 'The Scottish Iron and Steel Industry before the Hot-Blast', *Papers of the Iron and Steel Institute*, No 580 (1966–7), 10; A. Birch, *The Economic History of the British Iron and Steel Industry* (1967), 151

[1] R. H. Campbell, *Carron Company* (1961), 104 ff.
[2] K. G. Hildebrand, 'Foreign Markets for Swedish Iron in the Eighteenth Century', *Scandinavian Economic History Review*, VI (1958), 33; Mitchell Library, Chamber of Commerce Correspondence, Memorial for the Manufacturers of Iron in Scotland, Jan–Feb 1783.

My principal concern in this paper is not to explain the changing fortunes of the coke-based iron industry (already dealt with elsewhere) but to examine two related features of its development, capital formation and entrepreneurship.

I. *Capital Formation*

It is unfortunately the case that we are unlikely ever to derive exact details of every iron company's financial operations in this period, and thus we are concerned with establishing reasonable estimates based upon data fragments. Nonetheless, certain generalisations can be made both about the production of pig iron and also concerning other operations such as casting or bar iron manufacture. Although there were undoubted differences in the regional and chronological costs of investment, it would be mistaken to assume that furnace costs, for example, amounted to more in the 1820s or 1830s than in the 1780s or 1790s. There is some evidence to suggest the very opposite. The blast furnace at Glenbuck cost about £7,500, including the blowing engine c 1795,[3] and three furnaces at Muirkirk, two miles away, slightly less than £20,000.[4] The capital stock of Clyde ironworks amounting to £6,000 in 1786 was probably intended to cover the cost of the first furnace; yet in 1838 Shotts iron company added a new furnace at a cost of £3,000.[5] Inventories from the 1790s indicate that blast furnaces might represent as much as 30 and 40 per cent of total capital assets: in the case of Glenbuck 39 per cent and in the case of Muirkirk 37 per cent. Collieries and ironstone mines in both these examples were valued at about 20 per cent of total capital employed.

Where bar iron plant existed – as at Wilsontown and Muirkirk – an additional expenditure in the range of 15 to 20 per cent of capital costs was probably incurred. At Wilsontown the bar iron plant cost £14,000 c 1804, and the forge at Muirkirk, together with the water-driven equipment, cost slightly under £10,000, according to a valuation of 1793.[6] In general casting houses or foundries were very much less expensive to construct: at Glenbuck the foundry cost less than £2,000 and its equipment and stocks slightly more, the total approaching £4,000.[7]

Specialist foundries outside the ironworks, although numerous, were commonly much smaller in scale and therefore, relatively cheap to construct and to equip. For example, Joseph Cooper and Alexander Barker owned a foundry in Leith, which was valued in 1793 at £1,000.[8] From the 1820s the size and capital costs of the Glasgow foundries increased – that of Moses McCulloch

---

[3] Scottish Record Office [SRO], RH15/2593, Sederunt Book of the creditors of Glenbuck Iron Company.

[4] SRO, GD237, Box 151, Bundle 3, Tod, Murray and Jamieson Muniments, Abstract of Muirkirk Company's state, 31 Aug 1793.

[5] SRO, Register of Deeds 260/358 Dur.

[6] SRO, GD237, Abstract of Muirkirk Company's state, 31 Aug 1793; I. L. Donnachie and J. Butt, 'The Wilsons of Wilsontown Ironworks (1779–1813): A Study in Entrepreneurial Failure', *Explorations in Entrepreneurial History*, 2nd series, IV (1967), 163.

[7] SRO, RH15/2593.

[8] London Guildhall Library, Sun Fire Insurance Company Policy Registers, GH 11937/2, Policy 622337.

being valued at £4,500 in 1823[9] – but it is difficult to believe that this metal-using sector of the iron industry exceeded £400,000 in total capital assets in 1840. From the evidence of directories, contracts of copartnery and legal cases, it is clear that these units of production were generally small, labour-intensive and non-specialist.[10]

In all types of iron firm it was very common to build up the capital stock from profits. This policy ultimately posed few problems to firms established from 1830 for the following decade was one of relatively high profitability. Earlier, however, trade cycles exposed the weaknesses of businesses which were initially under-capitalised. The periodicity of foundations explains why so many firms encountered difficulties. For they were generally founded at the peaks of booms for capital goods, but economic circumstances had commonly changed before furnaces, foundries and forges came into production.[11] Thus, financial stability was difficult to achieve, since over-dependence on the credit structure was an inevitable consequence of under-capitalisation. One major difficulty, therefore, in compiling capital formation estimates for the industry rose from the constant revaluation of assets consequent on failures or business reorganisations.

The history of the Fife ironworks at Balgonie is paradigmatic. Founded in 1801 at the peak of a boom as the Leven Iron Company, this firm was bankrupt in 1803 before its buildings were completed. Some of the original partners continued the works on their own account, but by September 1803 were unable to meet the wage-bill. Restarted in 1804 once more with the aid of Alexander, 7th and 6th Earl of Leven and Melville (1749–1820), upon whose estate the works was located, the firm underwent financial reorganisation in January 1805, only to run into difficulties once more in 1808. Further financial manipulations accompanied the reconstitution of the business as the New Balgonie Iron Company, but this became bankrupt during the downturn of 1812. On each occasion of bankruptcy or reorganisation, the capital assets were revalued, unfortunately without improving basic profitability.[12]

Few firms in the industry, including Carron Company, were free from the difficulties inherent in initial under-capitalisation. Unlike the Balgonie Company, some businesses even before 1830 managed to achieve sufficiently long periods of profitability to sustain continued existence. But the success of Carron Company, heavily dependent as it was upon sales outside Scotland, was indicative of the industry's problems. Excess capacity presented insuperable difficulties in the twenty years after 1805 primarily because the level of Scottish domestic demand was not adequate to maintain sales of available output at profitable prices, and the London and Liverpool markets were glutted with iron from regions such as Wales with outstanding competitive advantages.

These underlying problems were partly consequential upon the investment

    [9] Ibid, GH 11937/146, Policy 1011071.
    [10] J. Butt, 'The Scottish Iron and Steel Industry before the Hot-Blast', *Journal of the West of Scotland Iron and Steel Institute*, 73 (1965–6), 208.
    [11] Ibid, 200 ff.
    [12] SRO, GD26/5/370–4, Leven and Melville Muniments; RH15/203, Sederunt Book of the Creditors of Balgonie Iron Company.

process, and until domestic demand caught up with supply, piecemeal productivity gains could only ameliorate without remedying a chronic economic condition. Yet in the deflation after 1815 the costs of capital investment fell, and thus new furnaces could be built in the 1820s and 1830s at costs approximately 20 per cent below the level prevailing in the 1790s. For example, Calder ironworks by 1830 had four new furnaces built at a cost of £20,000, including the price of two blowing engines, which, with the demise of Watt's patent, were also much cheaper.[13]

Caution commonly prevailed, even when technical changes made savings possible. Neilson's hot-blast process (1828) greatly reduced fuel costs, made possible significant gains in labour productivity, and since a greater throughput could be achieved in a given period of time economised substantially on capital and raw materials.[14] Yet it was applied relatively slowly and affected investment behaviour very little until after the boom of 1836 had revealed price levels which would have been profitable even if there had been no revolution in technique. Home and foreign demand in these circumstances was so buoyant that the lure of profitability enticed investment into doubling the number of furnaces and total capacity within four years.

Against this background of generalisations, one further characteristic feature must be set before attempting capital formation estimates. New capacity tended to be concentrated in Lanarkshire, thus reducing the likelihood of substantial regional differences in capital costs. Any estimates of capital formation are much more likely to be derived with reasonable accuracy from known capacity and furnace numbers, therefore, in the 1830s, but for the whole period the link between capacity and capital structure, in the absence of detailed financial statements for each firm, seemed the best guide. Table 2 is based upon that fundamental position, although land and colliery costs might be expected to vary even in the same county.

The bench years coincide exactly with those given in Table 1 and were selected because they mark significant features in the development of the pig-iron industry – in Scottish experience up to the 1870s much the most important

TABLE 2

CAPITAL FORMATION ESTIMATES (£) FOR BLAST FURNACE FIRMS

Year	Blast Furnace Investment	Other Investment	Total
1780	20,000	120,000	140,000
1796	100,000	480,000	580,000
1806	160,000	690,000	850,000
1828	225,000	1,340,000	1,565,000
1830	240,000	1,500,000	1,740,000
1836	550,000	2,800,000	3,350,000
1840	1,225,000	4,920,000	6,145,000

[13] Report of the trial of Neilson & Baird (1843), 160.
[14] C. K. Hyde, 'The adoption of the Hot Blast by the British Iron Industry: a Reinterpretation', Explorations in Economic History, X, 3 (1973), 282 ff.

sector. The 1780 figures represent investment at Carron and may err on the side of caution, since early furnace construction might be expected to be more expensive as design was applied in a strange environment.[15] However, it was deemed wisest to give a constant value of £5,000 for each 1,000 tons of blast furnace capacity throughout the period. This is unlikely to deflate the total estimates into the realm of wild inaccuracy and has the merit of emphasising the unrepresentative character of the Ayrshire examples of the 1790s, since for the industry as a whole, blast furnaces accounted for between 15 and 20 per cent of total capital. The 1796 figures give the story after the boom of the late 1780s and early 1790s was completed, and the statistics for 1806 indicate the broad outlines of the earlier boom peaking in 1800–1. In 1828 the hot-blast process was patented and its initial impact on capital formation was comparatively slight until the boom of 1835–6;[16] the late 1830s witnessed a substantial increase in investment, much of it planned during that earlier peak for prices.

Other investment in Table 2 includes the cost of land, collieries, mines and mineral leases, foundries and forges associated with ironworks, limekilns and coke ovens, steam engines, any social capital, and stocks. Rough checks against the experience of Carron, Wilsontown, Shotts and Balgonie suggest that a figure of 80 per cent or more of total capital was generally expended on investment other than blast furnaces.[17] In the 1820s those firms which survived from earlier periods as well as new firms founded in the boom of 1824–5 had disposed their capital more than usually (for the period as a whole) in such other forms of investment. This is probably explained by the related facts that under-capitalisation was ceasing to be a business problem, as the weaker firms left the industry or were reorganised on a sounder financial basis, and that excess capacity engendered caution in the creation of new furnace capacity without inhibiting the acquisition of cheaply priced mineral rights. Thus 85 per cent of total capital in the 1820s was represented by investment other than blast furnaces.

The figures for total investment were based upon the experience of the Shotts company, which in the period up to 1824–5 showed many of the weaknesses common to most firms. Thus, for the period before 1801 when Shotts was founded, two alternative techniques were possible: first, to use other data – from Wilsontown, Clyde and Carron, in particular – and second, to regress into the earlier period the initial experience of Shotts. Both methods were in fact used. For example, the experience of Clyde ironworks confirmed quite clearly that investment in land and minerals accounted for £27,000 in 1794 without any consideration of the capital costs of mining as against £6,000 on the first blast furnace.[18] Thus, figures of 15 to 20 per cent on blast furnaces for

[15] A number of statements to the effect that Carron Company had spent £150,000 on its plant were made, eg to the Royal Bank's directors in the 1770s. I am grateful for this reference to Professor S. G. Checkland.

[16] R. D. Corrins, 'The Great Hot-Blast Affair', *Industrial Archaeology*, VII (1970), 239–40.

[17] For help with the preparation of these tables and also for checks undertaken on individual companies, I am grateful to Mrs A. M. C. MacEwan, formerly my research assistant.

[18] SRO, Unextracted Processes, Currie Dal, C11/19, Clyde Iron Company v Dunlop, 1805–6.

the period 1780–1806 do not appear unreasonable. Having capital formation estimates for blast furnaces, which included information from Carron, Wilsontown, Muirkirk and Glenbuck, made it possible to establish the likely arithmetical limits on other forms of capital investment.

As already indicated in broad terms, the costs of capital investment in the 1830s tended to fall. However, from an assessment of Tables 1 and 2, it is apparent that total capital formation must have greatly increased; moreover, the proportion spent on furnaces rose compared with the 1820s but was rather similar in its proportions to experience in the period 1780 to 1806. With the general application of the hot-blast process by the late 1830s, greater quantities of raw materials were needed to keep furnaces in full production, even though fuel was a less significant cost in smelting. As competition for mining leases developed in the Monklands area of Lanarkshire, land costs tended to rise. For instance, the estate of Coltness with its rich mineral deposits cost £80,000 in 1836 before any furnaces were erected.[19] No doubt, the capital costs per 1,000 tons of output fell sharply in the 1830s· indeed the evidence from Shotts suggests that there was a decrease of over 50 per cent.[20] However, a great expansion of output and capacity was a consequence of a substantial increase in total investment.

Data about the metal-using sectors of the iron industry are much less in evidence. Malleable iron production was relatively unimportant before 1840, although a few firms producing goods reached capital sizes of £10,000 or more. Examples are the Smithfield, Dalnottar and Cramond companies, all of which combined to finance Muirkirk Iron Company.[21] In addition, there were about fifty small foundries not directly owned by blast furnace firms by 1813.[22] Mostly they were small and non-specialist, with little fixed capital. Their capital

TABLE 3

Capital Formation in Foundries, Forges and Malleable Iron Firms (Independent of Blast Furnace Firms)

Year	£
1780	100,000
1796	170,000
1806	190,000
1828	230,000
1830	255,000
1836	300,000
1840	400,000

[19] J. L. Carvel, The Coltness Iron Company (Edinburgh, 1948), 11 ff.

[20] A. M. C. MacEwan, 'The Shotts Iron Company 1800–50' (Unpublished MLitt thesis of the University of Strathclyde, 1972), 104.

[21] J. R. Hume and J. Butt, 'Muirkirk 1786–1802: the creation of a Scottish industrial community', Scottish Historical Review, XLV (1966), 166 ff; R. H. Campbell, 'Early Malleable Iron Production in Scotland', Business History, IV (1961); G. Thomson, 'The Dalnottar Iron Company', Scottish Historical Review, XXXV (1956), 10–20; T. M. Devine, The Tobacco Lords (Edinburgh, 1975), 37; Signet Library, Edinburgh, Session Papers 180; 8.

[22] H. Hamilton, The Industrial Revolution in Scotland (Oxford, 1932), 176.

size and numbers increased in the 1820s and 1830s especially in the city of Glasgow. Table 3 gives a series of capital formation estimates in this metal-using sector, taking into consideration the evidence of the *Statistical Accounts* and the directories.

Scottish foundries were able to take advantage of cheap pig-iron in the period after 1815, and this was the one circumstance which greatly aided their development. Another was the existence of abundant labour, including a sufficient supply of skilled labour. The gradual diversification of the economy associated with industrialisation widened the domestic market for cast-iron goods and, on long trend, increased the profitability of operations.

Some ventures were apparently grandiose. The Caledonian Iron and Foundry Company was established in Edinburgh in October 1824 'for the purpose of carrying on the business of smelting & manufacturing iron in all its branches'. The capital stock was fixed at £100,000, made up of 4,000 shares of £25 each. In fact, never more than £20,000 was called, and much of this, according to aggrieved shareholders, never found its way into productive investment. However, a foundry was established and valued with its equipment at just over £11,000 in 1828.[23] Most of the larger foundries were owned by the ironworks companies up to 1840, even though some of them were located in Glasgow and Edinburgh, miles away from the blast furnace plant.

Another feature of capital investment was its increasing concentration. The number of firms certainly increased in the 1820s and 1830s but not so rapidly as output. Bairds, for instance, by 1840 had twelve furnaces in blast and others at the planning stage; this single firm accounted for 17 per cent of pig-iron production.[24] The most important single explanation of this process was reploughing of profits. In general, the successful firms did not raise their rates of dividends; they increased their capital size and maintained dividends on a larger capital. The results were very much the same so far as partners were concerned, for greater profits were made and greater amounts paid in dividends. However, future profitability was safeguarded, as old plant was replaced and generous provision made for depreciation.

Estimates of aggregate gross capital formation in all branches of the Scottish iron industry (excluding the four charcoal-based firms) can, therefore, be compiled by uniting Tables 2 and 3. This is done in Table 4. Thus it seems likely that capital formation increased threefold between 1780 and 1796 and by a slightly larger margin in the 1830s.

After 1825 the great growth in the industry – which by the early 1840s accounted for 25 per cent of British output compared with about 5 per cent in 1830 – was aided by better technique and the abundance of blackband ironstone in the coal measures of Lanarkshire. Yet it would be a grave error of judgement to assign too much significance to a single technical process, even though the hot-blast was revolutionary in its implications, or to the prolific nature of factor

[23] SRO, Unextracted Processes, I Potts c 17/42, Caledonian Iron & Foundry Company v Scot 1831.
[24] R. D. Corrins, 'William Baird and Company 1830–1914', (Unpublished PhD thesis of the University of Strathclyde, 1974), 90.

endowments. A massive injection of demand from the United Kingdom and foreign markets stimulated the developing pace of capital formation in the 1830s. Weaker firms had been weeded out of the industry, and increasing profitability made the credit structure – and particularly the banks – more responsive to its capital needs. Ironically, reploughing of profits made external sources of finance less necessary.

II. *Entrepreneurship*

Commonly, the initial pressures to create iron firms were generated by the social and economic interaction of landowners and merchants. In the case of the Balgonie works, the initiative arose out of the financial embarrassment of David the 6th and 5th Earl of Leven and Melville (1722–1802), who in March 1800 had placed his estates in trust for the benefit of his creditors. His heir, Lord. Balgonie, who succeeded to the title in 1802, was equally short of funds, and the trustee, William Keith, advised him to increase his income and to eliminate his debts by developing the estate's mineral resources: 'It would be of very great Consequence to establish a Foundry & Ironworks upon your Estate provided a respectable Company with a sufficient Capital would undertake it.' The Devon ironworks was fostered by Lord Cathcart's 'man of business', who like Keith regarded such a project as the best outlet for his master's minerals.[25] Similar evidence could be adduced from Ayrshire, where Commodore Keith Stewart (1739–95) was active in sponsoring the development of ironworks at Muirkirk and Glenbuck,[26] or from Lanarkshire, where Colonel William Dalrymple supported the establishment of Omoa ironworks.[27] However, landowners generally adopted a passive rôle once industrial developments had been launched, unless they were compelled to intervene to safeguard their income from mineral royalties or their amenity.[28]

Joint ventures in the form of unincorporated companies were the most common forms of enterprise, although in the 1820s and 1830s Shotts Iron

TABLE 4

GROSS CAPITAL FORMATION IN THE SCOTTISH IRON INDUSTRY

Year	£
1780	240,000
1796	750,000
1806	1,040,000
1828	1,795,000
1830	1,995,000
1836	3,650,000
1840	6,545,000

[25] SRO, GD26/5/370, William Keith to Lord Balgonie, 1, 7, 14 July, 11 Aug, 3 and 12 Sept 1800.

[26] Hume and Butt, 'Muirkirk ...,' 162 ff and 179–80.

[27] Sir J. Sinclair (ed), *Statistical Account of Scotland* (Edinburgh, 1791–8), XV, 60.

[28] On this general question cf T. C. Smout, 'Scottish Landowners and Economic Growth', *Scottish Journal of Political Economy*, XI (1964), 218–34.

Company tried unsuccessfully to emulate the earlier example of Carron Company which had managed to obtain limited liability in 1773.[29] Family groups were frequently found within partnerships, but up to 1840 family firms represented a minority of the total businesses in the industry. The dominance of the partnership as the most common form of business enterprise can be explained both in legal and financial terms. At Scottish law the partnership's articles of association or 'contract' were legally enforceable, and the firm possessed a legal entity with rights to sue and be sued.[30] Thus, it was possible, in practice, to limit the financial risks of partners by specifying clearly within the contract of copartnery what borrowing rights managing partners possessed. Should they exceed these limits, they could be made personally responsible for the unauthorised loans. Further, the individual obligations of partners could be closely defined and fixed in proportion to shareholdings. In consequence, investing partners did not require to concern themselves in the day-to-day operations of the partnership. Equally, it was traditional mercantile practice in Scotland to disperse one's assets in a number of ventures in the hope of minimising risks and maximising returns. Larger than normal capital requirements, therefore, held few terrors for the commercial community, since they were met, in general, by extending the partnership rather than by increasing the individual shareholding.[31]

From time to time formal contracts of copartnery were not signed. Invariably in the period up to 1830 when under-capitalisation was a constant problem, this informality was a source of trouble and occasionally, of litigation. For instance, Wilsontown and Calder iron companies lacked formal contracts, and in resulting disputes it was impossible to apportion legal responsibility except in broadest terms.[32]

The sources of enterprise and of capital were much less obvious than the legal forms they took. English involvement was substantial, particularly up to 1806, and sometimes Scots in England invested funds, earned elsewhere, in Scottish ironworks. Carron Company and the charcoal-based companies had already established these traditions before 1780. Carron was founded in 1759 by Samuel Garbett, Dr John Roebuck and William Cadell of Cockenzie, only the latter being Scottish;[33] the York Buildings Company and ironmasters from the Furness district of north-west England had earlier built charcoal furnaces in the Highlands.[34] Wilsontown was founded in 1779 by three brothers, Robert,

[29] MacEwan, 'Shotts', 33 ff; R. H. Campbell, *Carron Company*, 24–5.

[30] R. H. Campbell, 'The Law and the Joint Stock Company in Scotland' in P. L. Payne (ed), *Studies in Scottish Business History* (1967), 136–51.

[31] These generalisations are based upon an extensive study of contracts of copartnery recorded in the Register of Deeds in the Scottish Record Office as well as in the Glasgow City Archives collection of Burgh Deeds.

[32] Donnachie and Butt, 'Wilsontown', 156–60; SRO, Unextracted Processes I McNeill C/7/16 Calder Coal Company v Calder Steel and Iron Company, 1804.

[33] R. H. Campbell, *Carron Company*, 7–10.

[34] D. Murray, *The York Buildings Company* (1973 ed), 61, 63–4; A. Fell, *The Early Iron Industry of Furness and District* (Ulverston, 1908), 343–415; SRO, GD1/168, Papers and Journals of Invergarry 1727–36 Ironworks; National Library of Scotland MS 993–5, Books and Papers of the Lorn Furnace Company 1752–1813.

John and William Wilson. They were natives of the parish of Carnwath in Lanarkshire, but John and William had accumulated the capital as a result of mercantile activities in Gothenburg and London.[35] The Wilkinson brothers, William and John, nibbled at the opportunity presented by Muirkirk before native enterprise established the works in 1787.[36] At Glenbuck the first firm operating between 1795 and 1805 was that of John Rumney and Company of Workington and was succeeded by another Cumbrian partnership led by Patrick and Peter Hodgson of Whitehaven.[37]

Perhaps the history of Balgonie ironworks will serve to emphasise the persistence of English enterprise. On 29 May 1801, for an annual rent of £1,300. George and William Losh, John Robinson and Joseph Wilson, partners in the Team Ironworks, Newcastle, Henry Martin, formerly of the London banking house of Hatton and Martin, Alexander Barker, Joseph Cooper and his son, Samuel P. Cooper, partners in Leith Walk Iron Foundry, secured the lease of ground and minerals, and the new works was begun.[38] The Losh family remained most constant, after this first partnership ran into financial difficulties. George (1766–1846) and William (1770–1861) were supported by their elder brother James (1763–1833), although he never did more than provide additional funds but was disappointed in the outcome.[39] 'Patience and fortitude are certainly Xtian virtues', he confided to his diary on 27 November 1809, 'and I pray to god that they may not fail me.'[40] In all, there were seven English partnerships at Balgonie, culminating in one dominated by Thomas Lewis, a London merchant, who gave up operations in 1814.[41]

During the great expansion of the industry in the late 1830s English enterprise was represented solely by the Coltness Iron Company. Founded in 1836, its moving spirit was Henry Houldsworth, who used his inside knowledge as a director of the Shotts Iron Company, to outbid that firm when it was seeking to expand. The capital was provided by Thomas Houldsworth of Manchester from profits made in the cotton industry, but the Glasgow Houldsworths had already acquired the Anderston foundry as their first step into the iron industry. Thomas and Henry Houldsworth were the senior partners, but it was Henry's sons, William and John, who undertook the active direction of the iron firm. Another partner was David Chapman who shared with Henry Houldsworth a cotton venture in Airdrie.[42]

Naturalised by domicile, the Dixons of Govan, principally coalmasters till

[35] Donnachie and Butt, 'Wilsontown', 150–2.

[36] Hume and Butt, 'Muirkirk', 164–6.

[37] J. Butt, 'Glenbuck Iron Works', *Ayrshire Collections*, 2nd series, VIII (1967–9), 68–75; SRO, Extracted Process, Decree exonerating John Sloan, trustee for Glenbuck Iron Company and RH15/2593.

[38] SRO, Leven and Melville Muniments, GD26/5/374.

[39] H. Lonsdale, *The Worthies of Cumberland* (1873), IV, 146 ff; SRO, Leven and Melville Muniments, GD26/5/371/2 Correspondence between James Losh and the Earl of Leven and Melville 1808–10; *The Diaries and Correspondence of James Losh*, ed E. Hughes (Surtees Society Publications 171 and 174, 1956 and 1959), I, xii ff.

[40] Carlisle Public Reference Library MS B320/8, Diary of James Losh, 1809–11.

[41] SRO, RH15/203, Sederunt Book of the creditors of Balgonie Iron Company, 1812; GD26/5/371/2–3, Correspondence and Memoranda relating to the ironworks, 1812–15.

[42] J. L. Carvel, *The Coltness Iron Company*, 11–20; MacEwan, 'Shotts', 88–9.

the acquisition of Calder ironworks in 1804, had their family origins in north-east England. After the failure of the Wilsons at Wilsontown, William Dixon I (1753–1824) acquired this works in 1821 and reopened it. Total costs of these purchases were under £12,000; for minerals alone this price represented two outstanding bargains.[43] However, Dixon of Calder was successful in 1830 in smelting iron with raw coal instead of coke, using Neilson's hot-blast process. Neilson and his partners in the hot-blast patent persuaded Dixon not to seek a patent for his new development and compensated him by granting him the right to use the hot-blast technique free of charge at two furnaces and by promising him a share in any licence revenue in excess of 5p per ton.[44]

Scottish enterprise was also well represented – increasingly from 1825 on-wards. Muirkirk Iron Company derived about 75 per cent of its initial capital from ex-colonial merchants, associated with the West Indian and American trades. Much the most significant influence in the early 1790s when the firm ran into financial difficulties was Neil Jamieson, formerly agent in New York for John Glassford and Company, the greatest of the tobacco trading companies. It was largely as a result of Jamieson's willingness to lend £11,000 on 2 May 1793 that the Muirkirk Company survived the financial crisis, especially since he exhibited to the Company's bond-holders a state of his personal affairs showing assets worth over £50,000. Furthermore, he agreed to place with the cashier of the Royal Bank a bond for £10,000, thus ensuring that working capital continued to be provided by the bank.[45]

About the early history of Clyde ironworks there are some elements of mystery. John Mackenzie of Strathgrave was associated with William Cadell and Thomas Edington briefly, but seems to have soon abandoned this connec-tion. Probably, he had technical experience of furnace building, since a man of the same name had been a technical consultant in the early years of Wilson-town ironworks. The minerals exploited by the partners at Clyde were owned by James Dunlop of Garnkirk, who was involved in many industrial enterprises before his bankruptcy in 1793. The Dunlop family retained an interest in mining on the bankrupt's estate through another James Dunlop, a London merchant who had been in the Virginia trade and resident in America.[46] In 1810 the Dunlops owned Clyde ironworks, and one can only conjecture that the London merchant's money had successfully triumphed over local capital.[47]

Francis and John Anderson, Leith iron merchants, were partners c 1796 in

[43] B. F. Duckham, *A History of the Scottish Coal Industry 1700–1815* (Newton Abbot, 1970), 129, 138–9, 181–4; Donnachie and Butt, 'Wilsontown', 166.

[44] R. D. Corrins, 'The Great Hot-Blast Affair', 239–40; James Condie who developed the Scotch tuyere c 1834, another element in the success of the hot-blast, was employed by Dixon at Wilsontown.

[45] SRO, Tod, Murray and Jamieson Muniments, GD237/151/3, Agreement and Supersedere betwixt the Dalnottar, Duntocher and Muirkirk Companies and their creditors, 1793; State of Neil Jamieson's estate, 23 Oct 1793 and accompanying letter of Jamieson to Tod, 21 Oct 1793.

[46] SRO, Unextracted Processes, Currie Dal, C11/19; Donnachie and Butt, 'Wilson-town', 152; T. M. Devine, *The Tobacco Lords*, 43, 47 and 180.

[47] H. Hamilton, *The Industrial Revolution in Scotland*, 176–7.

the Omoa ironworks, and they were replaced by William Young, a coalmaster, c 1810. Such a progression was fairly normal, for coalmasters became significant entrepreneurs in the iron industry from its inception. At Calder ironworks the initial partnership, formed in 1800, consisted of Alexander and David Allan, Glasgow merchants, James Burns and David Mushet, the latter being the managing partner. There was no formal partnership agreement, and the Allans attempted later to deny any association with the works. Initially, the coal for the furnaces was supplied by the Calder Coal Company which consisted of William Dixon and William Creelman, and as we have already noticed, Dixon purchased the ironworks in 1804 when Mushet and his partners ran into financial difficulties.[48]

Hugh and Robert Baird, founders and engineers of Port Dundas, inspired the formation of the Shotts Iron Company, taking a lease of land and minerals in 1801. They were joined by Walter Logan, George Munro, and their brother, John Baird, who were also partners in the Banton Coal Company. This co-partnery was a real marriage of convenience: the Port Dundas foundry required a regular supply of pig-iron, and the Banton Coal Company would have a good customer in the furnaces at Shotts. In the general depression of 1809–10 Hugh and Robert Baird encountered financial difficulties which caused them to withdraw from the Shotts Iron Company, but by 1811 all the partners were insolvent. The firm was only saved by the accession of new partners, John Blackburn and Robert Bogle, who cleared its debts amounting to £5,580. Logan, Munro, Blackburn and Bogle were all Glasgow merchants, the last two having made money in the West India trade.

When the Shotts Iron Company was re-organised with over thirty partners in 1827, its principal shareholders were Glasgow and Edinburgh merchants. Previously John Baird, the managing partner, had exercised most entrepreneurial functions, but by 1827 a new board of directors had relegated him to the rôle of production manager. The capital assets of the concern were increased from calls on shares and undistributed profits from £40,000 in 1824, first to £60,000 by 1826, then to £100,000 by 1836 and ultimately to £185,000 by 1840.[49]

The numerical size of the Shotts partnership from 1824 onwards was not typical of the industry as a whole. The Bairds of Gartsherrie developed a very substantial family firm which was founded on capital made in farming and coalmining by Alexander Baird, the father of a formidable iron dynasty which made profits of nearly £270,000 between 1833 and 1840.[50] John Wilson (1787–1851), managing partner at Clyde for Colin Dunlop and a shareholder in Neilson's royalty revenue, created, with Dunlop's backing, an ironworks at Dundyvan beginning in 1833. After Dunlop's death in 1837, Wilson became sole proprietor and greatly extended the works, incorporating within it a

[48] SRO, RH15/1925, Ledger of Omoa Ironworks and Bill Chamber Processes II, 19451; Unextracted Processes, I McNeill, C/7/16.
[49] MacEwan, 'Shotts', 28 ff.
[50] A. McGeorge, *The Bairds of Gartsherrie* (Glasgow, 1876), passim.

malleable iron plant, the total complex costing in the region of £300,000.[51] Summerlee Iron Company, operational in 1837, was founded with capital earned in the chemical and coal industries, for two of the four partners – John and George – were sons of John Wilson of the Hurlet alum works, and a third, Alexander, his nephew.[52] Carnbroe ironworks (1838) had only three partners – Alexander Alison, James Merry and Alexander Cunninghame, all of whom had prior experience in coalmining.[53]

Although most firms depended ultimately upon the capital made available by their partners, loan capital on bond or mortgage was commonly raised to eke out cash credits provided by banks. The Wilsons of Wilsontown had one cash credit with the Thistle Bank in Glasgow, and another for £10,500 with the Edinburgh bank of Sir William Forbes and Company. In addition, nearly £70,000 had been raised from London banks on mortgage.[54] Shotts Iron Company relied heavily on loans raised on bonds, over £12,000 being outstanding in 1830 and nearly £26,000 in 1838. Bank credit became more significant to this firm in the very last year of the 1830s.[55] Within that decade there was a significant movement of ironmasters on to the boards of banks, the Bairds being involved with the Western Bank, James Merry with the Clydesdale Bank and the Dunlops with the Commercial Bank of Glasgow.[56] Not only did enterprise reveal itself in the expansion of existing firms and the creation of new concerns but also in the more favourable reception given to ironmasters in financial circles.

It should be obvious from these brief remarks about capital formation and entrepreneurship that there was no fundamental shortage of either factor of production in Scotland by the 1830s. Structural changes in the economy could proceed but were generally dependent upon market changes outside Scotland. The external growth of demand for pig-iron and cast-iron goods was so rapid in the 1830s that factor endowments could be combined effectively with improved technology and advances in marketing and distribution to achieve massive growth in output.[57]

[51] T. B. Mackenzie, *Life of James Beaumont Neilson F.R.S.* (Glasgow, 1928), 31; A. Millar, *The Rise and Progress of Coatbridge and the Surrounding Neighbourhood* (Glasgow, 1864), 116 ff.

[52] Millar, *Coatbridge*, 120.

[53] Ibid, 122.

[54] Donnachie and Butt, 'Wilsontown', 160 ff.

[55] MacEwan, 'Shotts', 67 ff.

[56] Millar, *Coatbridge*, 34; Contract of Copartnery of the Clydesdale Banking Company, Glasgow (1838), 24; W. H. Marwick, *Economic Developments in Victorian Scotland* (1936), 62 ff.

[57] The research upon which this essay is based was conducted under the auspices of the Social Science Research Council. I am most grateful to the Council for their support.

JOHN BUTT

6

The Glasgow Cotton Spinners, 1837

Between 11 o'clock and midnight on Saturday 22 July 1837 John Smith, a cotton spinner, was shot in the back while out shopping with his wife in Glasgow's Clyde Street. Three days later he died from his wounds in the Royal Infirmary, but not before he had suggested that the reason for his assassination was the fact that he was continuing to work as a spinner during the strike of the Glasgow cotton spinners that had been going on since April. In the parlance of the time he was a 'nob'. On 29 July, Archibald Alison, the Sheriff of Lanarkshire, accompanied by Captain Miller, the superintendent of the city's police, raided the 'Black Boy' tavern in the Gallowgate and arrested the committee of the cotton spinners' association which regularly met there. In all, eighteen cotton spinners were arrested over the next few days. Most were held for periods ranging from two or three days to four or five weeks and then released without charge. But the officers of the Association, Thomas Hunter (aet 41), the president, Peter Hacket (36), the treasurer, Richard McNeil (28), the secretary and James Gibb (33), the assistant secretary, together with another spinner, William McLean (26), who was believed to have committed the actual murder, were charged and brought to trial in Edinburgh. The indictment against the five was a long one, involving illegal conspiracy, use of threats, intimidation and molestation against employers and workers, conspiracy to murder, and murder itself. In all, there were twelve charges against the prisoners. After what was one of the most lengthy trials to that date (the court sat for eight days from 10 am until 11 pm) the jury found, by a majority, four of the charges proved and, unanimously, the other charges not proven. The most serious charges of murder, and conspiracy to murder were found not proven, and they were found guilty only of being leading members of an association engaged in illegal activities. In particular, they were convicted of picketing, on two specific occasions, with intent to intimidate. The sentence was seven years transportation.

The trial and the particularly severe sentences imposed by the court were of crucial importance in the development of early Scottish trade unionism. The most powerful of Scottish unions was seriously weakened. The stigma of violence remained attached to unionism in the west of Scotland for years afterwards and it was decades before Scottish trade unionism recovered from this set-back.

Although well-known and frequently referred to by historians, the strike and trial have not in fact been examined in any great depth. In the records of the trial, in the reports of the Select Committee on Combinations of Workmen, which held its enquiry in 1838, and in the papers of the Government's law officers, one has a uniquely detailed collection of material relating to an early trade union. There are difficulties, of course. Firstly, it is not always clear who is speaking the truth. Can one trust the evidence of the accused, fighting for their lives or of the witnesses, well-paid for their services? James Moat, Robert Christie and James Murdoch, the key state witnesses, shared, with four others, the £500 reward offered by the cotton masters and the £100 paid by the government. Moat and Christie with their families were given free passage to Sydney, and the others to Quebec, with sums of money ranging from £141 to £317.[1] Secondly, it is never an easy task to understand a strike. As Alvin Gouldner, the author of one of the best-known studies of a strike, commented, 'a "strike" is a social phenomenon of enormous complexity, which, in its totality, is never susceptible to complete description, let alone complete explanation'.[2] To the participants in any system of industrial relations – the workers and their organisation, the management and the public authorities – a strike can look totally different. Each will stress particular events as being the significant ones and each will see some of the truth. In the case of the Glasgow cotton spinners the documentation exists enabling one to examine the issue through the eyes of all main participants. To look at all viewpoints does not guarantee total understanding: more likely it merely brings out the complexity and multi-facetted nature of industrial relations. In doing so, however, it is hoped that some useful insights can be provided into numerous aspects of the life, actions and thoughts of the participants.

I

The factory-based cotton industry had been introduced into Scotland at the ends of the 1770s, with mills at Rothesay and Penicuik, and was established in Glasgow in the early 1780s. By the 1830s, the industry was very much concentrated in the Glasgow area, with 98 cotton mills of about forty firms in the city and its immediate neighbourhood, employing about 10,000 workers. Of these about 1,000 were spinners who had under them three piecers, usually girls or boys from their own family, and there were about 3,000 card-room operatives and a similar number of casual carters, porters and labourers dependent on the mill.[3] Most spinners would have entered the mill as a little piecer at the age of eight or nine and gradually worked their way up to become a spinner, after about the age of seventeen, as vacancies occurred. As a little piecer, crawling

[1] S[cottish] R[ecord] O[ffice], Crown Agent's Papers. Balance Sheet.
[2] A. Gouldner, *Wildcat Strike* (1955), 65.
[3] [A. Alison], 'Practical Working of Trades' Unions', *Blackwood's Edinburgh Magazine*, XLIII (March 1838), 292; J. Butt, *Industrial Archaeology of Scotland* (Newton Abbot, 1967), 72.

under the threads and keeping the machine clear of dust, a child could expect to earn 2s 6d a week. At seventeen, as an experienced outside piecer, his earnings would be about 6s 3d. The piecer was paid by the spinner and, after the Factory Act of 1833, was made entirely the spinner's responsibility. Spinners' earnings varied according to the quality of the yarn they were producing, but a fine spinner producing 40 lb of twist per week could earn 40s gross.[4] The average was between 25s and 35s a week and this was less than spinners had been earning in the years immediately after the war. Nonetheless, their earnings compared very favourably with those of skilled craftsmen.

There is evidence of a union of spinners in existence in Glasgow soon after 1800, and by 1810 the union felt strong enough to demand that only union members be employed in the mills. The employers responded with a general lock-out and accepted back workers only after they had signed the 'document' renouncing their union membership. Enough organisation survived, however, for an attempted reduction in wages to be resisted for four weeks in 1811.[5] A reorganisation into the Association of Operative Cotton Spinners took place in 1816 and from then on there was a gradual building up of a powerful organisation. By the early 1820s wage-rates in Glasgow were higher than elsewhere and it was reputed that the skilled spinner could earn as much as 2 gns per week clear, after paying his piecers.[6]

The great concern of the spinners' association was to keep a firm control over entry into the trade, and to ensure that pressure of numbers did not destroy their earnings in the way it had those of the handloom weavers. According to the Articles of the Association, members were not to instruct anyone in the art of spinning except 'such as are the sons or brothers of a spinner'. These could be taken on as piecers, but any other piecers had to be women or girls. Members of the Association were specifically forbidden to teach male piecers, other than relatives, to spin. In addition to pressure from below there was also pressure from outside Glasgow. Initially, membership of the Association was confined to those who had served their time as piecers in Glasgow; then members of the Renfrewshire Spinners' Association were admitted on equal terms to the Glasgow Association; and later special terms were worked out for spinners from other parts of West Scotland. The aim was clearly to discourage the last, by demanding a £5 admission fee to the union from them as compared to the normal £1 3s, but it was also a recognition that the alternative to admitting them to membership was to have them working in Glasgow, but outside the Association. In a final effort to prevent the labour market becoming over-stocked, the Association had an emigration fund. The £3 necessary to pay the fare of an idle spinner from Glasgow to the United States was a small price to pay to prevent his wage cutting, and a shipping agent told the court, at the

---

[4] *Select Committee on Combinations of Workmen*, evidence of James McNish, QQ 1255–63.

[5] *Select Committee on Artisans and Machinery*, Evidence of Henry Houldsworth, p 476.

[6] The history of the Association can be found in Z. G. Brassay, 'The Cotton Spinners in Glasgow and the West of Scotland, c 1790–1840: a study in early industrial relations', unpublished MLitt thesis, University of Strathclyde, 1974.

cotton spinners' trial, that the Association regularly assisted people who were in debt quietly to remove themselves to the New World.[7]

Despite these efforts, however, an influx of new hands into the trade remained a major problem for the Association and a special committee on the matter was set up in 1836. This committee found that, in many cases, the employers were employing 'outsiders' in preference to Glasgow men, and especially in preference to union activists. One of the surprising features of the Glasgow situation was the way in which the Irish were able to find their way into spinning. This seems to have been the case since around 1800, stemming largely from an unwillingness on the part of the native population to go into factories. It was a situation in marked contrast to that in Lancashire, where few Irish men were able to become spinners.[8] The high proportion of Irish in the mills was reflected in the Association: Hunter, the president, had been born in Co Antrim and had come to Glasgow in 1814; Hacket was a native of Co Tyrone and had entered spinning in Glasgow in 1811; of more than fifty witnesses at the trial in 1838 at least a dozen had Irish names. The fact that there were so many Irish among the spinners is probably evidence of the limited success which the policy of restriction of entry had had.

It was of the methods used to get rid of the 'illegal men' that the prosecution in the subsequent trial made much play. The special committee recommended that 'No. 60', which was the short-hand for the idle members of the association, 'shall receive £5 for each of them they unshop; also £1 for every stranger which they shall keep from occupying wheels'. While the committee went on explicitly to deprecate any resort to violence or any attempt to violate the law, the authorities believed that this arrangement implicitly gave approval to violence and intimidation.[9] The committee also found that, despite the Association's rules, increasing numbers of boys were being employed as piecers, although they were not relatives of spinners, and were therefore constantly adding to the pool of potential spinners. Idle spinners were encouraged to take work as piecers rather than to allow the practice of employing boys. Finally, the special committee devised a plan by which three idle men and two working spinners each fortnight were assisted to emigrate or to move to another part of the country with a grant of £10.[10]

Yet another factor added to this problem of numbers. Most mills had attached to them a number of odd spinners, who had no mules of their own, but who took over mules when the regular spinner went off. Most spinners had one day off in six to clear their lungs of the dust which spinning produced, and to rest from work which required considerable exertion. A spinner might also

[7] There are three reports of the trial: A. Swinton, *Report of the Trial of Thomas Hunter, Peter Hacket, Richard McNeil, James Gibb, and William McLean, Operative Cotton Spinners in Glasgow* . . . (Edinburgh, 1938); James Marshall, *The Trial of Thomas Hunter* . . . (Glasgow, 1838); *The Trial of Thomas Hunter* . . . (Glasgow, 1838), published by William Tait and Peter McKenzie; Swinton, op cit, 152.

[8] *Royal Commission on the State of the Irish Poor*, 1836, PP 1836 XXXIV, p v; *Select Committee on Manufactures, Commerce and Shipping*, PP 1833 VI, p 313.

[9] Swinton, op cit, Appendix III, pp x–xiii.

[10] Ibid.

have a further half day off per week to collect the cotton and to return the spun yarn. So that the machines could always be kept going, odd spinners were there to take over, and the working spinner would pay them for working for him.[11] Finally, there was always the incipient threat of women spinners. These had been introduced first in 1818 when Dunlop & Co built their Broomward mill. The male spinners had responded violently, by mobbing the women, setting fire to the mill and with at least one shooting.[12] In spite of this a few survived, and in 1837 there were about seventy female spinners in Glasgow.[13] A Glasgow cotton spinner's position was then a fairly vulnerable one and there were plenty ready to replace him.

The governing body of the Association was a committee of twelve, consisting of a president, a treasurer, a secretary and nine directors. These were selected by delegates which every mill sent to a quarterly meeting. The delegate provided the secretary with the name of someone from his works qualified to act as a committee man. From the names submitted twelve were drawn by lot and, from the twelve, the delegates voted three office-bearers. The committee and office-bearers were changed each quarter. A member of the Association could not opt out of his part as a delegate or a committee man without risking a fine. At times of dispute other committees would be set up to deal with specific problems. For example, a finance committee was responsible for paying out strike pay and raising the necessary money. It consisted of members from the three districts of the Association, namely Calton and East Glasgow, Gorbals and South Glasgow, and Anderston, Duntocher and the West.[14] There would also be a supply committee responsible for arranging credit for strikers and, in the case of the 1837 strike, for actually buying and distributing oatmeal.[15] The authorities also believed there was a guard committee to organise picketing and, although this was denied by the leaders of the Association, there seems little doubt that some such committee did exist. In all these committees there was some overlapping of membership. As in any organisation a few activists shared the bulk of the work. However, it seems clear that a considerable number of the Association's members, willingly or unwillingly, played an active rôle in the running of the union.

The delegates from each mill were responsible for collecting the membership dues. These varied according to the needs of the Association. In theory, the funds were not allowed to fall beneath £1,000, and, if fortnightly expenditure was between £10 and £20, then the due was 9d per fortnight. When expenditure rose to between £20 and £30, the due was increased to 1s per fortnight, and, progressively, up to 2s per fortnight for an expenditure of between £60 and £70. Above that level of expenditure special arrangements had to be made with the agreement of the whole of the Association. In return a member received an allowance when he was out of work. This varied according to the number

11 *SC on Combinations of Workmen*, evidence of Angus Campbell, QQ 942–56.
12 Swinton, op cit, 74.
13 Ibid.
14 *The Sun*, 2 February 1838, speech of James McNish.
15 *Glasgow Argus*, 7 May 1838.

of members who were out of work, but usually it was 12s per week. Membership also entitled a man's family to £4 funeral benefit in the event of his death.

The Glasgow cotton spinners had for long had a reputation for violence against 'nobs'. During the struggle against the introduction of women spinners in 1819 and 1820, the mother of one of them was shot dead, presumably in mistake for her daughter. About the same time another 'nob' by the name of McQuarrie was shot and wounded. During the long strike and lockout of Glasgow spinners which took place in 1824 one John Graham was shot and John Kean was publicly whipped and transported for life for the assault. Ironically Kean was defended by the eminent Whig advocate, Henry Cockburn, and prosecuted by the up and coming Tory Crown Counsel, Archibald Alison, both of whom were to feature in the trial of 1838. There were other shootings during the strike, but most of the assailants seem to have escaped from Glasgow and were outlawed. In 1827 John Walker, a spinner, was transported for life for shooting into the bedroom of a new worker at Thomson & Son's Adelphi Mill. One of Walker's associates on that occasion, John McCaffer, was one of those arrested in August 1837 and later released. In 1832, the notorious case of vitriol throwing, in which Mary McShaffery was blinded, took place, reputedly because she had been mistaken for a women spinner. There are just a few of the best known cases. There were numerous other assaults of a less serious nature, or where no case came to court.[16] To the authorities, the murder of John Smith fitted into a pattern of assault and assassination that went back at least twenty years. Their concern was to show that the violence was organised by the committee of the spinners' association. They in fact failed to prove their case and since none of those charged in 1837 ever admitted responsibility or played the rôle of Broadhead of Sheffield and confessed all, the truth of the matter can never be known. It does not, however, require the presence of a tight-knit committee to explain the prevalence of the spinners to violence. It was 'nobs' who threatened their livelihood, and it was essential that these 'nobs' be got out. The typical method was to buy them out, and one witness to the Select Committee on Combinations of Workmen claimed that there were 'nobs' who could make about £100 a year by being bought out by unionists.[17] Strike breakers would be treated with drink and coaxed to leave a mill. Picketing, round a mill had the same end in view, and it has always proved extremely difficult to draw the line between peaceful picketing and intimidation.

Violence was not confined to the spinners and Archibald Alison was right when he declared that he doubted whether

> there had been so much as a single instance of combination, either before the Repeal of the Combination Laws, or since that time of a strike lasting any considerable time without threats or violence to the new hands . . .[18]

It was a violent society where arguments were traditionally settled by force. A few examples will suffice. In 1832 three miners had been transported for life

---

[16] The cases are well-documented in Brassay, op cit.
[17] SC on Combinations of Workmen, evidence of John McCaffer, Q 1553.
[18] [Alison], loc cit, 283.

for cutting off the ears of two strike breakers. In 1834, the calico printers resorted to all kinds of violent exercises to run the strike breakers out of town. There was a great deal of what, in Sheffield, was known as 'rattening' or industrial sabotage. An attempt was made to maim, if not kill, a manager by dropping a window-frame and blocks on his head. The strife culminated in the murder of a block-printer reputedly by a 'nob' and eventually troops were called in to protect the printworks.[19]

A great deal of violence was associated with drink. Drunkenness was common among some of the spinners and probably stimulated violence. Witnesses to the Committee on Combinations of Workmen – not necessarily unbiased, of course – claimed that 'nobs' were generally 'very low dissipated characters' who frequently 'got tipsified and abused the machinery' or were 'seen in a state of intoxication in the street'.[20] Such a pattern of behaviour was not confined to strike breakers. It is clear, that for many spinners, life centred round the spirit shop and there were plenty of these. One in every ten houses in Glasgow was a public one, compared with one in 56 in London. The bars sold porter, ale and ginger beer, but, as Sheriff Alison pointed out, such things were 'mere provocatives to the whisky'.[21] Although by July 1837 strike pay had been reduced to a mere 9d per week, McLean and his cronies spent much of their time in spirit shops drinking well into the night, unperturbed by the confinements of licensing laws. Robert Christie, the key witness for the prosecution, had owned a spirit shop while still working as a spinner, from 1834 to March 1837. There are also reports of drinking at work. Traditions more commonly associated with pre-industrial craftsmen seem to have been imported to the new factories: new hands coming in and a spinner getting his wheels or changing his wheels were all likely to involve celebratory drinking.[22]

One has an impression, therefore, that there was, among the spinners, a 'rough' drinking group, who would readily resort to violence against the strike-breakers or against managers whom they disliked. McLean, reputedly, had been involved in an assault on Robert Millar, the manager of the Lancefield Spinning Mill in 1832, though he denied it, and, on the evidence, it seems possible that he was involved in Smith's murder. However, alongside this group was a 'respectable' leadership. The manager of the mill at which McNeil and Gibb worked testified in court to their steady character, and that McNeil went to the same church as he. Both were members of the Mechanics' Institute.[23] Hunter and Hacket were Irish born, but there was never any suggestion that they were anything but respectable. They had frequently been officers of the Association, and the latter had played an active rôle in the factory reform

---

[19] A. Thomson, *Random Notes and Random Recollections of . . . Maryhill* (Glasgow, 1895), 22–4.

[20] *SC on Combinations of Workmen*, evidence of James McNish, Q 1181; evidence of John McCaffer, Q 1650.

[21] Ibid, evidence of A. Alison, QQ 1986–7.

[22] J. Dunlop, *Artificial Drinking Usages in North Britain* (Greenock, 1836); cf N. Smelser, *Social Change in the Industrial Revolution* (1959), 193; cf Thomson, op cit.

[23] Swinton, op cit, 93; *SC on Combinations of Workmen*, evidence of A. Gemmill, Q 2854.

campaign. Surprisingly, throughout all the evidence presented about the Association, there is never any suggestion that the Irish element among the spinners' which, judging from the names, was fairly large, was a factor contributing to the violence. Other leading figures in the Association had the credentials of respectability. Adam Sideserff, who was reputed to be a member of the 'guard committee', and Adam Dickson, who had chaired one of the meetings during the strike, were both members of Temperance societies[24] – and Dickson was an elder and Sunday School teacher in the Relief Church. A Calton magistrate and a minister testified to the good character of two of the spinners arrested in the original round-up by the authorities.[25] Finally, yet another leading member of the Association, Angus Campbell, had as his alibi for the time of the Smith murder that he was 'in the company of Mr Lamond, the law agent of Messrs. Monteith and Campbell, who were at the time candidates in the Conservative interest for the representation of Glasgow, at his house eleven miles from Glasgow'.[26]

These examples, in themselves, are not evidence of the existence of respectability, but they are at least an indication of a respectable element among the leadership of the Association. They are enough to cast doubt on the picture of a violent conspiracy organised and led by a tightly-knit secret leadership. At least some evidence does point to the leadership's trying to exert some restraint on the aggressiveness of the picketing. In May 1837, for example, they agreed to withdraw the pickets from the Oakbank Mills after troops had been called and arrests made. Circulars were issued dissociating the Association from any connection with violence and even the prosecution witnesses admitted that in the 1820s vitriol throwing had been condemned by the Association.[27] In spite of the case the authorities tried to make, picketing during the strike was in fact fairly sporadic. The crown's case rested largely on two violent outbreaks between pickets and strike-breakers – not many in a strike lasting four months.

II

The rôle of the employers in the events of 1837 was an ambiguous one. Having provoked the strike they appeared to be willing to let matters take their course and they were in no great hurry to seek a settlement. They were content to allow the sheriff to make the running against the spinners' association.

The employers had been associated in informal and semi-formal organisations since the beginning of the century. Most of the leading employers in the city were in an Association of Master Cotton Spinners in 1810-11, which sought to prevent the spinners' association getting legal recognition under friendly society legislation.[28] In the 1820s, a formal association of employers

[24] Swinton, op cit, 216.
[25] SC on Combinations of Workmen, evidence of A. Gemmill, Q 2798.
[26] Ibid, Q 2784.
[27] Trial of Thomas Hunter . . . (Tait and McKenzie), 21, 39.
[28] Glasgow City Archives, Minute Book of the Association of Master Cotton Spinners, 1810-1.

revived. During the early 1820s there were numerous strikes at individual mills. The great majority of these were over questions of management: insisting on the dismissal of foremen or spinning masters of whom the workers disapproved, protesting at 'too zealous managers' and seeking the exclusion of some 'obnoxious workman'. It would appear that these years saw an attempt by the employers to tighten up discipline within the factory – there were frequent protests at the use of fining – and this was resisted by the associated spinners. Bitterness between management and workers was exacerbated by the fact that many of the managers had in fact been themselves working spinners and were dependent for their jobs on proving their effectiveness in maintaining discipline.

It was to resist the strikes against managers than an employers' association was formed in 1823, and, in September 1824, there was confrontation with the associated spinners in a lock-out following resistance to a general reduction of wages. The strike and lock-out continued until February 1825 and there were riots, shootings and attacks on strike-breakers, but the spinners' association was not broken by the lock-out and, indeed grew in strength in the following years. The association of employers continued to exist and it was probably this that facilitated the working out of uniform wage rates throughout the Glasgow mills in 1827.[29] It is clear from the discussion of the delegates at the Isle of Man Conference of 1829, which resulted in the formation of the Grand General Union of All the Spinners of the United Kingdom, that the Glasgow spinners had few of the grievances that affected their Lancashire counterparts and were well content with the position the union had achieved.[30] The Factory Inquiry Commissioners of 1833 reported that the Glasgow association was very much in control of entry into the trade, was 'carrying things with a high hand' and had 'a complete monopoly of labour'.[31]

The Glasgow employers seem on the whole to have accepted the limitations imposed by the union, and there were no serious confrontations between 1825 and 1837. Nor did they introduce the major technological changes which both transformed and disrupted the industry in Lancashire in the late 1820s and early 1830s. The major changes in Lancashire had involved the introduction of greatly enlarged mules or the doubling or coupling of small ones. By the mid-1830s, 1,000 spindle mules were not uncommon in Manchester. In Glasgow, the largest mules – in only one mill in 1837 – were of 480 spindles. More typically, mules in Glasgow ranged from 200 to 360 spindles.

It is not at all clear why Glasgow employers failed to bring in large machines. One can think of a number of possible explanations. It may be that there was no shortage of skilled labour and therefore no incentive to innovate. This would tend to cast doubt on the extent to which the spinners were able to control entry into the trade and confirms their concern in 1836 when they sought to tighten control. One might have expected some innovation to try to break the hold of the spinners' association, as was to happen when the self-acting mule was

[29] SC on Combinations of Workmen, evidence of Angus Campbell, Q 673.
[30] A Report on the . . . Delegate Meeting of the Operative Spinners of England, Ireland and Scotland (Manchester, 1829).
[31] Factory Enquiry Commission 1833, First Report, 126, Second Report, 39.

brought in, in the following decades. Again the lack of innovation may suggest that the employers did not find the spinners' association a serious restriction. A further possibility is that once equality of wage rates had been accepted in 1827, there was no longer the competitive stimulus to innovation. It required the exceptional circumstances of 1837, when in much shrunken markets the Scottish manufacturers found they could no longer compete with their Lancashire rivals, to force upon them the adoption of technological developments. It might be argued that capital was lacking to bring about the necessary innovations since many of the Scottish firms, though by no means all, remained small and rationalisation came slowly. On the other hand, little investment was required, since small machines could be 'double-decked' without great expense. There was probably, however, a lack of machine makers in Glasgow to build enlarged mules.[32] Finally, a case could be made out for lack of innovation resulting from the very real strength of the spinners' union. Employers, knowing that technological change would bring confrontation with the spinners, postponed doing anything until their hand was forced in the crisis of 1837. Whatever the reason, the cotton industry of Glasgow basked in remarkable tranquillity for a decade.

The spring of 1836 brought 'extraordinary and unprecedented prosperity' and employers granted a 16 per cent wage increase.[33] By the autumn, prices began to tumble and the downturn persisted through the winter. Two major mercantile houses, deeply involved in the American trade, went down. It was at this point that the cotton spinners' association decided to support a strike against one of the largest cotton spinners in the area, Dunn of Duntocher. Dunn's mills in the North-West of Glasgow were outside the area covered by the equalisation of wages agreements of 1827, and, from time to time, there had been suggestions that action should be taken to push up wages in country mills to the level of those in Glasgow. In both 1834 and 1836 the Association had dissuaded its members from pressing for a rise.[34] However, at the end of October 1836, the 102 spinners at Duntocher struck work for increased wages and were backed by the union.

It was not very surprising that the Association should support a strike at that time. The boom conditions of August were passed, demand was beginning to fall off, but no one could yet see the full seriousness of the crisis that was about to hit the industry. Employers may well have blamed their reduced sales on undercutting by country manufacturers rather than on a general falling off of demand. At any rate, there is evidence that some employers actively encouraged the union to take action at Duntocher. It was claimed that both Peter Bogle and William Houldsworth, two of the leading Glasgow employers, specifically pressed for an agitation by the union against Dunn.[35] The strike lasted sixteen weeks, through to February 1837, and the spinners' association expended more than £3,000 backing it. In taking on Dunn, however, they were confronting the

32 I am grateful to my colleague Dr John Butt for this suggestion.
33 [Alison], loc cit, 288.
34 *SC on Combinations of Workmen*, evidence of Angus Campbell, Q 815.
35 Ibid, evidence of James McNish, QQ 1087, 1094.

largest employer in the area at a time when he too was likely to be feeling the effects of economic recession and the strike was broken. The union was left in a perilously weak state.

Six weeks after the end of the Duntocher strike, the Glasgow employers met under the chairmanship of Henry Dunlop. The meeting included most leading spinners in the city and neighbourhood – William Hussey, Peter Bogle, Daniel McPhail, William Houldsworth, Patrick McNaught and William Kelly and had the support of the firms of James Oswald and James Dennistoun. It was resolved to remove the advance of wages given the previous autumn. The meeting was on 5 April. On the 8th the spinners' association decided to resist and called a general strike of its members. Two weeks after the start of the strike there were signs that the spinners might be reconciled to their reduction.[36] But when the employers met again on 29 April they decided to impose yet further reductions. It was these that fundamentally threatened the position built up by the spinners over the previous decade.

The employers were concerned to assimilate their prices with those of Lancashire. They proposed to abolish the extra allowance paid for spinning 'pirn cops' or 'shuttle cops', which had been won in 1832, and which would have meant for some a reduction of 6s to 7s per week. More seriously, however, they reduced the piece-work earnings possible on a large machine. For a machine of 300 spindles the rate remained the same, but for every twelve spindles over 300 1 per cent was knocked off the piece rate up to 30 per cent. To take an example, a spinner working one pair of wheels with 300 spindles, making 40 lb of twist per week, could in 1837 earn 40s gross, out of which he would have to pay about 13s 6d to his piecers. A doubled machine, with 300 additional spindles would make 75 lb, but the spinner, under the new system, would not receive 75s but 25 per cent less than that, i.e., 56s 3d. Out of that, since additional piecers were necessary, he would have £1 5s 6d expenses, leaving 30s 9d clear. Therefore, for the much greater effort and responsibility required for doubled or large machines the spinner was only 4s 3d per week better off.[37]

It was clear that the technological changes which had come to Lancashire in the 1820s were now going to hit Glasgow. The enlargement of machines, which was clearly the intention of the employers, threatened technological unemployment for some spinners and for this alone was likely to be resisted. In addition, however, it brought to the fore the traditional problem of the pressure of numbers on the spinner's position. The enlarged machines required more piecers. It would not be possible for all piecers to come from the spinner's own family and it would be necessary to employ male piecers who, in turn, would expect to become spinners. The whole *raison d'être* of the spinners' association had been to prevent too many outsiders finding their way into the industry. Finally, it overthrew the equality of piece rates which had existed since 1827, thus again destroying a basic achievement of the association. A dispute over wages could have been settled through negotiation and compromise. From the end of April,

[36] Ibid, evidence of John Houldsworth, Q 432.
[37] Ibid, evidence of James McNish, QQ 1255–61.

the dispute altered its nature to one over the structure of the industry. This could only be settled by the victory of one side over the other.

The spinners naturally saw the actions of the employers in April 1837 as the closing of a trap that dated back to the strike at Duntocher during the preceding winter. By encouraging the Association to challenge Dunn in a long strike, the Glasgow employers effectively ensured that when they presented their own proposals the union would be in a financially weak position and, therefore, less able to resist. By the nature of the matter, firm evidence is unlikely to exist to prove or disprove the accusation, but there is some circumstantial evidence to support the spinners' case. One of the spinners' witnesses to the enquiry into combinations pointed out that the two or three employers who most actively urged action against Dunn, and even threatened a reduction of wages if nothing was done, were also the leaders of the associated employers in April.[38] Dunlop and Houldsworth both took an active part in the employers' associations and this was very much in keeping with their past actions. Dunlop had always believed in trying to break the union by confrontation; Houldsworth had always put faith in co-ordinating the activities of the employers and, as a result of his family contacts with Manchester, was well aware of innovations there. In their account of the troubles of 1824 the spinners association had claimed that these two were at the centre of it all:

It is still Mr Dunlop in every line of the history of the Cotton Mills. It is him in 1803; it is him in 1806; it is at his Mill, as he says himself, where all was in high violence in 1819; it breaks out in 1822 and 1823; and most disastrously in 1824. And it is remarkable, that the other Mills were never shut but in the quarrels of Messrs. Houldsworth and Dunlop.[39]

Both were strongly opposed to the union, keen to innovate and perfectly capable of laying long-term plans to break the union.

During the strike the employers made no attempt to seek a settlement. With trade stagnant there was no urgency about getting the mills moving again. There were only a few incidents of clashes between strikers and 'nobs' presumably because there was no widespread introduction of strike-breakers. Also, knowing the Association's lack of resources, the employers rightly saw that it was only a matter of time before the strike broke.

III

Public authority was represented by Archibald Alison, the Sheriff of Lanarkshire, and his part in the whole affair was crucial. Alison had worked in the Lord Advocate's office in Edinburgh for many years and had been tipped as a future solicitor-general in a Tory administration. However, in 1834, he decided to opt for the financial security of the Sheriffdom of Lanarkshire. In politics, he was a full-blooded Tory who believed that the first Reform Act had been a step towards democratic anarchy. He believed the Whig Ministry had carried the

[38] Ibid, QQ 1073–86.
[39] Narrative of the Late Occurrences at the Cotton Mills in Glasgow (1824), 23.

bill 'by means of popular intimidation and threatening meetings' and kept themselves in power 'by sedition, not infrequently aided by treason'.[40] His work on a History of Europe from the French Revolution confirmed him in his view that weakness on the part of the ruling class could be fatal.

To Alison, trade unions were 'an example of democratic ambition on a large scale', with the cotton spinners' committee playing the rôle of a committee of public safety.[41] Yet, in Glasgow, he found little that stood against them. There was no united upper class in the city, with, for example, no social intercourse between the sugar merchants and the cotton manufacturers or between either of these and professional men. In addition he believed, like Mirabeau, that a 'capitalist is the most timid animal in existence' and that there was little hope that the capitalists would effectively resist democratic advance. Further, Alison believed that there was little to be hoped for from the Government. It could not, he considered, be expected to stand against forces of sedition and treason and take the necessary coercive measures against people engaged in such things, since their activities were not so very different from those to which the Government's 'own elevation had been owing'. 'Anarchy was rapidly approaching', wrote Alison,

> and yet, such was the terror, selfishness, and supineness of the higher
> classes, that I found it impossible, even by the most strenuous efforts,
> to get them to combine in any defensive measures to meet the
> dangers with which all were threatened.[42]

The manufacturers had, for example, refused to sign a memorial to the Government seeking an extension of the police force to the rural areas of the county and to the suburbs of the city. The memorial drafted by Alison contained references to strikes and to unions and the manufacturers would not attach their names to something which seemed provocative.[43]

The existing police force of about 280 covered only the Barony of Glasgow and had no jurisdiction in areas like Anderston, outside the city boundary, where many of the cotton mills were. In those areas the Sheriff was dependent on the assistance of special constables to keep order and they were far from enthusiastic about their task. In May 1837, after some days of rioting around the Oakbank Mills, Alison had summoned 100 special constables from among 'the most respectable householders in the district'. At the time he believed the city to be 'almost in a state of insurrection', yet only one constable turned up and he had to depend on the military.[44] His use of a troop of horse to break up the pickets on this occasion was bitterly attacked in the radical press, but even some of the 'holders of property' questioned the legality of his action.[45] Yet such criticism merely convinced Alison that he was right to take a stand, if necessary alone, against 'the moral pestilence', as he described unions, that would

[40] A. Alison, *Some Accounts of My Life and Writings. An Autobiography*, edited by Lady Alison (Edinburgh, 1883), 374.

[41] Ibid, 350; *SC on Combinations of Workmen*, evidence of A. Alison, Q 2549.

[42] Alison, op cit, 373.

[43] *SC on Combinations of Workmen*, evidence of Alison, Q 2127.

[44] Ibid, QQ 1886, 1960.

[45] Alison, op cit, 376.

'overturn entirely the social state of the country', all of which was the 'fruit of the spread of Liberal principles'.[46]

There was, of course, some reason for Alison to be concerned about the public peace in the summer of 1837. It was not only the spinners who were on strike, but iron miners, iron moulders, coal miners, sawyers and many others. Indeed, Alison wrote, with some exaggeration, of the 'whole skilled trades of Glasgow, with the exception of the printers, hand and power-loom weavers' being on strike.[47] There was much bitterness outside the city during the iron miners' strike which lasted four months from June 1837. The bitterness was enhanced by the eviction of families from company housing and troops were used, on Alison's orders, to prevent attacks on new families moving to the vacated cottages. In addition, the iron masters equipped a large body of police to protect the new workers.[48] Since the beginning of 1837 there had been a standing committee of trades delegates in the city and the *New Liberator* news-paper, under the editorship of the loquacious radical, Dr John Taylor, sought to unite radicals and trade unions in a demand for universal suffrage. With unemployment widespread among a variety of workers, the times must indeed have seemed dangerous to someone immersed in the literature of the French Revolution.

As against that, however, even Alison admitted there was little, if any, co-ordination between the different trade societies.[49] The spinners' association had a great deal of difficulty in raising money from fellow workers and, by June, was already largely dependent upon pawned watches and small individual contributions.[50] It was only after the arrest of the spinners' leaders in August when the matter became a *cause célèbre* comparable to Tolpuddle, that united trades committees began to rally with financial and literary aid to the cotton spinners. In January 1838 as the trial got under way, Joseph Rayner Stephens and Feargus O'Connor did doubtful service to the spinners' cause when they talked of going forth 'with the dagger in one hand and the torch in the other' to 'wrap in one awful sheet of devouring flame, which no army can resist, the manufactories of the Cotton Tyrants'.[51] By then, however, the spinners had been back at work for nearly six months. Speeches like these confirmed Alison in his view of the spinners' association as part of a dangerous and wide-ranging radical conspiracy against property. Neither at the trial nor anywhere else, however, was it suggested that the leaders of the cotton spinners had sought to stir up wider class antagonisms. There was only one mass meeting during the strike and that was addressed by Dr Taylor, not by any of the spinners. None of the arrested spinners nor any of those who were regularly at the forefront of the Association displayed any demagogic ambitions. During the strike the Association looked to fellow spinners in Lancashire, with whom they had had some contact during the factory reform campaign, rather than to other groups

46 Ibid, 300; *SC on Combinations of Workmen*, evidence of Alison, Q 1977.
47 Alison, op cit, 300.
48 *SC on Combinations of Workmen*, evidence of Alison, Q 2390.
49 Ibid, Q 1863.
50 *Trial of Thomas Hunter* . . . (Tait and McKenzie), 23.
51 *New Liberator*, 6 January 1838.

of workers. At a time of very extensive unemployment and distress the strike was far from popular, as even the *Liberator* was forced to accept,[52] among the general working class population.

Early in July there were reports of a threatening letter having been sent to Alexander Arthur, the manager of the Adelphi mill in Hutchesontown. The mill produced mainly coarse cloth and, therefore, it had been relatively easy for Arthur to procure new hands to break the strike. Blood-curdling threats by mail were not at all unusual in these circumstances. However, with the murder of Smith coming about three weeks later, Alison was ready to accept the statements of two informants, attracted by the reward of £600 offered by Government and manufacturers, that this was the start of a campaign of murder against strike-breakers and employers. He saw the whole affair as reminiscent of the Cato Street conspiracy. The setting was right, as he and Captain Miller, the chief of police, pushed their way up through the trap door of the 'Black Bull' in the Gallowgate and arrested the astonished committee. A few days later. McLean was apprehended, thanks to some shrewd detective work by a police informant.

While it might have been possible to implicate McLean in the murder – all the evidence pointed to his being a fairly violent, though simple,[53] character – it was much more difficult to show that the murder was either instigated or approved by the spinners' association. Yet, from Alison's point of view this was essential. Both the Lord Advocate and the Crown Counsel were fairly doubtful about the weight of evidence against the spinners.[54] They pressed Alison and the Glasgow Procurator Fiscal to find further evidence. The action could have come before the Circuit Court at Glasgow in September, but the investigation was not complete. It came before the High Court in Edinburgh on 10 November, when the relevancy of the indictment was argued and upheld, but the actual hearing of the case was again postponed until 27 November. A few days before the 27th the authorities announced the postponement of the case for a fourth time. These delays brought a public outcry with petitions of protest containing 20,000 signatures being presented to Parliament. When the trial did eventually open on 3 January it was almost the last possible moment. After 8 January the case, under Scots law, would have lapsed.

The chief witnesses for the prosecution were James Murdoch, James Moat or Mowat and Robert Christie, The first had been refused strike pay by the Association in July, the second, who for a time had been a member of the committee, had a brother who was a strike-breaker, and the third felt aggrieved towards the Association because it had failed to pay him money he believed was owing to him. Murdoch and Moat were mainly used to show that there had been secret committees appointed by the Association in the 1820s and that these had been involved in murder and violence. Moat claimed that a similar committee had been appointed in 1837, the implication being that it too had planned murder and arson. Christie was the crucial witness against McLean in

52 Ibid.
53 *Trial of Thomas Hunter* . . . (Tait and McKenzie), 34.
54 Alison, op cit, 386–7.

that, according to him, McLean had actually confessed to the murder. The jury gave little credence to the evidence of any of these. They found only the publicly-known acts of mobbing and rioting proved against the accused. The seven-year sentences were harsh, though they have to be seen in the context of a tradition of exemplary sentencing in the Scottish Courts. Two years previously the ringleaders of religious riots in Airdrie had been sentenced to 14 years (for the Protestants) and 7 years (for the Roman Catholics) and a few days after the main trial, Lord Cockburn despatched yet another spinner (not a member of the Association) to Botany Bay for seven years for entering the lodgings of a strike-breaker and threatening him.[55]

IV

Sheriff Alison claimed to feel reasonably satisfied with the outcome of the trial. He continued to publicly justify his actions in statements at sittings of the Circuit Court and in anonymous articles in *Blackwood's Magazine*. Called before the Select Committee on Combinations of Workmen, which had been set up in the aftermath of the trial, he fared less well in face of hostile questioning and counter evidence. Andrew Gemmill, the Glasgow solicitor, who had, throughout the decade, acted as legal agent for the spinners' association, and for most other unions, presented a very effective case against Alison, accusing him of falsification of the facts and of partiality. The spinners' witnesses projected an image of quiet moderation. The employers with, only a couple of exceptions, left Alison to defend himself. There was no rush to corroborate the accusations against the union made by Alison, and the restraint of John Houldsworth's evidence is in sharp contrast to the sweeping denunciations of Alison. Presumably, with the spinners back at work and trade picking up, there was no desire to reopen old wounds – an attitude which no doubt confirmed Alison in his views of capitalists.

By the end of the strike and trial the spinners' funds were exhausted and members were pulling out rapidly. Two hundred and seventy-six men lost their places immediately after the strike and by January, 400 spinners were failing to pay the 2s 6d per week which the Association was levying to pay off debts.[56] In April, Andrew Thomson, a victualler, took out a summons against 433 members of the spinners' association, who had ceased to pay their contributions, seeking payment of a debt of £650 incurred by the Association during the strike in purchasing meal and bread to give to their members. Gemmill sought to get the recalcitrant members to bind themselves to pay the Association up to 11s a month until all unspecified debts were paid off. As was the practice in Scotland, the wages of the spinners were arrested until the case was settled. The proceedings were attacked in the press as an elaborate attempt by the Association to ensnare unwilling members for the rest of their lives.[57] In June, the matter came to court, and the arrestment of wages by the Association was declared to be 'nimious and oppressive', and the case was lost.

[55] Swinton, op cit, Appendix XIX.
[56] SRO, Crown Agents Papers. A. Alison to Lord Advocate, 2 February 1838.
[57] *Glasgow Argus*, 7 May 1838.

With the trial over there was the problem of what to do about the witnesses for the prosecution who had spent the last few months in protective custody in Edinburgh. In February two of them, Hassan and Cowan, reported to the Procurator-Fiscal that Christie had confessed to them that he had personally been involved in the shooting of Smith, along with McLean, Osborne, a mechanic in one of the mills, and a man named Brown. The last was reputed to have been 'intimate with' Mrs Smith. Alison questioned Brown and Osborne, but when both denied any involvement in the murder, he released them. At the end of May, Hassan and Cowan again approached the Procurator-Fiscal, who sent them to see the Crown Agent. This time they declared that Brown was willing to confess to involvement in the murder of Smith, provided that he was sent to America. James Todd, an umbrella maker, informed the Crown Agent that Christie had talked to him two days after Smith's shooting in a manner which indicated that Christie had been an accessory. Christie had denounced Smith as 'a damned blackguard' who had 'taken indecent liberties with and attempted to ravish the young girls who had been employed in the factories as piecers'.[58] Todd had made similar statements to the Procurator-Fiscal in Glasgow in the previous August when the spinners were first arrested, pointing out that Smith had in fact been tried and acquitted for rape a few years previously.[59] Although the accusations against Christie fitted with his behaviour immediately after the murder when he had hurriedly left for London, for a few days, none of these facts had been brought to the notice of the court.

No action was taken against Christie, Brown or Osborne. In July, the key witnesses and their families, 'all now much better off than before and than most families of their station',[60] were despatched to the colonies. The five prisoners were meanwhile languishing in the hulks on the Thames. Enough doubt and uncertainty and public agitation surrounded their case for their not actually to be sent to Australia and in August 1840 they were pardoned.

In the end, the truth remains obscure. The surprising thing is the extent to which historians have not been willing to accept a verdict of not proven, but have accepted, almost in its entirety, the prosecution's case against the spinners. In 1894 Sidney and Beatrice Webb concluded that

> The evidence given in court, and repeated before the Select
> Committee of 1838, leaves no reasonable doubt that the Cotton-
> Spinners' Union in its corporate capacity had initiated a reign of
> terror extending over twenty years, and that some of the
> incriminated members had been personally guilty not of instigation
> alone, but of actual violence, if not of murder.[61]

The most recent historian of cotton workers' unions, Professor H. A. Turner, has declared that 'there is little doubt that the Glasgow leadership set about achieving its aims not merely by a prompt use and support of mill strikes, but by systematic intimidation and hired violence'. The Glasgow Spinners' Associa-

[58] SRO, Crown Agents Papers, Declaration of James Todd, 23 May 1838.
[59] Ibid, 11 August 1837.
[60] Ibid, G. Salmond to D. Cleghorn, 22 June 1838.
[61] S. and B. Webb, *The History of Trade Unionism* (1920 ed), 171.

tion is described as a 'terrorist organisation', run by a 'directorate', using the methods of 'the guerrilla and Maquis'.[62] The evidence for such statements simply does not exist.

That there was a great deal of violence among the West of Scotland workers is not to be disputed. It was not, however, confined to the spinners. Miners, ironworkers, calico printers and building workers had all, at some time, been accused of using violence against strike-breakers. Handloom weavers had been responsible for using vitriol against individuals on at least one occasion in the 1820s. Violence among the spinners was a reflection of a violent society, passing through the trauma of industrialisation and heated by ample, cheap whisky. The evidence presented to the court in 1838 gives little backing to the suggestion that the violence was an essential part of the policy of the Association. In spite of the evidence, the assertions of Alison, that the union somehow had direct responsibility for the assassination of Smith and for such barbarities as the 'vitrioling' of Mary McShaffery, still seem to attract widespread acceptance.

The strike and trial served a useful purpose for the employers and the authorities. The spinners' union was effectively broken as a barrier against technological change. Enlarged machines and self-actors were introduced very rapidly after 1837, worked by youths and women, and the hand-mule spinners were in no position to resist. As a result, the Glasgow manufacturers avoided the ten years of turmoil which had accompanied the gradual introduction of enlarged machines in Lancashire in the 1820s and 1830s. An example had been made, guaranteed to discourage other unions. The heavy sentences also, no doubt, acted as a deterrent to any Chartists who might have had inclinations to advocate the cause of physical force. It was clear that the spirit of Lord Braxfield lived on on the Scottish Bench and it is hardly surprising that, from 1838, onwards, Scottish Chartism stayed, on the whole, well clear of the more violent streams of the movement.

The trial had its impact on future trade-union developments. Scottish unions remained notoriously weak bodies for decades mainly because they remained tainted with 'unrespectability'. The notoriety gained at the end of the 1830s stuck to unionism, and the new generation of leaders in the 1860s and 1870s went to tremendous lengths to create a fresh image. By the end of the 1860s no Scottish unions met in public houses. Some of the lessons of 1837–8 were well-learned.

[62] H. A. Turner, *Trade Union Growth, Structure and Policy* (1962), 91–3.

W. H. FRASER

7

The Episcopal Church in Helensburgh in the Mid-Nineteenth Century

This case study, mainly of one congregation but with some reference also to the Church of St Andrew-by-the-Green, Glasgow, attempts to discover how far the growth of the church kept pace with the growing population, and how its expansion was financed; whether it comprised only the middle class or the whole spectrum of society, and what contribution it made to the religious and social life of the area.

I

Helensburgh lies about twenty-five miles from Glasgow on the north bank of the Clyde. It was named after Lady Helen Sutherland, wife of the first Sir James Colquhoun of Luss who founded the town in 1776. The town grew only slowly, hindered partly by the lack of an adequate water supply and a good harbour, plans for which were dropped because local subscriptions were insufficient. In 1802, however, the town was made a Burgh of Barony by charter, with a Provost, two baillies and four councillors.[1] The first Provost was Henry Bell of steamship fame who in 1806 built baths 'with both *hot* and *cold*' in the town.[2] His widow continued to run the Baths Hotel even after his death in 1830.

There was virtually no industry. Apart from some fishing, the livelihood of the townsfolk depended largely on its visitors. From the beginning it was well laid out on a 'grid' plan with wide streets and large gardens and during the middle years of the nineteenth century it developed into a popular small watering place.[3] There were several steamers daily to Glasgow by mid century. Because of the influx of visitors the population was higher in summer than in winter. Helensburgh originally lay within the parish of Row (the church of which was two miles from Helensburgh). The population of Row was about

[1] *New Statistical Account* (Edinburgh, 1845), Vol VIII.

[2] Fowler's *Directory of Renfrewshire* (Paisley, 1836), 206. Henry Bell actually moved to Helensburgh from Glasgow in 1808.

[3] Not, apparently, without critics. A writer in *The Glasgow Examiner* of 11 August 1849 (quoted in *The Helensburgh and Gareloch Times*, 3 August 1881) speaks of 'the perils of the famous quay which ... affords excellent gymnastic exercises' and adds, 'we know no town that could be kept tidy and clean at less trouble, and yet we know none almost as dirty'. Nevertheless, 'Helensburgh is not the stinking place some would suppose'. The town council in the 1880s was much concerned with the pollution of the foreshore and other sanitary questions, hence the quotation.

853 in 1755 and about 1,000 in 1790–1.[4] It had doubled by 1831, being then 2,037. Most of this increase took place in Helensburgh and its suburbs, which had a population of about 1,400 in 1835.[5] By 1851 it was well over 2,800. The opening of the railway in 1857 connecting Helensburgh with Dumbarton and so with Glasgow resulted in a rapid rise in population, which had reached 4,770 by 1861, over 6,200 a decade later, and 7,585 by 1881 (including 395 in the training ship anchored off Row). There were 1,578 inhabited houses, many of those built after the opening of the railway being quite sizeable mansions whereas previously most had been of the cottage type, although even these were generally restricted to four, or even two, per acre. Even in the thirties and forties it was a flourishing little town with a public library and a reading room, a savings bank and a branch of the Western Bank. There were eight schools in the parish (and thirty public houses).

II

By the late sixties there were several places of worship in the town. The Established church had been built in 1847, originally as a chapel of ease to Row, but by then the parish church, seating 800 people. Even this was inadequate and in 1868 the West Established Church was opened, seated for 300. In 1852 the West Free Church had been opened on the site of a building put up in 1827 by the original seceders. By 1862 it was too small and Park Free Church was built.[6] The United Presbyterian Church had been opened in 1843 and was replaced by a new, larger one, in 1861. The Congregationalists had opened a Tabernacle as early as 1802; this building had been replaced in 1850. The Baptists also had a meeting house. The Roman Catholics met in a cottage, mass being said for the first time in 1865, a church not being built until 1879–80. There was also the Episcopal Church.

Table I gives some figures of membership and attendance in 1876, when 'on

TABLE I

CHURCH ATTENDANCE 1874

	Membership 1874	Attendance
East Established Church	505	418
West Established Church	114	167
Park Free Church	456	431
West Free Church	428	416
United Presbyterian Church	475	374
Episcopal Church	191	285
Congregationalists	98	199
	2,266 [sic]	2,280 [sic]

[4] Sir John Sinclair (ed), *The Statistical Account of Scotland* (Edinburgh, 1792), Vol IV.
[5] *Third Statistical Account* (Glasgow, 1962), Vol VI. The spelling of Row was changed to Rhu in 1927.
[6] The Park being a piece of ground set aside 'by the munificence of Sir James Colquhoun and several gentlemen resident in Helensburgh' for cricket, quoits etc, *Helensburgh Guide Book* (Helensburgh, 1863), 85.

the Sabbath, 16th April, enumerators appointed by *The North British Daily Mail* took a census'.[7] This represents over a third of the town's population, much more if 'membership' means 'adult membership'.

At the time that Helensburgh was founded, the Episcopal Church was still subject to the Penal Laws dating back to 1745. Although some surviving congregations had continued to meet, it was not until these laws were repealed in 1792 that the church could really expand. At that time there were only about forty priests in the whole of Scotland. Inevitably it would take time for new congregations to be built up, particularly in the West of Scotland where there was a weaker tradition of episcopacy than in the Highlands or the North East. Until the 1830s there were only six or seven congregations in the whole of Glasgow and south-west Scotland. Some of the country mansions had chapels, but there was also a strong covenanting history.[8] During the forties and fifties many churches were built, so that by the 1870s there were between forty and fifty in the Diocese of Glasgow and Galloway.[9] This rapid growth was partly financed by the Scottish Episcopal Church Society which in 1843, for example, reported that in the course of six years, seven congregations had been founded, four with the help of the Society. This growth was noted by the Rev Dr Gordon, minister of St Andrew-by-the-Green in Glasgow, in a pastoral letter read in church in 1868:[10]

> With one exception (the Nonjuring congregation of Mr Alex.
> Duncan, Minister of East Kilbride, rabbled out in 1688, which the
> present St. Mary's represents) the church in which we are assembled
> was the solitary Episcopal Church in the West of Scotland for
> nearly a century. During the last twenty years the Scottish Church
> has made marvellous advances, and no diocese has progressed more
> than Glasgow and Galloway. From Girvan to Ayr, all the way up
> the Clyde, there is scarcely a town on either side of the river, but
> where the Episcopal Church can be seen rearing its cross aloft, where
> 60 years ago, there was none.

A decade later there were forty-nine congregations in the diocese, including some private chapels, with forty-seven clergy, and seventeen schools.[11] Some of the new churches in Glasgow were built partly for the large number of

---

[7] Quoted in Pettit's *Guide to Helensburgh* (Helensburgh), 11. The figure for the Episcopal Church does not correspond with the church's own records which give 500 as the number of souls. It is nearer the 200 communicants figure.

[8] A report at the fifth meeting of the Scottish Episcopal Church Society in December 1843 comments, 'From a variety of circumstances, partly political and partly religious, a strong aversion to Episcopacy and to Liturgical worship existed in the south and western parts of Scotland and has continued until a very recent period. At present more enlightened sentiments prevail'.

[9] In the nineteenth century diocesan boundaries were being changed. Glasgow and Galloway were united in 1837 but their boundaries were not finally settled until 1888 when the counties of Peebles, Selkirk and Roxburgh were transferred to Edinburgh. See reference 17.

[10] Quoted in *The North British Daily Mail*, 20 April 1868.

[11] *Scottish Episcopal Church Directory* 1879.

English and Irish people moving into the city during this period of its rapid growth.[12]

According to early editions of the *Helensburgh Guide Book*, the episcopal congregation in Helensburgh dated back to 1814;[13] but there is no further record until twenty-seven years later when on 14 August 1841, the local episcopalians arranged for a room to be fitted up as a chapel. There Dean Routledge[14] of Glasgow conducted Divine Service for the first time on 22 August. Services continued and in October the first resident priest, the Rev J. R. Mackenzie, was appointed to the charge. Six months later, while the congregation was still meeting in this room, the first recorded baptism took place.[15]

It was clear that there was a need for a church building, and by July 1842 a suitable piece of land had been purchased. Building soon commenced and the church, described as 'a small, plain edifice in Tudor style'[16] was completed in the spring of 1843, less than two years after that first service. The Rector was inducted and the church, dedicated to the Holy Trinity, was opened on 6 April by the Rt Rev M. Russell, first Bishop of the United Diocese of Glasgow and Galloway.[17] Holy Trinity church had accommodation for between 180 and 190 worshippers, being intended to serve Dumbarton as well as Helensburgh, which it did until the consecration of an episcopal church in Dumbarton by Bishop Walter John Trower in 1848.[18] The Rev J. R. Mackenzie continued his ministry until 1844 when he was followed for a few months by the Rev R. Bruce. From 1845 to 1905 there were only two rectors: the Rev J. Bell, who officiated for the first time on Palm Sunday 1845 and continued until his death in 1861, and the Rev S. Syme, former curate at Stirling, whose ministry lasted from 1861 until 1905.[19]

[12] For example St Luke's Mission in the 1870s in Springburn, Glasgow, built according to the *Scottish Episcopal Church Directory* 1878 'for the English or Irish of artisan class'. Such developments were partly responsible for the Episcopal Church becoming known as 'the English Church' in the Glasgow area.

[13] There is also reference to an earlier place of worship at Kirkmichael where services were said to have been performed in the early part of the eighteenth century by 'an indulged Episcopal minister'.

[14] William Routledge, Dean of the Diocese from 1837–47, came orignally from St Bridges in Cumberland on his appointment as assistant at St Andrew-by-the-Green in 1795. See reference 19.

[15] Registers of Holy Trinity Church, Helensburgh.

[16] Battrum's *Guide to Helensburgh* (Helensburgh, 1864), 1st ed, 18.

[17] Michael Russell, rector of St James, Leith, was consecrated in 1837, continuing to retain the charge at Leith. (Between 1787 and 1837 Glasgow, once an archbishopric, was held with Edinburgh.) See reference 9.

[18] Walter Trower, rector of Wiston, Sussex, was Bishop of Glasgow from 1848 to 1859 and later Bishop of Gibraltar (the see established in 1842). He was the first Englishman appointed to a Scottish bishopric not having previously ministered in Scotland. F. Goldie, *A Short History of the Episcopal Church in Scotland* (London, 1951), 116.

[19] This pattern of long incumbencies is found in other mid-nineteenth century charges. St Mary's, Hamilton, for example, consecrated in 1847, had only three rectors between then and 1910; Christ Church, Mile End, Glasgow, only two between 1837 and 1903. St Andrew-by-the-Green, Glasgow, had equally long serving ministers with two exceptions (J. Riddock in 1750 and W. Norval, formerly a member of the established church, rector 1843–4). J. Falconer was rector from 1751 to 1807 when he died aged 80; W. Routledge from 1807 to 1843 and J. Gordon from 1844 to 1890.

III

The number of church members varied, but with the growth of the town, so the number gradually increased. With this rise there was a corresponding increase in the number of services it was possible to hold. From the very early days there was Morning and Evening Prayer every Sunday but few celebrations of Holy Communion. This, of course, was normal in the days before the influence of the Tractarians began to be felt. In 1841 (before the building of the church) there were three celebrations: in September, when the Bishop was celebrant and there were twenty-eight communicants; in October with twenty communicants and on Christmas Day with twenty-two.[20] There were just four celebrations in 1842, the number of communicants varying considerably, from fourteen to twenty-nine. In the following years with four celebrations recorded (probably not a complete list) the numbers were somewhat higher, varying between twenty-three and thirty-eight. In 1844, when there was no, resident priest for most of the time, the services being taken by visiting priests, the numbers communicating were between twenty-one and twenty-six.

This pattern of infrequent Communion services in the early nineteenth century was repeated in St Andrew-by-the-Green, Glasgow.[21] Before 1809 there are records of only two or three a year. From then until 1815 there were four celebrations recorded annually (Easter, Whitsunday, Michaelmas and Christmas). Good Friday was recorded from 1816 on (though always with fewer communicants that at the festivals). By 1839 there were also celebrations in July, September and November, making eight in all.[22] The membership was much higher than in Helensburgh and there could be 2–300 communicants at such festivals as Christmas at that time.

From August 1845 the newly appointed Rector of Holy Trinity, Helensburgh, began monthly celebrations of the sacrament. The congregation then numbered 136, forty-three of whom were communicants, the actual numbers at the various celebrations varying from thirteen to thirty-nine. Including the major festivals there were eighteen celebrations the following year, but on four occasions no one turned up, the smallest actual congregation was nine in February. By the mid-fifties the congregation had apparently grown considerably, being 250 in 1854. But by 1859 the 'number of souls' was down to 150.[23] Whether this drop was due to more accurate recording, to the omission of temporary summer residents and 'nominal' members, or to an actual loss of

[20] These and most other statistics are derived from the annual returns by the Rector to the Scottish Episcopal Church Society, the body most of whose functions were taken over by the Representative Church Council when it was set up in 1876. In the text it is referred to as the Church Society.

[21] St Andrew's was originally a 'Qualified chapel', built in 1750. It united with the Episcopal Church of Scotland in December 1805. It was variously described in the early nineteenth century, St Andrew, Willow Acre being common. St Andrew-by-the-Green later became the normal description.

[22] These figures are scattered among the various registers of St Andrew's church.

[23] The Episcopal Church seems to have been regarded by some as a haven from the strife of the disruption in the mid 40s. This tide may have receded towards the end of the 50s. J. H. S. Burleigh, *A Church History of Scotland* (Oxford, 1960).

members, perhaps to other churches, is not clear. The fifties were years of considerable controversy in the church and this may have adversely affected the congregation.[24] Certainly small numbers were recorded for several years, for example 140 in 1859–60. The number of communicants, however, remained much steadier in the low fifties.

But after this period, with the rapid increase in the population of the town and with something of a religious revival in Helensburgh, the number of members began to rise, reaching 250 in 1865 and 300 two years later. By this time the number of communicants was over 100. It would, in fact, have been impossible to accommodate all these members in the church. Until 1861 there was room for 182 people though more could be squeezed in in summer.[25] The average attendance in summer had long been much higher than in winter (150 compared with 70 in 1851–2, 200 compared with 100 in 1852–3. For the late fifties the summer average was 180, the winter 80).[26] There were by 1862 fortnightly celebrations of the Holy Communion as well as at festivals and on Saints' Days, Wednesdays during Lent and so on, perhaps a result of the Oxford Movement. The number of communicants still varied considerably. On a cold winter or spring morning it could be as low as eight or twelve (19 March and 15 January 1865) whereas at Christmas and Easter there were sixty to eighty.

By the early sixties the church was obviously becoming very crowded and consideration was being given to its enlargement. This was first mooted by the Rector at a vestry meeting in October 1863.[27] No action was taken for some years; until, in fact, it was clear that sufficient money would be forthcoming from the congregation to make it a feasible proposition. But by the summer of 1866 the demand for a larger church became general and several subscriptions had been promised. A committee was therefore set up to prepare plans for a building to cost not more than £2,500. (The eventual cost was nearer £3,000.)

The new church was opened on the site of the old in 1868, being consecrated by the Rt Rev W. Wilson[28] on 7 May and dedicated to St Michael and All Angels. This was clearly a landmark in the history of the Episcopal Church in Helensburgh. Some, apparently, regarded it as of even greater significance. The *Church Review* of Saturday, 27 June, quoted the *Scottish Witness* for June on the subject:

[24] Controversy over such matters as relationships with the Church of England (only in 1864, for example, were clergy of the Scottish Episcopal Church placed on an equal footing with those of the C of E); the use of the English or Scottish Liturgy; doctrinal questions raised by the Oxford Movement.

[25] The Annual Return for 1862 noted that there were 24 pews each 15 ft long 'accommodation really for 150'.

[26] A breakdown of the figure for seat rents for one year, 1844, illustrates the pattern. About 40 places were taken for the whole year, 10 for the season; others at varying amounts and therefore for various periods: 28 at 5/–, 29 at 3/6d, the rest mainly at 2/6d. So over 70 out of 122 places were let for the summer months. The number let for the whole year increased to over 60 in 1849. By the early 60s it was between 79 and 101.

[27] Vestry Minutes, Holy Trinity Church.

[28] William Wilson was consecrated in 1859. He was a Scot by birth, was educated in Scotland, and after ordination ministered in Montrose and then in Ayr, where he remained rector even after his consecration, the last of the Scots Bishops to do this.

> Thursday, 7 April [sic] will ever be remembered by churchmen
> who witnessed the consecration of the Church of St Michael and
> All Angels as a day of thankful remembrance and joy for our branch
> of the catholic church. We believe that . . . such an eventful day
> and of good omen for the church in this Diocese, has not occurred
> since the Reformation.

After the opening of the new building numbers continued to rise and by 1870 there were 395 souls, 139 being communicants. By 1875 the figures were 531 and 211 respectively.

IV

These church members represented a cross section of the community; many came from the middle or upper class,[29] but the working class was also represented. Helensburgh was not an industrial town, so 'working class' there would normally mean labourers, domestic servants and so on.

Some evidence of membership can be deduced from the Baptismal Registers, in which the father's occupation was recorded. In 1842, for example, there were five baptisms. The first was the daughter of a soldier in the Scotch Fusiliers; the second was the son of a labourer, the third the son of an accountant; the fourth the son of a mason and finally there was the daughter of Charles and Alice Edmonstone, landed proprietor.

This sort of pattern was maintained, as shown by Table 2. By the late forties, of course, the same names were re-appearing as siblings of the first child were brought for baptism. Seven of the twelve baptisms in 1849 were in this category. This is unlikely to make any significant difference to the analysis. Other factors might also distort the figures, for example the larger proportion of upper class or wealthy families who would have a house in Helensburgh for the summer; in any case these would presumably bring domestic staff with them. In fact in several of the above instances the home address was not Helensburgh. The lithographer came from Edinburgh, the surgeon, commission merchant and an esquire from Glasgow; the three glassmakers,[30] the lawyer, the blacksmith and a gentleman were from Dumbarton, the miner from Newton Stewart, the merchant and manufacturer from the Halifax area and the spirit dealer from Greenock. The bleacher came from Bonhill. In addition, different size of

[29] Such as the Dowager Duchess of Argyll who paid seat rents in the 1850s and in fact gave the book in which they were recorded. Similarly at St Andrew's, as for example in the late eighteenth century when the Duchess of Hamilton requested that a special seat with a canopy, be prepared for her in the proposed gallery. In 1787 she was sent a card with an account for £25 14s 0d to cover the cost, plus £14 for the seat rent for two years. Minute Books, St Andrew-by-the-Green. J. Sinclair in his *Analysis of the Statistical Account* (1831) wrote 'The Presbyterian form of religion has at present much to contend with from the increase of Episcopalians among the higher classes'.

[30] The Dumbarton Glass Factory which had closed in 1831 was re-opened between 1835 and its final closure in 1850. Not all the episcopalian glass makers travelled the eight miles to the church in Helensburgh. Some went to Glasgow. In 1842, for example, six out of the seven glass workers whose children were baptised at St Andrew's came from Dumbarton.

families in different classes might distort the figures. No attempt has, however, been made to obtain statistically satisfactory evidence on the basis of such small numbers.

TABLE 2
BAPTISMS 1843–9

	Fathers' occupation					
1843	1844	1845	1846	1847	1848	1849
Labourer	Labourer	Labourer (2)	Labourer (5)	Blacksmith	Labourer (2)	Labourer (3)
Lithographer and printer	Gentleman (2)	Accountant	Glassmaker (3)	Bleacher	Druggist	Gentleman (2)
Iron Moulder	Mason (2)	Colonel	Miner	Spirit-dealer	Colonel	Servant
*		Esquire	Plasterer	Tailor	Esquire	Commission-merchant
		Surgeon	Merchant and manufacturer	Commission-merchant	Gentleman	Colonel
			Lawyer		Captain (2)	Corn factor
			Colonel		Gardener	Druggist
			Incumbent		Mason	Mason
					Incumbent	Incumbent
					(Illegitimate)	

Numbers refer to number of instances the occupation occurs
* No occupation given

In the decade 1850–9 twenty-one occupations were recorded, the most frequently recurring being labourer (15 times) and mason (14 times),[31] merchants (5) and gentleman (4). Some of these were obviously the same families reappearing. The range of occupations apart from the above was wide: from medical doctor to carpenter, from quarrier to major, and included also a wright, a baker, a gardener and a coachman.

In the 1860s, although the overall pattern remained much the same, the occupations included some new ones, for example 'theatrical profession', butler, tailor, shipowner, schoolmaster, banker, carter, house painter, police officer, upholsterer, yarn twister, engraver, shoemaker, boilermaker, salesman, writer and joiner. The army was represented by a sergeant in the Royal Engineers and a Lieutenant Colonel. The places from which they came included Selkirk, Airdrie, Oxford and Liverpool as well as the Helensburgh area.

From these facts and figures it appears that, whatever may have been the composition of the permanent congregation, those who brought their babies to the Episcopal Church in Helensburgh for baptism represented a wide social spectrum. Evidence from the Registers of Baptism of St Andrew's supports this. The number of baptisms each year, 3–400 in the early years of the century and over 1,000 by the early 40s, and the very wide range of occupations, make it impracticable to do more than analyse the figures for a few selected years, from the surviving registers.

In 1805, for example, there were about 550 children baptised. 158 of them were children whose fathers were in the army;[32] in 97 cases their fathers were weavers, and in 32 cases they were labourers. For many years these three occupations were the largest. Back in 1802 for example, 23 per cent of fathers were weavers, 21 per cent army personnel, 12·5 per cent labourers; and in 1812 out of 847 baptisms 145 were weavers' children, 235 children of soldiers, 77 labourers' children. In 1805 four other occupations reached double figures: sailors (15), cotton spinners (13), potters (11) and merchants (12).[33] Four occupations were represented over five times: shoemakers, masons, smiths, servants. Miners, wrights and clerks each appear four times. The forty-three other occupations appear only three times or less and range widely, from the banker, the lawyer and the manufacturer to the pedlars, porters and bricklayers, and 'an African age 18', reflecting the socially mixed congregation.

In 1842, when Holy Trinity, Helensburgh, was being built, there were well over 1,000 baptisms at St Andrew's Church, representing seventy-nine (legible)

---

[31] The 2nd edition of the *Helensburgh Directory* (Helensburgh, 1865) lists twenty-six masons in Helensburgh.

[32] There were several thousand troops in Glasgow during the war years.

[33] The merchants included Robert Owen, whose daughter Ann Caroline was baptised on 22 February. All eight of his children were baptised at St Andrew's between August 1800 when David Dale was christened and August 1811 when Mary Dale's baptism took place: Robert Dale 25 January 1802; William 1 March 1803; Ann C. 22 February 1805; Jane Dale 19 January 1806; David Dale 8 September 1807; Richard 8 May 1810. This raises the question how far appearance in baptismal registers reflects committed membership. It is difficult to see why parents should bring children to a small, minority church unless they were so committed. Robert Owen's writings do not suggest such commitment. The Dales, of course, lived near the church.

occupations. Table 3 illustrates the pattern. Merchants were only represented twice, reflecting a big change in the make-up of the congregation. As indicated, the range of occupations was very wide and included such diverse jobs as umbrella makers, a street paver and a comedian, a physician and two foundry managers.[34]

By 1878 the picture had changed considerably, as shown by Table 4. There

TABLE 3

BAPTISMS IN 1842 AT ST ANDREW'S CHURCH

		Fathers' occupations Number of instances			
Over 200	50–100	20–49	10–19	7–9	4–6
Labourer (297)	Sailor	Spinner	Mason	Calico Printer	Dyer
Weaver (223)	Shoemaker	Printer	Painter	Cotton Spinner	Wright
Military (204)		Miner	Potter	Glassmaker	Blacksmith
		Collier	Baker		Ropemaker
		Smith	Hatter	Boilermaker	Bricklayer
		Tailor	Furnaceman		Hawker
		Engineer	Fireman	Ironworker	Pedlar
			Slater	Moulder	Dealer
			Bleacher	Founder	Carter
				Traveller	
				Police	

TABLE 4

BAPTISMS IN 1878 IN ST ANDREW'S CHURCH

		Fathers' occupations Number of instances			
Over 100	20–100	10–19	7–9	5–6	3–4
Labourer	Carter	Boilermaker	Constable	Weaver	Dealer
	Moulder	Joiner	Fitter	Bricklayer	Cloth lapper
	Mason	Baker	Rivetter	Hawker	Miner
	Shoemaker	Porter	Stoker	Printer	Miller
		Seaman	Slater	Blacksmith	Packer
		Tailor	Bolt maker	Driver	Planer
		Smith	Collier	Dresser	Servant
			Turner	Plasterer	Sawyer
			Clerk	Saddler	Tinsmith
			Flesher	Sweep	Fireman
			Painter		Cooper
			Steward		Plumber
					Rigger
					Sailmaker
					Brazier
					Dyer

[34] While the majority of families were from Glasgow, many came from the surrounding area (65 from Airdrie, for example, and 18 from Coatbridge). Some came from Ireland (22), specifically Belfast in 19 other cases and Dublin in 2. Several came from England, including 17 from Manchester and 16 from Liverpool. Quite a few came from further afield: 17 from America, 6 from New York, 3 from Canada for example.

were 690 baptisms in that year. The decline in the number of weavers and soldiers is very noticeable, there being only one of the latter. Apart from the occupations listed in Table 4 there were 100 others represented only once or twice, ranging from jeweller to ice cream maker, banker to ploughman, coachman to ham curer, auctioneer to stevedore, gilder to lamplighter. Merchants no longer appeared. The changing occupations were obviously as much a reflection of the changing industrial scene and the expansion of Glasgow as of the composition of the Episcopal Church; they also reflect the building of other Episcopal Churches so that St Andrew-by-the-Green was by then drawing on a much more restricted area, and so presumably a more restricted social group, for its congregation. The great majority of addresses in 1878 were within a small area of the centre of the city, very different in character from 100 years earlier.

From the baptismal registers of the two churches it thus appears that the occupational spread of episcopalians was very wide. Burials show the same picture. Records of burials at Helensburgh are incomplete, and only in 1868–9 were the occupations given (or, for that matter, cause of death). But this very scanty evidence also reflects a socially mixed congregation there. In 1868 there were nine funerals. In the early party of the year there were three: the 3 year old child of a ship-master (dying of consumption); a 64 year old spinster (dying of cancer); and a mason's wife (who died of dropsy, aged 55). The first three burials after the opening of the new church were labourers' children (9, 14 and 16 years old respectively, one dying of brain fever, two of consumption). Dysentry was the cause of death of the 63 year old wife of a builder and of a 39 year old widow. The other cause of death was bronchitis; nothing else was recorded. Only three burials were recorded in 1869: two babies, the youngest son of the incumbent aged 2½ months, and the daughter of the local printer at 2 years 8 months. There is no information about the third. There were eighteen funerals in 1870 but no information was given except age.[35]

St Andrew's records of burials are much more comprehensive, but after the very early years of the nineteenth century stop giving much information about occupations. The occupations represented from 1800 to 1802 are shown in Table 5. In each case there were several with no occupation entered: nine in 1800, five in 1801, eight in 1802. Burials seem to represent a wide cross section of the population at that period.

In later years only a small percentage of the occupations can be ascertained: army personnel are sometimes identifiable, as in 1825 when 'Captain Sutherland, 33rd Regt. Foot', and Mrs Sutherland were entered, having drowned in the Comet steam boat (on their honeymoon); merchants were sometimes so described, for example in 1839 three appeared;[37] their identification is possible

[35] Eight were under 3 years old, four between 19 and 22, only three were over 65.

[36] In all these statistics the occupation has been counted each time it occurs, even when it is the same individual re-appearing either in his own right or, for instance, as a parent, largely because it was not always possible to identify any one individual with any degree of certainty. Sometimes it is, as in the table when the merchant in each case was Humphrey Colquhoun whose wife was buried in February, his '½ year' old son in July, his 3 year old son in October. He himself died the following year.

[37] These were 'Alex. B, son of Thos. Slater, 11 months'; 'Matthew Lowry 45 years'; 'Thos. D. son of Wm. Bently, 5 months'.

when the name is known,[38] for example in 1817 'Isabella Graham, wife of Ambrose Dale', and 'John, son of Ambrose Dale', or 1842, 'Mrs. Mary Dale, wife of Ambrose Dale'.[39] But such evidence is far too scanty to be informative about the make-up of the congregation and in any case gives a biased picture. Moreover, by the middle years of the century the number of burials recorded had fallen to a mere handful, sometimes one or two or even less each year. Age and cause of death continued to be meticulously recorded, but little else.[40]

The marriage registers are a further source of information. Such records in Helensburgh before the opening of St Michael and All Angels church in 1868 are virtually non-existent. Some examples from the late sixties and early seventies do, however, provide evidence that people in a wide range of occupations or representing a wide range of social classes belonged to, or at least chose to be married in, the Episcopal church. Presumably the religious affiliation of the bride was more important in making this choice than that of the groom, but only in a few cases can her occupation or class be ascertained. One may, however, assume that they would tend to come from the same background.

In the two weddings recorded in 1868 the grooms' occupations were gentleman and saddler.[41] In 1869 all three brides were domestic servants, the

TABLE 5

OCCUPATIONS RECORDED IN REGISTER OF BURIALS, ST ANDREW'S CHURCH

1800	1801	1802
Doctor of Medicine	Cork cutter	Cottar
Carver and gilder	Grocer	Saddler
Rope maker	Fidler	Bottle blower
Blacksmith	Innkeeper	Labourer
Grocer	Bottlemaker	Surgeon
Cotton spinner	Tanner	Merchant (3)[36]
Surgeon	Minister of Religion	Weaver (3)
Flesher	Army (2)	Potter (3)
Merchant (2)	Weaver (3)	Army (5)
Weaver (3)		
Army (15)		

[38] This also applies to the marriage registers as when in 1816 for example the Rev H. H. Stewart married Mary Dale of Rosebank, Glasgow. Both Robert Owens (father and son) signed the register as witnesses at this wedding.

[39] Ambrose Dale, merchant, married Mrs Mary Danby in 1821. He was elected a manager of the church in 1834. He does not appear to be related to David Dale.

[40] As in 1833 when cholera caused three of the fourteen deaths recorded. If there was no service this was noted, eg in the case of unbaptised babies, or, as in 1854 'No service, because she died a "Mileite" ', or 'No service because she was a "methodist" ', or in 1856 'Of course, no service because she died in connection with Miles of St. Jude's' – a reflection of the religious controversies of the period: Rev C. P. Miles was minister of St Jude's, Blythswood Square, from 1843–58. After a violent controversy with the Bishop his benefice was withdrawn and St Jude's became a Church of England establishment.

[41] The marriage register gives the ages of bride and groom as 26 and 28, 21 and 23, respectively. 20 was in fact the lowest age recorded in any wedding before 1875 when ages ceased to be given. 30 was the oldest. 23 was the most popular age for men; most brides were 20–6. Young marriages were obviously not in vogue in Helensburgh in this period.

grooms being a butcher, an engineer and a carter. The grooms in 1870 included a gentleman from Ireland, whence also his bride, two joiners, a surgeon major and a pitman (who married a domestic servant). In 1873 the bridegrooms were merchants in two cases, a gentleman, a slater who married a greengrocer, a tailor and a labourer, the last two both marrying domestic servants. The range of occupations and classes was equally wide in the following year; the vice-consul of the Netherlands from Lisbon married a Cardross girl; a local shoe-maker married a dressmaker; a moulder from Stenhousemuir married a domestic servant, and a local labourer also got married. Other examples from the late seventies show the same picture; the Welsh baronet, the Ceylon coffee planter, the Glasgow oil manufacturer and the Liverpool merchant contrasted with the plumber who married a governess, the music teacher and the medical student, the coachman and the fishmonger's assistant. Labourers did not appear, though hawkers do.

Similar evidence is available from St Andrew's church and may be illustrated by a few examples. 1821 was fairly typical of the early period. Twenty-four weddings were recorded, no occupations being entered in six cases; seven were soldiers,[42] one a sailor, three were weavers and there was also a labourer, gunsmith, tailor, shoemaker, butler (who married a waiting maid employed in the same household), a mason and a merchant. Of the nineteen marriages in 1840 there was one with no occupation recorded, one where the groom was described as 'Esq.' (from Cork). There were nine occupations otherwise: a blacksmith, five labourers, a clerk, a printer, three soldiers (one specifically referred to as a private), three hawkers, a surgeon, an iron worker and a comedian [sic]. After the middle of 1848 the 'Register' consists of the actual certificates of proclamation of banns, hence the details depend on the various session clerks who filled them in. In 1857 for example those residing in the Barony of Gorbals were generally not described. Of the rest a wide range of occupations was to be found: surgeon and seaman, merchant and musician, engineer (twice) and steam boat labourer, traveller and tailor, cloth lapper and cook ('a man of colour'), hawker and smith, draper and glassmaker, and two labourers and comedians.

The Pew Rent Books of St Andrew's for 1817–45, and details of pew rents in Helensburgh, provide further information about membership, but as occupations were not given they have not been referred to in this study.

From the various registers it thus appears that all classes were represented. This is supported by the more direct evidence of successive Helensburgh rectors in their annual returns in which the information was for a time specifically asked for. From 1851 to 1854 one third of the Helensburgh congregation was described as 'working class' and between a third and half the communicants were described as 'poor'. The description changed in the mid-fifties.

---

[42] 'Soldiers' may in this connection include all ranks and represent all classes. One of them, for example, was Robert Douglas, Captain, who married Mary S. Douglas of the Parish of Bothwell, youngest daughter of the Rt Hon Lord Douglas of Bothwell Castle. The latter family appears elsewhere in the marriage registers, list of seat renters, managers, etc.

By 1855–6 a third of the congregation was described as 'poor'; the following year a third were 'working class'; in 1857–8 a third were perhaps more accurately described as 'operatives and labourers'. By the end of the fifties half were in this category. Since the rector would presumably know members of a fairly small congregation pretty well, considerable reliance may be placed on these estimates. They certainly do not suggest a middle class church, nor in fact the 'English church', since the majority of members were local people.

Direct evidence from the rector of St Andrew's also illustrates the social mix of the congregation. An appeal for funds in 1853 includes this paragraph:

> Moreover situated now (which twenty years ago it was not) in a
> neighbourhood rampant in fearful wickedness, the most choice
> locality (though disadvantageous to itself as to worldly interests)
> where a House of Prayer ought to appear, Saint Andrew's has become
> *the Church for the Poor*, the full half of the seats (in toto 640) being
> *free*, or, at least, occupied gratuitously, by intinerant and irregular
> worshippers.

Then follows

> For many years, the chief and more aristocratic congregation here
> assembled, although now the empire of fashion no longer reigns in
> the Saltmarket, Bridgegate and Goosedubs, neither in their environs.

This was very different from the old days when, according to articles written by the Rev Dr Gordon, the Rector, in 1861 and 1863, 'powdered-headed flunkies ... marched along the passages with their masters and mistresses prayer books', and 'white whigged aristocrats filled the body of the church'. There would then be 25–30 carriages at the gates, and many people would wait 6–12 minutes to obtain seats. But even in earlier years, 'the Episcopal congregation of Glasgow consists of people of various ranks of society. The poorer sort, who are chiefly tradesmen and labourers from England and Ireland, are very numerous and can afford to pay little or nothing for their seats' according to a report by the Rector, the Rev W. Routledge, dated 31 August 1815. He also noted, incidentally, the difficulty of providing a place of worship for the English troops when quartered in Glasgow.[32]

V

The actual day to day running of the church, its fabric and finance, was obviously in the hands of a much smaller group. These managers appear to have been appointed by the trustees in Helensburgh, and at St Andrew's to have been elected by the congregation.[43] It was a much more restricted group than the congregation as a whole.

---

[43] More accurately, those men who paid seat rents. (An unsuccessful attempt was made in 1825 to give some voice to ladies 'who, though by the constitution of the chapel are restrained from giving a vote, yet whose feelings ought to be one of the first objects of our solicitude in this particular instance' (the appointment of an assistant minister), St Andrew's Vestry Minutes.

In Helensburgh there were often only four to eight people involved and the same people remained in office for a long period. It included a high proportion of well-to-do business men.[44] Military men also appeared; for example at a meeting of the managers in 1849 two of the five present were army officers, presumably retired. When land was originally bought in 1842 the property was vested in a group of trustees including a Glasgow banker (sometimes described as an accountant), a major and a surgeon. Formal meetings of the vestry and trustees were often infrequent. The meeting of April 1851 was apparently followed by one in October 1857, the next being February 1862: membership was not an onerous task! This meant that deaths and removals in the interval could leave the actual business in the hands of few survivors, as in 1862 when Mr A. Yuille of Darleith was the sole surviving named trustee. When Mr Thomas Watson died in 1901 he had been a trustee for forty years. He was described as a writer. Others appear to have been merchants like Mr John M. Smith, shipowners like Mr James Aitken, or bankers like Mr W. Nimmo. Some were wealthy and able to contribute very generously to their church. Mr Alex Dennistoun, for example, gave the west window of St Michael's church. There were individual gifts of £100 or £200 towards the new building in 1868, and large gifts like those of vestryman R. D. Jackson Esq (of Stanhope Street, Hyde Park Gardens, London) who gave the chancel window (as an Easter offering, according to the *Helensburgh and Gareloch Times* 20 April 1881), having previously given the glass mosaic reredos; he also gave the alabaster pulpit. Several of them were JPs, for example A. B. Yuille, on the vestry from 1850, and Alex Dennistoun of Golfhill, appointed to the vestry in 1862. The latter was Deputy Lieutenant of the county and also an MP. None, however, seems to have reached the heights in local affairs; none appears to have been Provost of the burgh during the period under review.[45] Several of the vestrymen and trustees appear to have been connected by marriage (for example the Buchanans, Yuilles, Dennistouns). It is evident, therefore, that the actual management of the affairs of the church was in the hands of a fairly restricted group, mostly Glasgow businessmen. Many of their meetings, in the 60s at least, appear to have been held in Glasgow.

St Andrew's was also administered by managers and these too represented very largely the well-to-do merchants and bankers in the city, especially during

[44] Vestry minutes of the two churches. Not all were successful businessmen. For example, Mr Booth, resigning his trusteeship, wrote in August 1851 'In consequence of misfortune I shall be obliged to go abroad'. Similarly at St Andrew's: a general meeting of the congregation was, for example, called in February 1831 because of the insolvency of 'Mr. Ellis the late Treasurer'. In his hands were over £150 he was holding to pay off church debts, and also the proceeds of the seat rents. 'From the state of his affairs these sums are not forthcoming, therefore very heavy loss may be contemplated.' The following January the amount owed was reckoned to be over £381. He had been a manager on and off since 1796. In earlier days Mr Niven had in 1781 'not withstanding his misfortunes declared his intention to pay the chapel managers money due to them'. John More of the Royal Bank was hardly 'successful' either. He was manager from 1806 to 1818 when he left Glasgow. See S. Checkland, *Scottish Banking* (Glasgow, 1975), 296 f.

[45] Most of the provosts between the mid 30s and the mid 70s were in fact members of the Free Church or the United Presbyterian Church.

the church's early years. Of the first nine managers,[46] four were described as merchants, the others being bookseller, sugar baker, dyer, vintner and tobacconist. At least one early manager – Patrick Colquhoun, appointed treasurer in 1781 – was Provost of Glasgow. The number of managers was later raised to twelve and then in 1828 reduced to nine. Provision was made both for change and continuity as some had to retire each year, but as these were often re-elected, the management remained within a small group, many of whom served for long periods. James Fyffe, for example, first elected in 1800 was still a manager in 1828. Bright Langley, merchant, was a manager from 1799 until his death in 1817. James Kipple, merchant, elected in 1829 was still a manager (together with his son John) in 1849; the records then stop. The next entry in February 1876 is 'No minutes have been engrossed since the last entry of 23rd March 1849'. Evidence of the management of the church during the middle years of the century is therefore lacking. But for the period for which records are available merchants and bankers, army officers and doctors like Charles Wilson and his son David, the surgeon, were the backbone of the management.

In each church much of the day to day work was delegated to sub-committees, presumably a reflection of current business practice. This was particularly true of St Andrew's, where at, or soon after, every annual general meeting of the congregation not only the managers but other sub-committees were elected. These were responsible for the music, for the poor and for taking up the collections at the church door. Ad hoc committees were also set up periodically for specific purposes.

VI

Most of the money needed to run the church had to be raised by its members, although some was available from central church funds to which, of course, contributions had also to be made. After 1856 the biennial parliamentary grant to the Scottish Episcopal Church, the Regium Donum, of £600 a year, voted since 1814, was withdrawn,[47] being replaced by a fund raised by subscription.[48] No public money was available after that date.

Most of the church's income was obtained from seat rents. In the early years

[46] The merchants were Alex. Oswald, James Dennistoune ('one of the merchant princes', S. Checkland, op cit, 169), David Dalyell, David Cochrane. Andrew Stalker was the bookseller, Caspar Clausen (the Dutchman) the sugar baker, Robert Parr the dyer, Robert Tennent the vintner and George Sangster the tobacconist. Alex Speirs, one of the major tobacco merchants, was added in 1751 to the list of managers. See T. M. Devine, *The Tobacco Lords* (Edinburgh, 1975).

[47] The Rt Hon W. E. Gladstone was largely responsible for the ending of the Regium Donum. His presence appears frequently in Scottish Episcopal Church history. See reference 49.

[48] While many episcopalians were in favour of this change, some were opposed to it, like Mr Erskine D. Sandford who, speaking at the 1855 meeting of the Church Society when this was announced said, 'I must say I think that has been done in a spirit of oppression which savours more of the eighteenth than of the nineteenth century, when no Scottish Episcopalian could worship God after the manner of his fathers, without being subjected to penalties and persecution'.

in Helensburgh this represented something under half the annual income. In 1849, for instance, the accounts show an income of £139 13s 11½d, £40 9s 0d of which came from seat rents, £41 0s 7d from ordinary collections. (Special collections had raised £25 5s 6½d, and subscriptions towards the debt on the church were £13 5s 0d. The Diocese had contributed £5. The remaining £15 comprised collections for the Church Society and the poor.) In the following year, rents raised over £40, collections over £44. By 1868 the proportion had changed. Seat rents then raised over £162, collections more than £234. Collections during the early 70s remained higher than seat rents except in 1873. For example, by 1876 collections totalled £214, rents £149. There was an elaborate scale of rents, periodically modified, and always some free seats. In 1855–6 for example, the Annual Returns show 76 sittings let, 21 free, 8 allocated to the Rector, 7 for choristers and the remaining 70 unlet.

As already indicated, Sunday collections brought in most of the remaining revenue and became increasingly important. Detailed figures are only available for the 1850s. In 1851–2 the Rector reckoned that the average collection was £1 4s 5d. After this it fell to 15s 0d by 1856–7 and then rose to 17s 0d by the end of the decade. Communion offertories between 1848 and 1851 were recorded in detail. They could be as low as 2s 1½d, the amount contributed by fifteen communicants on the ninth Sunday after Trinity 1850, that is under 2d on average, or as much as the £5 13s 10d contributed at Christmas 1848 by forty-two communicants. There was in fact little correlation between numbers and offertories, so average figures would be meaningless. For example, in 1849 on one occasion 25 people contributed 15s 7d, on another 27 people gave 7s 9d. One Sunday 18 people gave 10s 10d, on another 16 people donated 5s 4d. In 1854–55 the total of such offertories was about £24. Later figures are not available.

And St Andrew's the pattern was somewhat different. Back in the 1780s seat rents and collections each raised about £50. But gradually the proportion coming from seat rents went up; as in Helensburgh the scale was periodically modified and raised. The accounts for the year ending January 1815, for example, show collections bringing in about £229, seat rents £389. These figures had fallen by the early 30s; about £77 for collections in 1830, for example, and about £340 from seat rents, partly presumably a reflection of the changed state of the economy. The last accounts recorded in the period under review, 3 January 1846 to 3 January 1847, show seat rents from permanent sitters raising over £157, temporary ones over £40, and collections down to something over £56.

Collections 'at the Sacrament' were presumably for the poor in both churches; specifically so at St Andrew's after 1820. 'Wine and washing' also were paid from this account in the early 40s. The amounts here also varied considerably. The offertory in February 1842, for example, was 15s 0d, on Good Friday over £3 and more than £5 at Easter, over £6 at Christmas. On other occasions, five of them, it varied between 14s 5½d in August and £2 6s 2d on Whitsunday.

Collections and seat rents could not, however, meet all the expenses.

During the middle decades of the century the relatively small congregation in Helensburgh built two churches, a parsonage and a school. In each case it had to borrow money and then raise enough to pay off the loan and interest; this burden remained a heavy one until the late 70s. Various methods of raising funds were adopted.

No evidence remains of the method of financing the first church, which cost about £1,000. Some was certainly borrowed, £24 12s od being the amount of the debt outstanding at Whitsunday 1849. Subscriptions towards the debt in the previous financial year were £13 5s od. The debt appears to have been cleared by 1850, seven years after the church was built.

Raising money by obtaining subscriptions was a normal way of meeting these large items of expenditure. In 1857, for instance, when it was decided to construct a parsonage at a cost, according to the 1858–9 Return, of £730, a subscription list was opened. Amounts varying from 5s od to £10 were collected; £2 2s od was contributed by the Chancellor of the Exchequer.[49] £47 7s od was thus collected between November 1861 and August 1862. About £170 was still outstanding and a bazaar was therefore held. This, with further subscriptions, raised £147 which was paid into the Clydesdale Bank, opened in Helensburgh in 1857.[50] By February 1863 the balance had been paid off and a surplus built up, nearly £55 being paid into the National Bank (the church seems to have had accounts with both banks for a time).

The question of building a new church was raised in the same year that the debt was paid off and, as already noted, a decision to go ahead depended on finance being available. By 1866 it seemed feasible and plans were made. £300 was borrowed from the Church Society and some also from the bank; in May 1867 it was agreed that the cash credit was 'now to be handed to the Clydesdale Bank so that it might be operated on'. The repayment of these debts remained a burden for thirteen years. £35 a year had to be paid to the Society, for example. Each year money was set aside for paying off the debt. In 1869 over £59 was so allocated, over £88 the following year. It fluctuated from £75 in 1871 to £84 in 1872 to nearly £99 in 1873 and then, perhaps a sign of financial stringency during the 'Great Depression' it fell between 1874 and 1876 from £78 to £63. Special collections were also made periodically for the reduction of the debt, generally three times a year. A collection on the day the church was opened raised over £60. In 1871 further money was borrowed from the Church Society to reduce the debt at the bank, which fell from its October 1870 figure of almost £1,013 to about £410 in December 1872. In 1880 the debts were finally settled, £38 being paid to the bank and £27 to the Society, special subscriptions having been collected for this purpose.

The rest of the money for the new church was raised by subscriptions. A list of subscribers dated 1868 shows donations varying from 2s 6d to £200. The Rector himself gave £200. Non church members contributed. Provost Breingan, for example, gave £2. James Smith (ex-provost), the Jordanhill

---

[49] The Rt Hon W. E. Gladstone. See reference 47.
[50] In the same premises as the Western Bank which had opened in Helensburgh in 1841, and under the same manager who had run it until that bank's failure in 1857.

banker, gave £5. The net was cast widely enough to include the Bishops of Glasgow, and Gibraltar (formerly of Glasgow), the Dean of Argyll and the Isles, and the Rt Hon W. E. Gladstone, who gave £3. Some 140 contributions appear, some several times. The total given according to this list was £1,254 2s 6d.

At St Andrew's it was also necessary to borrow money and to appeal for subscriptions. Financial difficulties were foreseen as early as the 1780s and subscriptions asked for. Although the church was not rebuilt it was several times enlarged, galleries and vestry being constructed; the organ had to be paid for and heavy expenses were incurred, for instance, after the floods in 1782 (£30 in that year's accounts) and 1816, and for other reasons. The roof was by 1813 reported to be in a bad state because of an error in the original plan and also because of the bad state of the wood,[51] and in 1824 the walls of the vestry showed signs of giving way and had to be strengthened. Real financial stringency can be traced back to 1802 when the treasurer was authorised to draw money from the Ship Bank. Before 1810 there were bills outstanding on the Royal Bank. By 1812 the 'Balance due to the Treasurer' in the annual accounts was about £406; two years later it was £647. To meet the debt subscriptions were collected and in 1828 it was reported that £890 had been raised. Thirty-nine subscribers were listed, most giving £10 or £25, though some, like Lord Douglas, gave more (£50). There was a further appeal in 1849 because 'the interior of the Edifice is in quite a decayed state and urgently requires to be renovated'. £700 was needed; apparently only £230 was raised. The minutes of an earlier suggestion, in 1847, that subscriptions should be raised by a committee has a pencilled note by Dr Gordon in the margin, 'All of whom did not raise one shilling'. The managers therefore found it necessary to borrow from the Edinburgh and Glasgow Bank; a cash credit of £170 was granted in March 1849. But it seems that the books still would not balance and in December 1852 it was agreed at a meeting of managers and qualified members that 'seeing the managers and other members were sorry that they were not in a position to make payment of the debts due in the accounts submitted to them, they henceforth entrust the charge of the pecuniary affairs of the Church to the Rev. J. F. S. Gordon. . . .' A further long and impassioned appeal for funds was issued in 1853. Most of the contributions paid, according to the list appended to the appeal, were between £1 and £5, though a few were smaller and some larger. The Church Society gave £40, James Kibble Esq gave £10 as did Sir H. C. Pollock, Bart, the Bishop of Glasgow and Galloway and the Marchioness of Lothian. The Duke of Buccleuch donated £25, W. E. Gladstone Esq MP gave £2 2s 0d.[52] The gap in the records after this date makes it impossible to trace the church's financial position for the next few years.

Seat rents and collections, supplemented by loans and subscriptions then, were the main sources of revenue. There were only a handful of legacies

[51] One critical nineteenth century comment on St Andrew's finances said, 'The most extraordinary thing is how not hundreds but even thousands of pounds were frittered away upon a building of poorest design', 'Senex' (J. M. Reid), *Glasgow Past and Present* (Glasgow, 1884), Vol III.

[52] His donations to Helensburgh have already been noted.

bringing in a little interest. Virtually all the running costs had to be met from these; cost of heat and light, insurance, wages, cleaning, maintenance and repair bills and so on had all to be met. Communion plate, prayer and office books had to be bought,[53] and choir robes provided at St Andrew's.

The major item, however, apart from the building projects already referred to was the priest's stipend, though in the very early years in Helensburgh small amounts were received to augment this from the Church Society funds (eg, £10 in 1851–2). The original arrangement there with Mr Bell was that once the debt had been paid off, he would receive the amount of seat rents and ordinary collections after deducting normal running expenses. The vestry had the power to make extraordinary collections for church funds. In 1849 he appears to have received about £40, the following year over £63. There had been an attempt in 1850, the year the debt was cleared, to change this system but in fact it remained the same until October 1857 when it was modified. In future 'ordinary collections and seat rents were not to be burdened with the expenses incurred in church' but these should be paid for out of subscriptions and collections made for that purpose. In other words it was clearly recognised that the congregation's first responsibility was to pay the Rector's stipend. By this time, of course, money was being raised to build the parsonage.

Mr Bell died in November 1861 and when the Rev J. S. Syme was appointed in February 1862, it was agreed that he should receive £100 a year plus the parsonage free of rent, the £100 to be paid monthly 'out of the first end of the seat rents, collections and communion offertories'.[54] He was also to receive anything thus collected over and above the £100 after deduction of the current expenses of the church, on the understanding that he should pay the interest on the £120 debt on the parsonage: a rather complicated arrangement but one that seemed to work. The accounts in February 1863 showed that he had received £166 14s 9½d and that £51 was still due to him. By the end of that year 'Mr Syme appeared entitled to £197 5s 1d' according to the vestry minutes – considerably more than the £100 minimum agreed. His stipend varied during the next few years. It was about £198 in 1864, £200 the following year, then £193, down to £185 in 1867, perhaps because of the cost of the new church, up to £234 in 1868.

With the opening of the new church with its burden of debt, new arrangements were made. He was to receive £200 a year (if the income allowed this after paying expenses); a third of any balance would also go to him, the remaining two-thirds going towards paying off the debt. In 1869 he received over £229 under this formula, over £244 the following year. His stipend varied

[53] Coal, eg cost £1 10s 0d in Helensburgh in 1849. £8 1s 9d was paid the following year for gas fittings. By 1867 the gas bill was 13s 9d. Insurance cost £1 7s 9d in 1849, £2 7s 6d by 1867. The gardener in 1850 received £2 5s 0d, the organist and choir cost £5. The organist appointed in 1857 received £12 a year, and by the early 70s the cost of the organist and choir was over £20.

The accounts for 1846 at St Andrew's show salaries (excluding the Rector) costing over £57; repairs over £17 and such incidentals as coal, insurance, gas and an umbrella stand totalling over £8.

[54] Quoted from a letter to Mr Syme from the Bishop telling him of his appointment and recorded in the Vestry Minutes.

between £237 and £249 over the next four years but then, with the onset of depression, it fell from £239 to £238 and then £232 for two years. Only in 1878 did it recover to nearly £248. From 1877 he did, however, also receive an Easter offering which varied in the region of £32 to £46 at this period. By 1878, the first £500 loan having been paid off, the arrangements were again modified, two-thirds of the balance over £200 was to go to him and only one-third to paying off the debt. When this was finally achieved in 1880 the original salary arrangements were restored.

The Rector, then, was assured of an income, even if a fluctuating one, out of members' contributions through collections and seat rents; an income, incidentally, well above that paid to many other priests in the Episcopal church. In the mid-sixties the church was aiming at a minimum stipend of £100 for incumbents, a minimum not completely achieved until the 1890s. The vestry would seem to have been able to give a good account of their stewardship.

As St Andrew's church the records of 1781 (resumed after a gap of nearly thirty years after 1751 'when no further proceedings appear to be recorded') show the Pastor's salary as £60. By 1795 Mr Routledge had been appointed as an assistant at £50, by which time the Rector's salary was augmented by a £5 annuity and a £10 'present'. Mr Falconer, at a general meeting that November, asked for an increase, noting that 'all kinds of provisions and family necessaries have become much dearer . . . particularly since Whitsunday 1795 . . .'; a reflection of the wartime inflation. Although some members suggested dismissing the band, selling the organ, or doubling the seat rents, little was done and a year later he wrote that 'ye must all know that no man will sell me the smallest article of food, raiment or other family necessaries one farthing cheaper than to them'. After this there were increases so that by 1807 the combined salaries were £250.[55]

When, after Mr Falconer's death, Mr Routledge was appointed as Rector his stipend was fixed at £100 and £100 as a present. By 1810 the combined salary and present was £230, £250 by 1811, then £275, £300 by 1814, presumably to keep pace with the current inflation. But after the war things became difficult and by 1822 the most that they could offer as a 'present' was £150. By 1824 the total was down to £200. Unsuccessful attempts were being made to find an assistant; one reason for the lack of success was that the clergy were elected annually. In 1825 the Bishop asked for this to be expunged from the constitution. In 1843 Mr Norval, and then in 1844 Dr Gordon followed Mr Routledge as rector. Their stipends still appeared to be £100 with various irregular supplements, some, like the interest on an annuity, causing throughout the period a good deal of controversy between rectors and managers.

It is quite clear, therefore, that while the Rector of St Andrew's was assured of a stipend, and one that never fell below £100, nevertheless the managers faced considerable financial problems and perhaps met with less success than their counterparts in Helensburgh. There is no reason to suppose they were less capable as managers; a major factor must be that the church in Helensburgh was sited in a growing, wealthy community whereas St Andrew's was in an

---

55 Vestry Minutes, St Andrew's Church.

area of Glasgow from which the wealthier members were moving out, and moreover, it was in a sense increasingly in competition with other episcopalian churches, which Helensburgh was not.

Not all the money raised by these congregations was used to meet their own expenses. Donations were made to outside charitable causes. In Helensburgh in May 1850, for example, it was decided that there should be a collection for the SPG on Ascension Day and in September for the Church Society. Other special collections were for church funds. Various similar arrangements were made from time to time. In 1877 for instance £25 was collected for the Indian famine and £3 for the Chanda Mission started in the central provinces of India by Rev G. Carruthers. In 1871 the Bishop of Calcutta backed his appeal to the Episcopal Church to support this mission. Some examples may also be drawn from St Andrew's. In 1809 and 1813 there were collections of about £51 and £35 respectively for the lunatic asylum. The Magdalene Asylum got £48 in 1813, £32 three year later. The Aged Woman's Society received £181 in 1815, the Royal Infirmary £60 in 1818. In 1819 £27 was collected for the Fever Hospital, £33 for the Jews Society, £33 for the Aged Women's Society. The Deaf and Dumb Asylum received gifts in 1824 and 1826, of over £50 altogether.

Each church also collected money for the poor. Data for the early years in Helensburgh is very scanty, but evidence survives that from 1868 to 1875 between £16 and £29 was set aside each year for the poor. For some years there are more detailed records at St Andrew's. Until 1762 there was no money available for the 'poor of episcopal persuasion', except charitable contributions made periodically by members of the congregation. This was thought troublesome and so a separate fund was established. By 1783 this amounted to £150 which was loaned to the 'Town of Glasgow's Chamberlain to lye at 5%'.[55] About 20/- a month was distributed to the poor from this interest plus subscriptions and an Easter collection. Details are not available until 1823 when a full record was started, partly in an attempt to prevent imposters from depriving the deserving poor of their share. It was reported in January of that year that 'Impositions have often been attempted on the Treasurer and in some instances where seeming wretchedness had excited compassion and obtained relief, the object has been found unworthy of it'. It was agreed that the fund was primarily for the 'virtuous' poor of the congregation in need because of sickness or other misfortune not caused 'by their own fault or misconduct'. It was proposed that a person should be a member of the congregation for two years before he was eligible. The managers – or the sub-committee which dealt with the poor – were obviously torn between their 'humane' desire to relieve suffering and the need to keep the fund going without frittering it away. Each one was allocated a district near his residence so that he could visit the poor in his area to assess their need; how far this was ever carried out is not known. The records show that in the 1820s there were about thirty-two regular poor, most receiving 3/- a month. In 1823 over £90 was paid out, including a few pounds for the occasional poor. The majority of recipients (twenty-three in all) were widows. Ten years after the records started there were twenty-eight regular

55 Vestry Minutes, St Andrew's Church.

poor, mostly still receiving 3/- though in December they only got 2/-, presumably because money was short. There were still some occasional poor. The total given was between £74 and £75. The last full account is that for 1841, by which time the regular poor were down to twenty-two, still normally receiving 3/- a month. Only c £65 was paid out. There had been occasions when they received more or less than the 3/-, for example 5/- in February 1838, 2/6d in December 1839. There were always some who got more, presumably because of dependants or in cases of sickness. The capital of the fund was eventually all used up.

VII

The connection between the churches and education in the nineteenth century was, of course, very close, and the Episcopal church was no exception. As early as 1841 the Church Society was helping to finance thirteen schools with about 1,800 children on the books. Payments had been made by the Society to schoolmasters in Glasgow, Paisley and the Highlands. Donations to the funds came not only from Scotland but also from England, Ireland and as far away as India. In 1862 Helensburgh contributed £3 1s 0d.[56] The fund had been set up at the 1838 synod as a fund firstly for aged and infirm clergy, salaries for assistants, and aid for congregations. The minimum stipend in 1841 was £80, and thirty-two charges were assisted to reach this figure. Secondly, it was for candidates for the ministry to help their studies; thirdly, for episcopalian schoolmasters; books and tracts for the poor, and finally diocesan libraries. It was in fact an extension of the fund established as far back as 1806 to make 'moderate additions to the incomes of Bishops and the most necessitous of the inferior clergy.'[57]

By 1843 between 800 and 1,000 children in the Glasgow diocese were apparently receiving Christian education in church day or Sunday schools.[58] The number of schools the Society inspected rose from 37 in 1849 to 120 a decade later. Not all the children in Episcopal church schools were episcopalians. For instance out of over 6,000 on the rolls of 74 such schools surveyed by the Argyle Commission, under 2,000 were episcopalians: quite a significant contribution to the educational service available. Since the late forties the church had also been active in providing higher education. Glenalmond, for instance, founded in 1847,[59] was to be both a school and a theological college, although this dual rôle soon ceased. By 1850 there was a training college for men teachers in Edinburgh, to which women were later admitted.

In Helensburgh the church school seems to have been started in the very early days, there being, according to the returns to the Church Society, thirteen boys and ten girls on the roll in 1845. In 1850 it was decided to build a school, apparently a two-roomed building. The larger room, described as the boys' school in the returns to the Society in 1851-2, seems in fact to have held a

---

[56] The Rt Hon W. E. Gladstone again appeared, giving £20, presumably in addition to his normal annual donation of £5.
[57] *Representative Church Council Report 1903* (p 55).
[58] Report of the Scottish Episcopal Church Society, December 1843.
[59] Mr Gladstone was once again actively involved, being one of its founders.

mixed class. The girls' school met in the smaller room. The return to the govern-ment inspectors in 1856 gave age and sex distribution as in Table 6. The list of subjects taught appears very impressive but smacks of window-dressing,[60] being essentially the four Rs. All pupils learnt scripture, catechism and liturgy. All in the larger school did history, all in the girls' school geography and grammar, and all the girls learned to sew. Books and visual aids were provided: Bibles, testaments, maps and historical charts, pictures, charts of the kings of England, geographical and astronomical diagrams, plaster of Paris models and so on. Fortunately not all the returns were as detailed, but all give a picture of a reasonably full and varied curriculum.

It was reckoned that the school had room for about 200 scholars, with between 116 and 175 actually in attendance in the late fifties and early sixties. In 1862, for example, the average attendance on weekdays was 106 out of a possible 161 (75 boys and 86 girls). When the new church was built the old school was taken down to make room for it and another built with accom-modation for ninety pupils. The number on the books from then to 1875 varied between 33 and 58 boys, and 39 and 65 girls, plus 15 infants before 1870. The average attendance in the early seventies was in fact well below these figures. In 1874, for example, there were 55 boys and 60 girls on the books, 32 boys in attendance on the average, and 45 girls. The school would obviously have been seriously overcrowded had they all turned up. Reactions to the 1872 Education Act were not recorded!

It appears that the contribution of the Episcopal church to the educational life of Helensburgh was not confined to the school for, according to the *Scottish*

TABLE 6

CHILDREN ON BOOKS, 1856. HELENSBURGH

	Boys	Girls	Girls' school	
Under 4	2	6	Under 7–8	4
4–5	2	3	8–9	5
5–6	2	5	10–11	3
6–7	1	3	12–13	4
7–8	2	1	over 14	10
8–9	4	3		—
9–10	1	2		26
10–11	9	4		
11–12	2	1		
12–13	2	1		
13–14	1	0		
over 14	1	0		
	29	29		

[60] In the mixed school the subjects included: letters, syllables, narrative, books of infor-mation, writing on slate, writing on paper, dictation on slate, addition, division, compound addition, proportion, as well as geography and grammar. The girls' school also had multi-plication, practice and fractions, music, drawing and French. The report a few years earlier had included Latin.

Episcopal Church Directory (1879), evening classes were held by the incumbent in the school room, and there was a working men's institute connected with the church.

The church provided education for some of the children of the rapidly growing town. But financing the school was a continual problem. The original building cost about £260. By the time it was built £96 had been raised by subscriptions, and a member of the vestry had been delegated the job of obtaining further subscriptions from acquaintances in Glasgow. The Church Society was approached for a £50 grant. But even when the building was paid for the school was never self-supporting. It did charge fees, varying from 1/- to 3/- a quarter in 1851, but some children paid nothing. Ten boys and twenty-three girls received free education that year, twenty-two boys and twenty-five girls in 1852. The income from fees in the school's first year, 1851, was £8 15s 0d. Subscriptions brought in £25 and the Society contributed £15: a total of under £49. But costs were higher, over £66 in fact. The master's salary was about £36, the mistress received £20. Coal, cleaning and so on cost a further £10. The deficit had to be met by calling on this small congregation for further subscriptions. In 1852 these amounted to £52. By 1856 the school's own income was £51, subscriptions and grant raising it to the £95 required to cover the salaries, by then £88, plus £5 for fuel and repairs. (It was realised as early as the mid-fifties that salaries were too low and the master's was raised to £52, the mistress's to £36.) At that date thirty-two children paid 1d a week, thirty-six paid 2d, fifteen paid 3d a week. Every year collections were made regularly in church for the school. By 1865, for instance, these totalled £17. When the master resigned in 1863 it was thought that, 'for £70 per annum a school master of efficiency could be had'.[61] At this generous salary it was assumed that he would be willing to assist with the church music.[62] The advisability of continuing the school unless it could be 'self-sustaining' was discussed at that time, but continue it did.

The debt on the school was financed at least in part by the use of bills. This was authorised by the vestry on 26 March 1865. The accounts show an entry on 31 March 'To loan by bill from Clydesdale Bank, Helensburgh, £50'. The interest paid at the end of December was £1 3s 0d. This bill was either renewed at intervals, or cancelled and replaced by a new bill, as in February 1866 when it was renewed for £45, or January 1868 when it was cancelled and one for £54 granted. Early in 1869 the bank requested that the debt in connection with 'the late school' be settled. It then stood at £54 3s 9d and was met out of church funds.

Evidence of educational provision at St Andrew's is scanty, though there are references scattered among the registers particularly during Rev W. Routledge's ministry. There was certainly a Sunday school, with sixty children attending on average in 1829 for example, forty-five a year later. There was a lending library with between forty-five and fifty-seven people using it in these years. Approxi-

[61] Vestry Minutes.
[62] The Parochial and Burgh Schoolmasters' Act 1861 had increased the stipend of such teachers to between £35 and £70, school mistresses to a £30 minimum.

mately sixty children would be catechised in Lent at that period, and presented to the Bishop for confirmation, mostly 15 and 16 year olds. Collections were made in church from time to time for the Sunday school and library, raising £28 in 1836 for example, but nearer £18 for the next few years. The Sunday school account for 1834 shows expenditure of nearly £56, much of the money to cover this being the proceeds of an oratorio. Church members gave not only money but also gifts of books to the Sunday school or library.

VII

No general conclusions can be drawn from this very limited study. What is evident is that in Helensburgh at least the membership of the local Episcopal church between the 1840s and the 1870s grew at approximately the same rate as the town's population, that is about four fold. While the management of the church both there and at St Andrew's was in the hands of a very limited group of people, the congregation as a whole represented a fairly wide cross section of the local population. While it received some money from outside sources by way of grants or gifts, most of the income was raised by the congregation itself. From this it managed not only to pay its day to day expenses, in particular the Rector's stipend, but also to pay off the debts incurred on the various building projects, to support charitable causes and maintain a poor fund, and to make a reasonable contribution to the educational facilities of the burgh. By the end of the 1870s, in spite of added difficulties during the depression years, it was free of debt.

St Andrew-by-the-Green was set in a quite different milieu and of course had a much longer and more varied history, so the two churches are not strictly comparable and in fact no such comparison has been attempted. But what is evident is that there also the congregation was socially 'mixed', although by the middle of the nineteenth century it had become much more an English or Irish working-class church. It faced considerable difficulty of inherited debt from its earlier, wealthier days but still managed to make some contribution to the poor and other charitable causes and to continue until its eventual closure in 1975.

BARBARA M. THATCHER

8

The Performance of the Standard Life Assurance Company in the Ordinary Life Market in Scotland 1850–75

From humble beginnings in Edinburgh in the spring of 1825, the Standard Life Assurance Company in little more than a quarter of a century had come to hold 'the highest position in Scotland [among indigenous offices] ... estimated by the amount of its annual business'. Indeed 'with one, or it may be two exceptions', it could by 1850 claim to transact 'the largest business in Great Britain'.[1] Yet its rise to this position of lofty eminence had not been a smooth and untroubled progression, marked from its inception by a well defined secular increase in the volume of its new whole life proposals. Particularly during 1825–30 when it shared the same managerial staff and premises as the Insurance Company of Scotland – the fire office from which it evolved – its results betrayed no marked pattern of growth and, equally important, it had become dangerously over-dependent upon the granting of personal loans as a means of stimulating business. By January 1829 one-fifth of the Standard's whole life liabilities were a direct product of this type of 'high risk' transaction. Even after, however, the break with the Insurance Company of Scotland in 1831, there was little immediate indication of a spectacular improvement in its fortunes, although the level of new annual returns recorded during the period of James Cheyne's occupation of the managerial chair – 1831–7 – was, with one exception, consistently above the best result – 1827–8 – which had been attained in the 1820s.

It is clear, therefore, that the 'take-off' phase of the Standard's life underwriting activities came relatively late and only after William Thomas Thomson, its youngest as well as its longest-serving manager, had assumed – subject always to the over-riding authority of the board – control of its fortunes in November 1837. In 1838–9 £200,000 of new assurance was secured for the first time within the compass of the company's financial year. In 1843–4 this total was to be decisively eclipsed when almost £380,000 of new contracts were sealed, while in the Investigation year of 1849–50 the temporary setback

[1] *Annual Report of the 25th Annual General Meeting of the Standard* (1850).

to this strong upward trend which had occurred in 1847–8 in the aftermath of the collapse of the 'railway mania' was quickly forgotten when the £500,000 barrier was breached, setting a new peak performance in the office's recent history. In some measure, of course, the contours of these returns can be seen as a vindication of the painstaking work of Cheyne who in little more than a quinquennium carried through a series of mundane but much-needed reforms of the Standard's existing administrative infrastructure. Nonetheless while that contribution was real enough, the principal credit for these results clearly belonged to the expansionist plans which W. T. Thomson had designed for the company in the 1840s. By persuading his directors to penetrate decisively the English and Irish ordinary life markets; by extending the spatial coverage of the agency network; and by embarking upon a take-over strategy which would enable the Standard to inherit the 'good will' and existing connections of the three companies it absorbed between 1844 and 1850, Thomson had provided a firm foundation from which the office could, and did, prosper.

But, as he realised, it was not sufficient, if the impetus for growth were to be maintained in the future, to cling blindly to traditions and practices which had served the company well in the immediate past. As competition between the major life offices intensified in the post-1850 world, it was essential to adapt well-tried techniques and to innovate in order to maintain the company's competitive edge in changing market conditions. It was to this end that the Standard during the third quarter of the nineteenth century was prepared, under Thomson's guidance, to sanction fundamental discontinuities in policy and to press ahead with changes which involved a significant slackening in the terms of the assurance contract. In the 1850s and early 1860s, for example, the proprietors and directors approved of the manager's proposals to ease restrictions on foreign travel; to make arrangements for the revival of policies which had lapsed through the non-payment of the appropriate premium; and to bring the office's commission rates paid to its agents more nearly into line with those of its major English and Scottish rivals. Similarly when in the 1860s a decline in the tontine reversionary bonus to its policyholders under the office's original 'with profits' scheme threatened to exercise a braking effect on the growth of new premium income, the board approved of Thomson's strategy, finalised in 1865, for a new participating plan which, hopefully, would resolve the immediate crisis. Finally, the idea of extending its geographical horizons was warmly endorsed when in 1865–6 the Standard acquired the Colonial Life Assurance Company with its network of representatives and local boards in virtually every part of the British Empire. It was largely as a result of these developments, together with the take-over of the Minerva (1864) and the Victoria (1865), two London-based life offices, that the company was able to emerge in the 1860s as the premier company in the United Kingdom. After a period of sluggish returns in 1855–63, the Standard was never to obtain less than one million pounds of new annual business in any year between 1864–75, with the high-point of £1,509,528 8s 4d being reached in 1874–5 itself.[2] The concern

[2] This section is based upon Chapters II–IV of a forthcoming study of Scottish life assurance by J. Butt and J. H. Treble.

of this article, however, is not with analysing the broad contours of new premium income from disparate life markets, but rather with examining in depth the office's performance in Scotland during the third quarter of the nineteenth century.

I

Surveying the broad pattern of economic development in Scotland during the period 1850–75, it can be argued that the socio-economic climate was particularly conducive to a further expansion of ordinary life business. For the most part the economy was relatively insulated from major shocks, although such events as the 'cotton famine' of 1861–5 had adverse repercussions upon a significant, albeit localised, sector of the slowly broadening spectrum of Scottish industry. Similarly the failure of the Western Bank in 1857 could only have exercised a retarding influence on the growth prospects of all life offices seeking proposals from the middle-classes in and around Glasgow.[3] Apart, however, from these sharp but geographically circumscribed checks to prosperity, Scottish industries – particularly linen, iron, engineering and the factory-based production of cotton fabrics – enjoyed a considerable measure of good fortune, interrupted only by the commercial crises of 1857–9 and 1866–8 which affected the whole of the United Kingdom's economy. Advance in industry was paralleled by progress in other areas of the economy. A programme of heavy investment in land and agricultural improvements, which was another feature of this quarter of a century, enabled life assurance companies, including the Standard, to extend their life underwriting activities since in many cases the *sine qua non* of the loans they made to Scottish landowners was the sealing of a policy, often for a sizeable amount. Lastly, the tertiary sector of Scottish industry – including banking, retailing, wholesaling and commerce – experienced growth, albeit at an uneven rate, while between 1851 and 1861 there was a 30 per cent increase in the numbers employed in full-time education and a 50 per cent rise in those who ministered to the religious needs of the Scottish population.[4]

These trends, coupled with the numbers employed in domestic service in Scotland – in 1851 10·5 per cent of its occupied population was classified under that generic heading, in 1861 12 per cent and in 1871 10·7 per cent[5] – indicated clearly enough that, as in England and Wales, Scottish middle-classes were growing at a faster pace than the overall rate of increase in population and that the share of the National Income accruing to these elements in society was almost certainly proportionately greater than in the decade 1841–51. As J. A. Banks' work has demonstrated in an English context, however, it is dangerous in this period to postulate the idea of a homogeneous 'middle class', possessing common socio-economic characteristics; for much of the material gains made by

---

[3] Committee Minute Book III, 14 October 1858.
[4] G. Best, *Mid-Victorian Britain 1851–75* (1971), 86. But in both cases numbers in education and the churches remained stationary during 1861–71.
[5] Ibid, 104.

the English middle-classes went to the tax-paying elements who earned incomes in excess of £200 per annum. The same probably held true for Scotland, although that hypothesis has yet to be rigorously tested. But what in Scottish society is not in dispute is that the years 1851-71 were characterised by an expansion in the numbers of those who could be labelled the lower middle-class, including clerks of all descriptions, schoolteachers and the 'shopocracy'. It was amongst this class, rather than the more socially elevated taxpayers that life offices could expect to secure proposals for essentially modest sums of money.

Significantly enough, the extant data of its 1860 Investigation strongly suggest that the Standard had derived a considerable portion of its more recent business from precisely those who could be placed in this broad social grouping. At that date, out of a total of 3,677 'with profits' policies still in force in Scotland, no fewer than 743 were for less than £100 and another 672 for between £100 and £200. In aggregate terms just under 40 per cent of its participating contracts in 1860 covered sums of less than £200. But in addition to the support of the lower middle-classes, the company was also heavily patronised by their more affluent brethren, since no fewer than 776 proposals were for between £400 and £500 and a further 466 for between £900 and £1,000.[6] Moreover, there is no reason to believe that the pattern revealed by these returns was unrepresentative, since all the available indicators, qualitative as well as quantitative, confirm that the demand for the services of ordinary life offices was widely diffused in social terms. The Standard's English-based officials, for instance, were quick to draw attention to the sharp contrast which existed between the responsiveness of Scotsmen to the message projected by an assorted collection of mutual and proprietary companies and the situation obtaining in England. As William Bentham, its Inspector of English Agencies, wrote in May 1856, 'it is impossible to overestimate the difference between Life Assurance in Scotland and in England. In the former country the value of the sound education which is highly prized and easily attainable even in the lower Classes of Society becomes apparent when brought into conjunction with Life Assurance. The number of intelligent Scotchmen acting for respectable Companies in this Kingdom is surprising and it is rare indeed to find one recommending a Company the pretensions of which he has not thoroughly sifted'.[7] Although this generalisation could not be legitimately applied to all parts of Scotland, the claim itself could be statistically verified since as early as 1852 Scotland, assessed on a *per capita* basis, possessed twice as much life cover for its population as England.[8]

Reinforcing the positive influence of these exogenous variables favourable to growth was the well-documented fact that Scotland escaped relatively unscathed from the flotation of 'bubble' life companies which proliferated in England during the late 1840s and early 1850s, and which gave rise to fears, largely unjustified, for the reputation and future stability of the assurance industry. This theme, which stressed the responsible and cautious quality of the

---

[6] 1860 Investigation, IX, Final Results. (Deed Box No 4, 1860 Investigation.)
[7] Sederunt Book XIV, 2 May 1856.
[8] B. Supple, *The Royal Exchange Assurance* (Cambridge, 1970), 112.

management of Scottish offices, was strongly emphasised by the Standard's directorate during the first half of the 1850s. The board's case for urging the indigenous population to assure their lives with Scottish companies was perhaps most eloquently stated in its *1855 Annual Report* when it dwelt at length with the situation in Scotland where 'a fair emulation' between itself and its Edinburgh- and Glasgow-based competitors provided 'a wholesome stimulant, beneficial to the public, and inspiriting to the Offices themselves'. In England on the other hand 'the daily increasing evil which presses on the English public by the wholesale manufacture of new offices, calls loudly for legislative interference; but although a Committee of the House of Commons reported, eithteen months ago, on the necessity of some check being instituted, the evil still continues, one hundred and four new offices having been projected, and fifty-six founded, during the last two years alone (the last Scotch Office founded was in 1846)'.[9]

For the most part, therefore, it can be concluded that external constraints on the development of life underwriting in Scotland were relatively few and that their retarding influence was more than offset by the growth-inducing forces which have just been discussed. Indeed, apart from the checks to trade which occurred in the late 1850s and the second half of the 1860s, there were only two general decelerating exogenous forces which can be described, in a Scottish context, as of some significance for the individual office. In the first place the failures of the Albert and European Life Assurance Companies in 1869 administered a much more profound shock to the assurance world than the earlier collapse of such 'rogue' offices as the West Middlesex in 1841.[10] For although the impact of these events was most fully felt in England, all parts of the United Kingdom were to some extent affected by the failure of two institutions of major standing. In the wake of these disastrous events, it was scarcely surprising that the Standard – along with other offices – embarked upon a concentrated advertising campaign which sought to assuage the fears of potential assurers by stressing the strength of its financial resources and the prudence with which it managed its funds, to the mutual benefit of proprietors and participating policyholders alike.

Of more importance, however, than this short-lived crisis was the increasingly fierce competition between rival companies which was one of the salient characteristics of the history of the assurance industry in Scotland during the third quarter of the nineteenth century. Already by the late 1840s the larger Scottish offices had extended their horizons from their initial preoccupation with canvassing and 'working' those areas within easy reach of their Head Offices – covering, according to the geographical location of the individual company, roughly the towns and hinterland in and around Glasgow, Aberdeen or Edinburgh – to creating a network of agencies embracing all the major areas of population in the United Kingdom. In Scotland this development meant that at the start of our period all the major indigenous companies had

---

[9] *Annual Report*, 1855.
[10] The failure of the Albert and European Companies led to government intervention in the life assurance industry when it passed the 1870 Life Assurance Act.

representatives in the principal towns of the heavily settled central belt and in the most important centres of social and economic life in the more sparsely populated Highland zone. But in addition to the ferocity of the struggle between themselves, they were also confronted by a challenge of formidable proportions from most of the English life offices which were attracted to Scotland by the prospect of an expanding market.

The Standard's assessment of the dimensions and severity of outside competition can be amply illustrated from its surviving records. In 1849, for example William White, its first Inspector of English agencies, presented a graphic picture of the problems confronting the company during a tour of Scottish towns. In Kirkcaldy he was compelled to acknowledge that the office suffered from its 'want of local influence . . . as contrasted with other Companies . . . particularly 'the Scottish', 'Union' and the 'North British'. These offices command a greater influence than the Standard in consequence of a number of shareholders being resident in the Neighbourhood'. At Dundee Ogilvie, the company's agent, met the argument that he had achieved little on behalf of the Standard – during 1845–8 he had forwarded a token total of £1,700 of new proposals – with the assertion that 'complaints as to want of Business' were 'made by the agents generally . . . and indeed if all the Offices get a share of business the individual amount cannot in any instance be great, for almost every door in the leading streets exhibits the name of an Assurance Office'. Finally in Stirling the Standard was called upon to meet the challenge of the Scottish Widows' Fund which 'has done a good business' in the town and the Scottish Equitable, while in Dunfermline it had to contend with the last-named office and the Scottish Provident Institution which 'have succeeded best'.[11] During the course of the next twenty-five years, as the pace of competition accelerated, the Standard's principal agents were to protest loudly that 'when it came to a question of results few could promise much, and none a great deal. They all complained of the enormous competition for assurance business in Scotland, and undoubtedly the field has been very much worked of late years. As an example of this, Mr. George Gray of Perth told me that when he first represented the Standard [in the late 1820s] there were three Agents of Assurance Companies in Perth, now [October 1870] there are forty-eight, also that in one November he sent in £37,000 of new assurances, while now he finds difficulty in getting any, although equally anxious as formerly to do so, and having a connection with the younger generation through his Son'.[12]

That there was an element of validity in these contentions cannot of course be disputed, for an identical picture, couched in similarly lugubrious language, had been presented to the Edinburgh board at an even ealier point in time in relation to its operations in England. Nevertheless, having conceded that point, the historian should beware of accepting it uncritically as a convenient monocausal explanation for the contours of the Standard's Scottish new business during the years 1850–75. For if the formidable nature of these outside pressures were a reality, they should not disguise the fact that competition was taking

11 Committee Minute Book II, 10 July 1849.
12 Ibid, IV, October 1870.

place within a life market which on trend continued to grow, and, of equal significance, that the proportionate share of that market which accrued to a given office depended in large measure upon the degree to which it had attuned its organisation and its assurance 'package' to meeting the needs of an increasingly sophisticated public. It is against this backcloth that the detailed analysis of the Standard's run of annual statistics has to be set.

II

Tables 1 and 2 embody the returns by country for the office's total United Kingdom business during the twenty-five years under review. Drawn exclusively from policy registers, they record – where a direct comparison can be made – a level of business slightly in excess of the published statistics in the Standard's *Annual Reports* since they include all whole life transactions, whether sealed by single or annual payments, and do not necessarily take into account contracts which lapsed during their first year. Nevertheless this difference should not be overemphasised, for it in no way distorts the overall pattern of

TABLE 1

NEW UNITED KINGDOM BUSINESS 1850–75 BY COUNTRY

Year	Scotland £	England £	Ireland £
1850–1	206,694	—	68,871
1851–2	222,198	182,042	60,008
1852–3	188,637	182,372	102,441
1853–4	221,997	237,430	70,291
1854–5	235,780	272,266	102,478
1855–6	219,447	210,449	107,229
1856–7	229,189	265,061	92,839
1857–8	189,347	216,954	112,121
1858–9	218,195	227,300	82,601
1859–60	193,900	387,162	132,525
1860–1	158,396	239,360	128,580
1861–2	199,802	228,357	87,301
1862–3	183,779	349,020	124,050
1863–4	221,598	468,382	142,488
1864–5	213,990	596,064	182,075
1865–6	178,342	390,496	152,609
1866–7	134,623	429,090	123,676
1867–8	126,365	443,364	157,083
1868–9	164,023	—	89,085
1869–70	139,786	—	115,991
1870–1	133,208	359,245	138,946
1871–2	186,803	362,754	—
1872–3	246,023	385,113	—
1873–4	179,695	406,960	—
1874–5	347,857	601,004	—

Source: Policy Registers of The Standard Life Assurance Company, 1850–75

the company's life underwriting activities. In broad terms, it can be confidently concluded that the Standard's Scottish performance can be assessed with a reasonable degree of accuracy from these data.

Even the most cursory examination of these statistics reveals that the level of returns from Scotland was profoundly disappointing compared with the comparable achievements recorded in England and Ireland. Assessed on a quinquennial basis, the volume of new Scottish business fell consistently between 1850–70, while even the revival of the office's fortunes in 1870–5 owed much to the 1874–5 figure which was by far the best annual Scottish result in the whole quarter of a century. Conversely, it seems likely – although the historian cannot be dogmatic on the point in the absence of data for 1868–70 – that between 1850 and 1870 the company's quinquennial record in England was one of unbroken advance, while the quinquennial experience in Ireland between 1850 and 1865 conformed to a fundamentally similar pattern. Switching from global totals to percentages the Scottish outline remains equally bleak. Whereas during 1851–60 Scotland in no fewer than four years produced over 40 per cent of the office's United Kingdom business, that statistic was not to be surpassed in any one of the post-1860 years for which calculations can be made. Indeed in

TABLE 2

NEW UNITED KINGDOM BUSINESS, 1850–75: PERCENTAGE SHARE OF EACH COUNTRY

Year	Scotland	England	Ireland
1850–1			
1851–2	47·86	39·21	12·93
1852–3	39·84	38·52	21·64
1853–4	41·91	44·82	13·27
1854–5	39·20	45·26	16·54
1855–6	40·86	39·18	19·96
1856–7	39·04	45·15	15·81
1857–8	36·52	41·85	21·63
1858–9	41·32	43·04	15·64
1859–60	27·17	54·26	18·57
1860–1	30·09	45·48	24·43
1861–2	38·76	44·30	16·94
1862–3	27·98	53·14	18·82
1863–4	26·62	56·26	17·12
1864–5	21·57	60·08	18·35
1865–6	24·72	54·13	21·15
1866–7	19·58	62·42	18·00
1867–8	17·39	61·00	21·61
1868–9	—	—	—
1869–70	—	—	—
1870–1	21·10	56·89	22·01
1871–2	—	—	—
1872–3	—	—	—
1873–4	—	—	—
1874–5	—	—	—

1867-8 and 1870-1 Ireland contributed on a larger scale to new premium income than the Standard's country of origin.

In mitigation it can of course be argued that, within the framework of the United Kingdom, the ultimate hegemony of England as the principal source of new proposals was inevitable, given its greater population base, greater wealth and the strenuous campaigns which were mounted by Head Office to tap the fertile English market from the mid-1840s onwards.[13] Moreover, even if the Scottish results were a source of anxiety to the Edinburgh directorate, it should still be remembered that in *per capita* terms Scotland continued to perform markedly better for the company than England throughout the 1850s, 1860s, and early 1870s, and that the volume of new annual Scottish proposals was higher than that of most of the Standard's rivals. But when full allowance has been made for this type of special pleading, it still cannot mask the secular decline in Scottish business which occurred in successive quinquennia until after 1870; nor can it shed any light on factors which powerfully shaped the size of that fall during a period when the lack of significant external checks might have led the historian to have anticipated a much more favourable outcome.

It is in fact only when the data which have just been analysed are related to the broad parameters of growth of the Scottish economy in general and of the ordinary life market in particular that it becomes possible to start to define, and isolate, the nature of these retarding influences. Viewed from this perspective, three conclusions can be safely drawn. In the first place it is clear that the principal sources of the Standard's difficulties were to be located within the company. Deficiencies in its administrative infrastructure and practices rather than adverse exogenous restraints were largely responsible for its failure to exploit more effectively its home market. Secondly, although one or more of these endogenous variables might have exercised a decelerating effect in England and Ireland as well as in Scotland, the contours of new annual business indicate that either their presence was recorded with more devastating impact in Scotland or that there was at least one factor which operated in an exclusively Scottish context. Finally, whole areas of the company's management of its internal affairs can be specifically exempted from any responsibility for this trend, including its proven and long-established record of wise allocation of its funds in the sphere of investment, its innovating rôle in the 1850s and 1860s in the whole term field, and, assessed overall, the quality of its salaried officials. Indeed, of all the managers of the major Scottish life offices during these decades it would be most difficult to support a thesis purporting to demonstrate that W. T. Thomson was the victim of entrepreneurial fatigue. During his tenure of the managerial chair – 1837-74 – his ability to discern where the true interests of his employers lay; his awareness of the need to promote rational change in the company's practices; and his building up, after 1865, of a growing overseas business enabled him to bequeath to his son and successor, S. C. Thomson, an inheritance of exceptional strength and vitality. Yet if his total contribution to the economic health of the Standard in beyond dispute, it is impossible, when the focus of attention is switched from a United Kingdom,

[13] Butt and Treble, op cit, Chapters II and III, passim.

and British Empire, perspective to the more narrowly circumscribed horizon of Scotland, to avoid the conclusion that in at least one area W. T. Thomson and the board must shoulder a major part of the responsibility for the post-1850 contours of new Scottish business. That area dealt with such sensitive, but inter-related, topics as the quality and efficiency of its Scottish network of agents and the effectiveness of the degree of supervision which Head Office exercised over the execution of their duties.

III

Any analysis of the workings of the office's agency system must begin by acknowledging that in certain respects the directorate and management tried to ensure that it was properly attuned to meeting the challenge offered by its principal competitors. To this end the Agency Committee of the board, whose origins can be traced back to the early 1830s, was entrusted with the task of revising the lists of the company's accredited representatives in the light of their ability to secure 'first class' risks. This involved its members – as in the pre-1850 period – in the complex process of evaluating both the scope of the local market in which the individual agent was working and identifying the presence of any unfavourable constraints on life underwriting which might be of only parochial significance or of much wider dimensions. In the wake of that information decisions had to be taken as to whether or not to dismiss the agent; whether the problem of results might simply be circumvented by appointing a second representative to canvass for business in the same town as the existing agent; or whether – as in the cases of Inverness and Aberdeen in 1858[14] – merely to rely upon exhortation to secure improved returns. Ranged alongside this necessary work of revision was the task of extending the spatial coverage of the office's agency network in the Scottish mainland. This last undertaking might – as in certain areas of the East of Scotland in 1858[15] – be discharged by the Committee itself; alternatively it might be delegated to one of its salaried staff. This latter expedient was actively employed in 1852 and 1855 when representatives from Head Office were despatched to the Highlands, while in 1858 a temporary Inspector of Agents was sent to cover the same area to complete this process.[16] Reinforcing these developments the Agency Committee, with the approval of the full board, did not hesitate, where market potential seemed to justify the experiment, to extend the system of Local Boards of Directors – usually consisting of influential businessmen – from their pre-1850 bases in Glasgow, Inverness, Dumfries, Aberdeen and Perth to Paisley in 1856 and Greenock in 1852.[17] Lastly, since the smooth working of the relationship between the typical agent and the company was, in money terms, determined by the attractiveness – or otherwise – of its commission payments, it was important that the directorate should pay attention to the advice tendered to them by their officials on the

14 Committee Minute Book III, 14 October 1858.
15 Ibid.
16 Sederunt Book XII, 21 June 1852, XIII, 28 May 1855; Committee Minute Book III, 15 December 1858.
17 Sederunt Book XII, 25 October 1852, XV, 9 December 1856.

important question of rates revisions. On the whole the evidence indicates that this is precisely what happened throughout this period. In 1851, in addition to the existing commission rates, the board tried to stimulate business by offering rewards, on an ascending scale, to those of its representatives who secured more than £1,000 of with profits proposals in any one of its financial years.[18] In 1855 matters were taken further when, after a detailed examination of its commission structure by H. Jones Williams, its President Secretary in London, it was agreed to bring its system of remuneration more nearly into line with those of the major English offices by substituting payments of 10 per cent on new, and 5 per cent on renewal, premiums for its former flat rate of 5 per cent on all premiums.[19] This concentrated programme of reform was completed in 1856–7 when the office sanctioned slight changes in the terms it offered to its 'occasional agents' – largely members of the legal profession who, as the designation suggests, would from time to time send a proposal from one of their clients to the Standard – by allowing them for the first time to receive commission upon 'assurances . . . in connection with loans in Scotland', although in relation to this concession it was stipulated that no such benefits would be paid 'on any Assurance exceeding the sum the Company retain on their own risk, on first class lives £7,000'.[20]

Yet if this record of endeavour appears outwardly impressive, it is impossible to overlook certain fundamental flaws in the operation of the agency system in Scotland which emerged over time. Prominent among them were the increasing difficulties which the company encountered in exercising effective control over its scattered representatives as the multitude of demands made on the time of Head Office staff expanded *pari passu* with the growth of business. This damaging development was, it must be stressed, largely the product of features in the Standard's organisational infrastructure which were unique to Scotland. In England by the mid-1850s the essential work of agency overhaul and extension had been largely devolved upon the shoulders of two Inspectors, while other essential administrative duties of the office's English operations were left to the London board, aided by a full-time staff. In Ireland on the other hand the Resident Secretary in Dublin was expected to undertake periodic tours of outlying agencies and to submit his findings on their competence to the directors in Edinburgh. Since, however, the scale of the company's commitments in Ireland was of much more modest dimensions than in Scotland and since Local Board in Dublin was never entrusted with any executive powers, it is scarcely surprising to discover that this skeletal system worked relatively well in the 'Sister Isle'. But in Head Office things were somewhat differently ordered.

Both before and after 1850 it was the custom in Scotland to expect the 'chief officers' of the Standard – usually either Thomson himself or, as in 1855, G. H. Todd, who filled the post of Secretary – to tour the major centres of population and the more thinly settled areas of the Highlands, with a general

---

[18] Committee Minute Book II, 6 May 1851.
[19] Private Minute Book II, 12 February 1855.
[20] Sederunt Book XV, 13 February 1857.

mandate to seek out, where required, new agents; to jolt the complacent into activity; and to recommend the removal of those who had consistently failed to bestir themselves. By the late 1850s, however, it was already recognised that the formidable burden of work within Head Office drastically reduced the prospects of senior officials being long absent from Edinburgh and of having much opportunity of conducting personal inquiry into the suitability of potential representatives in towns of any distance from the Scottish capital.[21] As W. T. Thomson commented in 1863, 'it was not the practice to visit regularly the Agencies in Scotland but that he or some other official of the Company took advantage of any convenient opportunity that presented itself to see certain of the Agents'.[22] Yet at a time when the number of Scottish representatives of its competitors continued to proliferate, it was widely accepted that 'the only effectual way of maintaining a steady interest on the part of an agent was to visit him very often'.[23] Reluctance or inability to follow this rubric – for motivation in terms of results mattered little – could only lead to the retention of the inefficient long after they had furnished convincing proof of their ineptitude.

In the Standard's case the working out of this process can be traced in some detail from the extant records. It is clear, for instance, that a systematic and concentrated visitation of the major agencies was rarely undertaken by top management during these years, to the company's detriment. In this context Todd's visit to the Highlands in 1855; the brief given to W. T. Thomson to overhaul the agency system in the summer and autumn of 1863; and S. C. Thomson's evaluation of the office's principal urban representatives in 1870 stand out precisely because they ran counter to the general trend.[24] But what was equally serious for the life underwriting experience of the office was the fact that criticisms, advanced at the conclusion of such tours, might fail to produce prompt remedial measures. Todd, for example, was moved to comment that if 'the ... Agents generally [in the Highalnds] are gentlemen of respectability and influence and well qualified for the duties of their Offices', there was 'at the same time ... room for a greater exertion on the part of some of them' and – as if highlighting their past neglect of opportunities for business in their area – 'a wide feild [sic] for their operations'.[25] This point was to be underlined in 1870 when S. C. Thomson drew attention to the fact that notwithstanding the legitimate pride the Standard could derive from having recruited its representatives in the largest towns from the ranks of individuals of the 'highest local standing', the contours of new business remained obstinately static.[26] On neither of these occasions, however, was any positive action forthcoming from the Edinburgh board, although S. C. Thomson had gone to some

[21] Committee Minute Book III, 14 October 1858.

[22] Ibid, IV, 28 May 1863.

[23] W. Brown, Life Branch Work, *Journal of the Federation of Insurance Institutes of Great Britain and Ireland*, I (1898), 17.

[24] Sederunt Book XIII, 28 May 1855; Committee Minute Book IV, 19 January 1863, October 1870.

[25] Sederunt Book XIII, 28 May 1855.

[26] Committee Minute Book IV, October 1870.

lengths to suggest that one source of the Standard's poor Scottish results might be the infrequent personal contacts between Head Office and its field-workers. As he wrote, 'Other Companies seem more constantly to inspect their Agencies, cancel unprofitable ones, and make new appointments where there is an opening and the Standard, I think, must do something more in this way'.[27]

But quite apart from the deleterious general effects of such indecision upon the office's fortunes in Scotland, the Agency Committee did little to help to reverse the trend of declining quinquennial new business in the 1850s and 1860s by its cautious approach in two specific areas where reform was long overdue. In the first place it failed to grapple decisively with the problem of poor returns from Glasgow. Throughout the period Glasgow was bound to determine in a very direct way how well or how poorly a company performed in the Scottish ordinary life market not merely because it was the industrial and commercial hub of the West-Central belt but also because, in terms of population, it assumed a position of even greater dominance in the demographic experience of Scotland than London did in England. Whereas roughly $10\frac{1}{2}$ per cent of Scotland's total population lived within the city's boundaries in 1841 – 275,000 out of 2,620,000 persons – that figure had risen sharply to slightly more than $16\frac{1}{2}$ per cent – or 522,000 out of 3,360,000 – three decades later. Expressed in another form, while the overall rate of increase of the Scottish population between 1841 and 1871 was 35·4 per cent, the comparable statistic for Glasgow was fractionally less than 90 per cent.

Nevertheless, despite the opportunities which a growing middle-class afforded for building up a lucrative and expanding life underwriting business in the city, the qualitative and admittedly fragmentary quantitative data which have survived demonstrate conclusively that the Standard's board had genuine grounds for its frequent lamentations about the unfavourable pattern of its Glasgow returns. As Table 3 illustrates, the aggregate volume of new proposals forwarded to Edinburgh from its Glasgow headquarters fell away sharply during the period 1846–55, although it is important to note that for the post-1848 years these returns tend to exaggerate the company's difficulties since they exclude the contribution made to city business by a burgeoning system of sub-agents. Unfortunately, without an exhaustive analysis of Policy Registers the parameters of that contribution cannot be defined with any accuracy; but at least one indirect indicator – roughly £65,000 of assurance still in force in Glasgow in 1855 had been won by the Standard's four sub-agencies during the course of the previous five years – points to the inescapable conclusion that it was not insignificant. Yet even when this caveat has been entered, it seems certain that in no single year between 1850 and 1855 did the amount of new assurance remotely approach the 1846–7 figure when almost £100,000 of new contracts were issued, while it remains doubtful whether – with the possible exception of 1852–3 – the record of 1847–8 was surpassed. After 1855 runs of statistics for the city only again become available for the 1870s. In the intervening years, however, little real growth appears to have occurred. In 1860, for example, the appointment of a deputation from the board of directors to

[27] Ibid.

visit Glasgow and to explore ways of improving the office's efficiency indicates that the bleak pattern of the early 1850s had continued.[28] More than a decade later – in December 1872 – the small amount of business in relation to the cost of the Standard's operations in Glasgow resulted in W. T. Thomson being despatched on an identical mission with instructions 'to report, with any recommendations which might occur to him as to the more successful working of the Agency for the future'.[29] Finally, as the data covering the years 1873-7 make abundantly clear, there was every justification for S. C. Thomson's complaint that 'the business since 1873 ... is inconsiderable for such a place as Glasgow and the district around, and from the Messrs. Sloan's own Agency [the Sloan brothers were the office's principal Glasgow Agents] the business has fallen off almost year by year'.[30]

It only remains for the historian to identify those forces which promoted this end. In broad terms they can be listed under two headings. Firstly there were certain external influences which, although for the most part of only local significance, acted in either spasmodic fashion or continuously, to inhibit growth. Among these exogenous variables were the loss in 1850 of a valuable connection with a local bank which had hitherto placed a considerable volume of new business with the Standard; the disadvantageous position in which any Edinburgh-based life office found itself when it was brought into competition in Glasgow with rivals whose headquarters were located in the industrial capital of the West of Scotland; and the fact that struggle for 'first class' risks

TABLE 3

GLASGOW NEW BUSINESS

Year	Glasgow Head Office Returns	Glasgow Sub-Agents' Returns
	£	£
1846-7	96,800	—
1847-8	49,300	—
1848-9	32,500	—
1849-50	Not available	Not available
1850-1	22,549 10s 0d	Not available
1851-2	18,049 13s 0d	Not available
1852-3	35,049 14s 0d	Not available
1853-4	19,725	Not available
1854-5	14,750	Not available
1872-3	10,450	10,050
1873-4	11,050	12,850
1874-5	9,900	37,050
1875-6	5,950	20,550
1876-7	4,700	21,650

Source: Sederunt Book XIV, 22 September 1855; XXIV, 17 September 1878

[28] Sederunt Book XVII, 4 September 1860.
[29] Ibid, XXIII, 10 December 1872.
[30] Ibid, XXIV, 17 September 1878.

was at its fiercest in the major conurbations.[31] But there were other retarding forces at work which can be traced to deficiencies within the company's internal organisation. The record, for instance, of new proposals won through the personal exertions of William Brown, who was Glasgow Resident Secretary from 1848 to 1869, strongly suggests that although he possessed many sterling personal qualities – his assiduity and integrity were never in dispute – an ability to advance the company's name among his social peers and equals was not prominent amongst them. In like manner his successor, A. J. Sloan, despite his connection with the business classes through his stockbroking activities, was acknowledged to be 'rather a slow man', and as S. C. Thomson pointed out in 1878, 'a man of different temperament in the same position might do more for us in the way of actively going about to seek business'.[32] But compounding the problem of lack of dynamism in successive Resident Secretaries was the fact that Head Office, by insisting on remunerating its senior Glasgow officials on a commission, rather than salary, basis – although Brown for a brief period at the start of his career was placed on a fixed income – tended to encourage them to cultivate outside interests.[33] Thus, by refusing to contemplate speedy action against officials who had scarcely distinguished themselves in the ordinary life market or to follow the lead of some of their competitors by appointing a full-time branch secretary, entrusted with considerable powers of control over his sub-agents, the Agency Committee and W. T. Thomson guaranteed that the Glasgow pattern would conform in most respects to that policy of institutional conservatism which it followed in other parts of Scotland. Given this response, it was perhaps inevitable that the steps which were taken in the city – including periodic reviews of the branch; the creation of sub-agencies within the city; a proposal, later abandoned, to seek sub-agents in such adjacent towns and villages as Rutherglen, Milngavie and Balfron; and the belated appointment of the company's Scottish Inspector of Agents, based in Glasgow, in 1873[34] – could offer little scope for any dramatic or sustained upsurge in new business.

The second area of organisational neglect can be treated more summarily. Unlike the situation in England where it was freely admitted that 'our best Agents have been Shopkeepers', the majority of the office's Scottish representatives were overwhelmingly recruited from the ranks of lawyers and bankers. Yet by concentrating almost exclusively upon men who were located in the higher echelons of the professions, the company did not reach as effectively as it hoped the swelling number of potential assurers who were located in the ranks of the *petit bourgeoisie*. In the view of H. Jones Williams, for example, assessing the Scottish agency network from his London office, the Standard in Scotland had for long sought representatives 'of too high a [social] class, so to speak, to

---

[31] Ibid, XIV, 22 September 1856; Committee Minute Book IV, October 1870.

[32] Sederunt Book XXIV, 17 September 1878.

[33] It is clear from the surviving records that the Sloan brothers actively prosecuted their stockbroking activities at the same time as they acted for the Standard.

[34] Sederunt Book XVII, 4 September 1860, XXIII, 10 December 1872; Private Minute Book II, 24 August 1849; Committee Minute Book II, 15 April 1850; Sederunt Book XXIII, 16, 30 September 1873.

work actively for us'. Whereas 'the Shopkeeper sees more people, and has no scruple in pressing people to assure, . . . the high class banker or lawyer will positively decline to do it'. The validity of this type of criticism was duly acknowledged in October 1870 when S. C. Thomson argued that in the larger towns – Edinburgh, Dundee, Glasgow, Aberdeen, Perth, and Paisley – the Standard should consider appointing 'energetic canvassing Agents, selected from the higher class of Shopkeepers', although even once this recommendation had been made, after two decades of disappointing results, there is no firm evidence to show that it was fully implemented.[35]

Administrative weakness, however, was not solely to blame for what, in 1878, was described as 'the falling off in business from Scotland from some time back'.[36] As early as 1855 W. T. Thomson had recognised that the aggregate total of new premium income within the United Kingdom could be affected by the manner in which the Standard's original 'with profits' plan had been organised. Following the lead of the London Equitable, the company had adopted the tontine principle under which it was pledged to paying bonuses, at the conclusion of the quinquennial divisions of profits, for each year the individual policy had been in force. As long as the bonus was on trend rising, little criticism was to be expected of what was, even in the medium-term, an 'exhausting' mode of distributing the available surplus. Nevertheless since its operation would over time make heavy demands on company profits, a point would be reached at which the bonus would inevitably decline.[37]

That point finally came in 1850 when a tontine reversionary bonus of 21/- per cent per annum was declared compared with the corresponding figure of 25/- at the 1845 Investigation. By 1855 a further fall to 18/- per cent per annum had occurred, while the figure for both the 1860 and 1865 Investigations was 14/- per cent per annum. Yet, in W. T. Thomson's words, the continuation of this trend 'may influence the amount of new business transacted by the Company', since 'rival Offices will of course point to the decrease, and hint at a further reduction, making the most of it'.[38] Nor would such an outcome be surprising since the tontine scheme possessed two distinct drawbacks: it exacted higher premiums from its assurers than some of the participating plans of other companies and its rewards were heavily weighted in favour of those families who had good longevity records.[39] In other words, once its principal strong point, its hitherto substantial bonuses, was undermined, it would by very definition appear a less attractive proposition to whole sections of the assuring public.

What therefore was to be feared in the immediate future was a deceleration in the rate of growth of, rather than a decline in, the number of new United Kingdom proposals. It was for this reason that W. T. Thomson tried to persuade his board – although he himself was to have misgivings about the utility

[35] This paragraph is based upon Committee Minute Book IV, October 1870.
[36] Sederunt Book XXIV, 17 September 1878.
[37] See for this point, Butt and Treble, op cit.
[38] Minute of the Meeting of the Investigation Committee, 17 April 1856. (Deed Box No 3, 1855 Investigation.)
[39] See Butt and Treble, op cit.

and propriety of the step in 1860 – to introduce an 'Equal Scheme' which would combine the advantages of a more competitive rates structure with the prospects of better bonuses during the early years of a contract's life. Rebuffed in 1855 and 1860, this proposal was finally sanctioned in 1865, largely on the grounds that further delay could prove harmful to the long-term prospects of the office. Even then, however, these new incentives failed to arrest the downward movement in Scottish business during the ensuing quinquennium. If any further proof were needed by the directorate, these results could only serve to underline the point that a falling tontine bonus had been of marginal significance in influencing the company's performance in Scotland in the previous two decades and conversely that an indispensable precondition for a sustained recovery was a comprehensive overhaul of its agency and inspection system.[40]

[40] This point is clearly made, for instance, in Sederunt Book XXIV, 17 September 1878. For the debate about the Equal Scheme, see Butt and Treble, op cit.

J. H. TREBLE

9

Some Aspects of Working-class Conservatism in the Nineteenth Century

A neglected feature of nineteenth-century politics is the continuing and periodically influential involvement of working men in Tory politics. Such 'angels in marble' are sometimes explained in terms of the 'politics of deference', and churchmen, monarchists and patriots aping their social superiors – though modern investigations disprove such simplistic (or polemical) views.[1] Inevitably, the spectre of Tory proletarians incensed devotees of a vast, amorphous and imaginary 'working-class movement'. Consequently, 'deviants' from pre-determined models of political behaviour are either ignored or denounced as 'traitors'. The easiest option is to deny their existence altogether. G. D. H. Cole asserted (of the 1840s) that 'it is doubtful if such a creature as a "Conservative working man" had ever been thought of'. While such factory reformers as Richard Oastler and Joseph Rayner Stephens[2] 'might describe themselves as Tories' (and certainly did), according to Cole,[3]

> their followers would not have accepted the label as applicable to
> their own convictions. They were Chartists, or Ten Hours men, or
> Socialists, or Radical Reformers, not Tories. Only as these
> movements died away, and the Liberal and Conservative Parties
> began to assume their modern forms, did it become possible to
> discover such a person as a "Conservative working man".

Cole was wrong. Not only was the Parliamentary and Northern leadership of the factory campaign predominantly Tory, but many local campaigners fully shared their leaders' views. Such Tory working men as Squire Auty, Matthew Balme and John Wood – and Radicals who later became Tories, like John Hanson, Joshua Hobson, John Leech and Alexander Taylor – played important roles. Only in Scotland, it seems, were Tories conspicuously absent.[4]

---

[1] Robert Mackenzie and Allan Silver, *Angels in Marble* (1968); cf E. A. Nordlinger, *The Working-Class Tories* (1967).

[2] C. R. Driver, *Tory Radical. The Life of Richard Oastler* (New York, 1946); J. T. Ward, 'Revolutionary Tory: The Life of J. R. Stephens', *Trans Lancs & Cheshire Antiq Soc*, LXVIII (1958).

[3] G. D. H. Cole, *A Century of Co-operation* (Manchester, 1945), 73.

[4] J. T. Ward, *The Factory Movement, 1830–1855* (1962), 'The Factory Movement', in *Popular Movements, c 1830–1850* (1970), 'Matthew Balme', *Bradford Antiquary*, ns XL (1960), 'Squire Auty', ibid, XLII (1964), 'Leeds and the Factory Reform Movement', *Pub Thoresby*

But in addition to 'Tory-Chartists' and factory campaigners, there were also organised bodies of Tory working men, defying the cherished tenets and conceptual frameworks of many subsequent historians of the working classes. Practical politicians found it easier to appreciate electoral realities. Chartist support for Tory candidates at the elections of 1841 was recognised by Whigs and Liberals. 'Radical and Chartist votes were courted wherever there was a contest by the Tories', observed Henry Cockburn, 'to whom these votes were almost invariably given'. The *Morning Chronicle* noted that 'the Chartists, such as are voters, have almost to a man supported the Tories', and the *Bradford Observer* asserted that local Chartists 'had been chiefly instrumental in throwing out Mr. Busfeild', the Whig.[5] In 1868, when Lancashire workers voted Tory, Engels told Marx that 'once again the proletariat had discredited itself terribly'.[6] It still disappointed theorists when Hugh Gaitskell bluntly asserted that '3 out of 10 male trade unionists and 4 out of 10 of their wives vote Tory'.[7]

The present paper is an attempt to examine the attitudes and organisations of a sizeable body of working people. It seems desirable to commence by asserting the reality of its existence.

I

Tory groups existed among working folk long before the formal establishment of societies in the thirties. Loyalist 'Church and King' bodies were at least as active as radical organisations during the French wars from the late eighteenth century.[8] For many years boozy patriots had banded together to provide 'friendly society' or exclusive 'craft unionist' benefits for Right-wing freemen of old boroughs.[9] In Liverpool, for instance, the shipwrights exercised considerable political influence.[10] Convivial 'True Blue' dinners, 'patriotic' celebrations of royal or Pittite anniversaries and rallies to defend the Church from papist or protestant attack regularly attracted many working men. The Reform Act of 1832, however, made further organisation necessary. Registration societies and professional election agents gradually usurped the older influence of county oligarchies and the Tadpoles and Tapers of the metropolitan clubs – though the process was slow.[11] Party organisation in a recognisable form

Soc, XLVI (1961), 'The Factory Reform Movement in Scotland', *Scottish Hist Rev*, XLI (1962), 'Bradford and Factory Reform', *Bradford Textile Soc J* (1961), 'Some Industrial Reformers', ibid (1963), ' "Old and "New" Bradfordians in the Nineteenth Century', ibid (1965), 'The Factory Movement in Lancashire', *Trans L & C Antiq Soc*, LXV–LXVI (1969).

[5] H. Cockburn, *Journal* (Edinburgh, 1874), I, 297; *Morning Chron* quoted in Oastler's *Fleet Papers*, I, 30 (1841); *Bradford Obs*, 1 July 1841; cf *Scottish Patriot*, 16 May, 6 June 1840.

[6] (18 Nov 1868) *Marx and Engels on Britain* (Moscow, 1953), 499.

[7] *Report of the 60th Annual Conference of the Labour Party* (1961), 153.

[8] See G. S. Veitch, *The Genesis of Parliamentary Reform* (1948 impr); cf P. A. Brown, *The French Revolution in English History* (1918), ch 9–10.

[9] See R. L. Hill, *Toryism and the People, 1832–1846* (1929), 47–51.

[10] S. and B. Webb, *The History of Trade Unionism* (1950 impr), 39–40, 71.

[11] Norman Gash, *Politics in the Age of Peel* (1960 impr); Robert Blake, *The Conservative Party from Peel to Churchill* (1970), passim.

started to develop, under such expert political manipulators as Francis Bonham.[12] Among the plethora of clubs, societies and associations which emerged were numerous working-class groups, many of which were Tory; indeed, the Conservatives were more successful than their rivals in forming workers' organisations.

The first Operative Conservative Society was established at Leeds in March 1835, after preliminary planning by three individuals in February. Its manifesto of 2 March adopted Oastler's motto of 'The Altar, The Throne and The Cottage'. Progress was initially slow, but the Society had energetic leaders in its president, William Beckwith, and its secretary, William Paul (an employee of Messrs Hives & Atkinson's flax mill). A powerful ally was Robert Perring, editor of the Tory *Leeds Intelligencer*, who was 'Constitutional and Conservative – attached to the Monarchy and the Church . . . [and] would apply the hand of reform wherever reform was really wanted'. A great dinner in the Corn Exchange Inn on 25 November led to a large increase of membership, Perring's speech, it has been suggested, 'put the Society on its feet'.[13] But other speakers included the pugnacious Bradford Anglican priest George Bull, the local Tory leader Robert Hall[14] and the 'Factory King' Oastler – who proposed the toast to Church and State and urged operatives to prefer a Tory to a Conservative title.[15]

The 'Corn Exchange' meetings gradually grew in size, partly, no doubt, because of the aid of Sir John Beckett, MP, Hall and Perring. On 1 March 1836 Beckwith and Paul presented an optimistic first report. 'Our motto is "Onward"; our watchword is "Persevere"', they wrote, drawing attention to the formation of similar societies of Tory workers in Ashton, Blackburn, Bolton, Liverpool, Manchester, Oldham, Preston, Sheffield, Wakefield, Warrington and other towns.[16] Benjamin Matthews presided over the general meeting, attended (on a wet night) by over half of the 200 members.[17] Paul boasted of the extension of Operative Conservatism in a pamphlet in 1839 – and in a fourth edition in 1842 reported a Leeds membership of over 600, meeting weekly, with a library of some 300 volumes and a reading room (that regular symbol of Victorian 'mutual improvement'). New societies were mentioned in Barnsley, Bradford, Dudley, Huddersfield, Hull, Ripon, Salford, Stockport, Tamworth, Walsall, West Bromwich and Wolverhampton.[18] Paul's lists were incomplete, but surely demolish one myth.

Operative Conservatives' purposes varied considerably. Largely Anglican,

[12] Gash, 464, and 'F. R. Bonham', *English Hist Rev*, LXIII (1949).

[13] M. A. Gibb and Frank Beckwith, *The Yorkshire Post. Two Centuries* (Leeds, 1954), 17–9.

[14] J. C. Gill, *The Ten Hours Parson* (1959); Susan Brooke, 'Some Notes on the Hall Family', *Pub Thoresby Soc*, XLI (1954); Frank Beckwith, 'Introductory Account of *The Leeds Intelligencer*', ibid, XL (1955).

[15] *Leeds Intelligencer, Leeds Times*, 28 Nov, *Blackburn Standard*, 2 Dec 1835.

[16] William Paul, *A History of the Origin and Progress of Operative Conservative Societies* (Leeds, 1839), 10. The Manchester Society's first dinner was noted in *The Times*, 29 July 1836.

[17] *Leeds Intelligencer*, 5 March 1836.

[18] Paul, op cit (Doncaster, 1842), 11–27.

Protectionist and traditionalist, they initially spread a Tory message among working people, especially by canvassing and registering those entitled to vote. The Leeds men, we are told,

> acted as the stormtroops of the Tory cause, crowding into vestry
> meetings, heckling Liberal gatherings, swelling the signatures on
> Tory petitions and performing the leg work of canvassing.

Such operative 'packing' of the 1837 vestry elections led to the return of a Tory majority on the Improvement Commission.[19] A contemporary observer – probably the Manchester barrister and journalist Robert Scarr Sowler[20] – pertinently observed that[21]

> My acquaintance with the Operative Conservative Societies has
> taught me that active employment is highly necessary to their
> prosperity, if not to their future existence. Like a giant machine they
> must be kept continually in motion . . .

Tory working men were generally fervent followers of local Conservative leaders. Leeds operatives loyally cheered the barrister Hall, editor Perring, merchant Thomas Blayds and banker Beckett. Sir John (MP in 1835–7) and his brothers William (MP in 1841–52) and Sir Edmund Beckett Denison (MP for the West Riding from 1841) always sympathised with Tory operative attitudes; Oastler 'somehow . . . liked that breed'.[22] At Bradford the operatives' hero was John Hardy, a self-made lawyer, squire and industrialist, who (like Sir John) had moved over from Whiggism. The local Society was founded in July 1837 by one Bob Waterhouse in Bank Street and was subsequently led by William Coates, the borough's postmaster, and James Wade, landlord of the 'New Inn', a traditional Tory-Radical haunt. It helped to elect Hardy in 1841, after failing in 1837. And it continued to be supported by such leaders of the Constitutional Association as squire Plumbe Tempest of Tong, the ironmasters Charles Hardy, Joshua Pollard and Henry Wickham, the worsted masters John Rand, J. G. Horsfall, William Walker and G. W. Addison and (oddly enough) by the returning officer, John Crofts – all of whom attended its dinner of January 1846. Middle-class Tories – generally men prominent in the factory and Poor Law campaigns – widely encouraged the growth of Northern operative Conservatism. At Pudsey, for instance, Tempest was the patron and the chairman was the Rev David Jenkins, the curate.[23]

Nevertheless, to Oastler's disappointment, the Leeds men did not instantly support his stance on industrial reform. Oastler had tried, as he told the London Radical journalist Henry Hetherington in 1835, 'to persuade a few labouring men – 1st. To trust in God. 2d. To look at *principles*, not *names*'.[24] But in May 1836, when even the 1833 Factory Act was menaced by Poulett Thomson's

[19] D. Fraser, 'Improvements in Early Victorian Leeds', *Pub Thoresby Soc*, LIII (1970).
[20] On whom see J. H. Nodal, 'Obituary Notices, 1861–81' (MS in Manchester City Library).
[21] 'R. S. S.', *Thoughts on the State and Prospects of Toryism* (1837).
[22] Paul, 11; *Fleet Papers*, I, 30 (1841).
[23] William Scruton, *Pen and Pencil Pictures of Old Bradford* (Bradford, 1889), 185; *Daily News*, 21 Jan 1846; Ruth Strong, *The Story of Pudsey Church* (Mirfield, 1975), 28–9.
[24] *Poor Man's Guardian*, 29 Aug 1835.

amendment and when Beckett seemed to have deserted the 'Ten Hours' cause, Oastler urged the Leeds men to maintain their promise to defend factory reform. Paul denied that his Society was thus pledged, whereupon Oastler retorted that unless operative Tories aided the cause (since 1830 a major factor in the politics of the textile areas) their party would sink.[25] Oastler never liked Peelite Conservatism and was later bitterly to assail its 'Free Trade' proclivities. But it was obviously galling to be deserted by natural allies, however temporarily and even in a town whose factory reform loyalties had long been doubtful. In 1833 Oastler told the Radical journalist John Foster (a later renegade) that 'in Bradford they are red hot and even in Leeds united and firm – nay, even enthusiastic. We have gained much in Leeds by recent defalcations – we know our men'. But within weeks he told the Keighley leader Abraham Wildman that 'we are all right at Huddersfield, Holmfirth, Manchester, &c, &c. Leeds is divided, I believe, as indeed it always is'.[26] The 'Factory King' remained, as he told ultra-Radical friends, an 'old-fashioned ultra Tory', explaining that[27]

> I admire the ancient *varied* suffrage much more than the new-fangled "£10 suffrage". I believe the men let into Parliament by the "£10-ers" are more ignorant, more tyrannical, more selfish and more blood-thirsty than those who formerly occupied their seats. I should rejoice to see the suffrage extended upon the *ancient* and *varied* plan – because, then, no *one* class would be able to rule *all* the others.

Such 'Radical' postures, such traditionalism, such religious and monarchist loyalty did not appeal to all Tory operatives, in the days of the 'Tamworth Manifesto'. But most Tory workers seem to have been Protectionist men of the Right.

Inevitably, opponents often condemned such Tory organisations. Leeds Radicals assailed 'the Leeds Operative Conservative Society's Dinner – So Called', sarcastically noting Paul's schoolmaster rôle. Chartists initially found it 'rather astonishing' that 'a poor devil depending on his day's work and obliged to give a portion of that to the support of the Church and other Institutions should rank himself as a Conservative Operative'. Glasgow Liberals mimicked the formal address of local Tory operatives to Peel in 1836. 'Oh, shades of Pitt, Castlereagh, Liverpool!', complained Sheffield Liberals, 'are these the men who inherit the blue mantle of Toryism?' Leeds Liberals had long been warned about 'operatives of that nondescript and mongrel class betwixt Ultra-Radicals and Ultra-Tories' (which was not a bad description of many O.C.S. attitudes) and later Lancashire Liberals were told of combinations of 'Eldonites, Cobbettites, O'Connorites, Stephensites, Oastlerites'.[28] But operative Toryism certainly spread; Manchester's third dinner was attended by that hero of so many

[25] *Leeds Times*, 14, 21, 28 May 1836.
[26] Oastler to Foster, 23 June 1833 (London University Library, Goldsmiths' Collection), to Wildman, 25 July 1833 (*Keighley News*, 9 Apr 1870).
[27] *Weekly Police Gazette*, 5 March 1836.
[28] *Leeds Times*, 28 Nov 1835; *Northern Star*, 21 Apr 1838; *Glasgow Argus*, 29 Dec 1836; *Sheffield Independent*, 7 Feb 1835; *Leeds Mercury*, 8 Sept 1832; *The League*, 23 Dec 1843.

Radical campaigns, Sir Francis Burdett, and a Salford tea-party attracted over 3,000 people.[29]

The Societies generally aided the campaign against the Poor Law and the defence of Irish Protestantism. Indeed, there was an 'Orange' element in operative Toryism (most notably in Auty's Bradford and in some Lancashire towns), which was regularly affronted by Peel's attitudes. Furthermore, most Societies were Protectionist and bitterly opposed to the Government's moves towards Free Trade.[30] One parliamentarian in particular represented the combination of virtues most admired by Tory operatives. William Busfeild Ferrand, the heir to an estate near Bingley, was a stentorian Oastlerite MP for Knaresborough in 1841–7, who founded the Bingley association in 1836.[31] He had served his political apprenticeship as a militant speaker at factory reform rallies; he loathed the Poor Law and was forever 'exposing' its misdeeds; he hated the Anti-Corn Law League (and especially its industrialist leaders) and attacked it in its own habitat; he was strong, noisy, litigious and argumentative; and he rejoiced in the title of 'the Working Man's Friend'.

Ferrand (then called Busfeild) had unsuccessfully contested Bradford in 1837 against his uncle (confusingly, another William Busfeild). He was never forgotten by local Tory workmen. His speeches and pamphlets struck an authentic note of traditionalist Tory Radicalism, and in March 1843 Auty (a self-made printer, who had started work at the age of 6) presided over an Operative Conservative Association meeting in the 'New Inn' to thank 'that champion of the working classes'. James Wade meticulously recorded operatives' gratitude for Ferrand's

> bold, unflinching and persevering conduct, in successfully opposing
> the introduction of tread-mills into the accursed union bastiles [sic],
> and thereby frustrating the wicked designs of the three despotic
> 'Kings' [Poor Law Commissioners] of Somerset House, and their
> master (or servant) Sir James Graham, and likewise for exposing to
> the world, through the British House of Commons, in full glare,
> the Addingham factory case, with all its horrors and cruelties, in
> connection with the New Poor Law.

Wade, Auty and their colleagues particularly welcomed Ferrand's[32]

> manly and straightforward conduct in support of the Working
> Classes of the community, and his energetic condemnation of the
> attempts made to introduce into the Union Workhouses machinery
> inconsistent with the Laws of this Country, and offensive and
> degrading to humanity.

Such working-class support for a young squire was scarcely 'deferential':

[29] The Times, 20, 23 Apr 1838.

[30] Hill, op cit, 59, 66–7.

[31] J. T. Ward, ' "Young England" at Bingley', Bradford Textile Soc J (1966); Leeds Intelligencer, 6 Feb 1836.

[32] Wade to Ferrand, 5 Mar 1843 (Ferrand MSS, by courtesy of the late Col. G. W. Ferrand, OBE); cf The Times, 20, 24 Feb. Benjamin Gomersall of the Birstal O.C.S. wrote similarly on 12 May (Ferrand MSS), as did L. K. Royston of Leeds on 30 Mar and James Banks of Pudsey on 31 Mar (ibid).

the operatives were bitterly attacking the Conservative Home Secretary, Graham.

In April 1845 the Dublin Protestant Operative Society went further, by asking Ferrand to support the impeachment of the Prime Minister, Sir Robert Peel, because of his proposal to increase the grant to the Roman Catholic seminary at Maynooth. 'I rejoice to say', replied Ferrand,[33]

> that a strong Protestant feeling is spreading through the country
> against Sir R. Peel, who, in my opinion, is the greatest traitor who
> has existed since Judas Iscariot. I purpose presenting your petition
> on the second reading of Peel's Popish Bill.

In August 1847 Ferrand almost became a candidate for Dublin, where he was a hero to the Protestant operatives.

II

The Glasgow Operative Conservative Society was established in December 1836, with the support of the local Tory Press and the Church of Scotland journal, the *Scottish Guardian*. Its character was thus established, as Tory and Presbyterian. A recent writer suggests that this pioneering Scottish group 'never possessed any effective strength'. However, its appearance certainly startled local Radicals, like Peter Mackenzie, editor of *The Loyal Reformers' Gazette*, who regularly fulminated against 'the pitiful Glasgow Tories' and 'this abominable gang, the Orange Tories', past and present. A new committee of trades delegates was established in January 1837, to provide 'a nucleus round which the trades of Glasgow might rally on any future emergency'.[34] The immediate cause of the formation of the first Scottish Society was (two days before Christmas in 1836) to offer 'cordial congratulations [ultimately signed by over 2,000 operatives, to Peel] on [his] election to the Lord Rectorship of our Venerable University'. The workmen explained their beliefs. They were 'warmly attached from principle to our glorious Constitution in Church and State, under which the nation had been elevated to a pitch of unexampled prosperity'. And, no doubt trying to amend the meanness of the civic authorities, they praised the 'sagacity, prudence, fidelity and independence' displayed in Peel's 'exertions to purify and perpetuate that Constitution'. 'We are friendly to the well-considered reform of every abuse which our Institutions may have contracted in the lapse of years', they declared:

> but we desire to see them reformed only through the means which
> the Constitution itself provides, It is our earnest hope that an over-
> ruling Providence may long avert from the British Legislature the
> introduction of such changes as would inevitably destroy the
> salutary influence of one of its Branches, and lead to the virtual
> overthrow of another.

The Glasgow Tory operatives 'regarded the interests of the Working

[33] Ferrand to W. C. Espy, 3 Apr 1845 (Ferrand MSS).
[34] Alex Wilson, *The Chartist Movement in Scotland* (Manchester, 1970), 35; *Reformers' Gazette*, 26 Sept 1835; *Glasgow Argus*, 29 Dec 1836, 9, 12, 16 Jan, 20 Mar 1837.

Classes as identified with, and inseparable from, those of the Aristocracy, and should consider any infraction of the rights of the Peers, as the presage of an ulterior violation of the liberties of the People'. And, typically, they welcomed Peel's reported plan to support the Kirk financially:

> Sir, we love the Church of Scotland, for all it has suffered and all it
> has done, to provide the poor with religious instruction, and to
> afford their children a Bible education in its Parish Schools; and we
> long for the time when its boundaries shall be so enlarged as to
> become again commensurate to the wants of the population.

Peel replied in similar terms to this message of 'warmest gratitude': 'there was', he wrote, 'no portion of society more deeply interested in the maintenance of peace and order, in the protection of property, in the respect for constitutional privileges, than the working and industrious classes'. And he maintained that[35]

> the ancient monarchy and mixed form of government under which
> we live, give infinitely greater security in a country and society
> constituted like ours, for the continued possession of these advantages,
> than any that would be offered, at least that would be realised, by
> institutions purely democratical.

A committee started to plan the constitution and programme in February 1837, in Wright's coffee house, under Hugh Hamilton. It was agreed that the Association's motto should be 'Fear God; honour the King; and meddle not with those who are given to change'. The objects were

> to maintain . . . the British Constitution as established at the era of
> the Revolution in 1688; . . . to defend the interests of the
> Ecclesiastical and Educational Establishments of Scotland . . . and
> . . . to promote the purity of administration . . .

Membership was open to Tory workers in the city and suburbs on payment of 6d 'entry money'. Management was entrusted to a president (Hamilton), two deputies (James McNab and William Anderson), a treasurer (Robert Graham, a printer) and secretary (William Keddie), aided by a 22-strong committee (including two wrights, three warehousemen, four clothlappers, a fringe-maker, a shopman, a sawyer and seven printers). It was proposed that an annual rally should be held around 13 January, 'being the anniversary of the Glasgow Banquet to Sir Robert Peel', but the first general meeting was a dinner attended by 270 men in the Town Hall on 17 March.[36]

The Glasgow Association soon threw itself into election work for the Conservative R. J. I. Monteith and established a sub-committee to watch the activities of the 'Practical Trades Committee', which supported the Liberal John Dennistoun. It offered to help the Registration Committee 'in promoting the purification of the Roll of Electors, and in increasing the number of Conservative Voters' and was asked to canvass 'the wards of the city considered to be the worst, viz, the 1, 2, 3, 4, 6, 10, 11 and 12'; and it helped to raise funds to

---

[35] 'Minutes, Glasgow Conservative Operatives' Association', by courtesy of Mr Andrew Strang, MBE, who kindly provided me with a photostat copy (23 Dec 1836); *Glasgow Courier*, 3 Jan 1837.

[36] Ibid, 8, 10 Feb, 17 Mar 1837; *Regulations of the Glasgow Conservative Operatives' Association* (Glasgow, 1837).

contest the validity of some Irish elections. From early venues in coffee houses officials moved to the session houses of the Albion, Gaelic and Tron churches. At the general meeting in the Town Hall on 30 January 1838 Anderson became president of a growing organisation, supported by a committee of 35 men. In March it was decided to collect an annual subscription of 6d, to cover growing expenses. The Association had a varied programme. It heard papers on Ireland, Chartism and current politics; it congratulated Graham on defeating the Duke of Sussex as the University's Rector;[37] it held a dinner 'in honour of Conservative principles' in the Trades Hall (subsequently reprinting the speeches); and its general meeting of 1839 was 'crowded by workmen', who elected James Brown as president, backed by a 45-member committee; when Brown moved to Manchester he was succeeded by John Taylor. A new venture was planned from August 1839, when it was resolved to open a reading room. But old interests continued to attract members. In November Taylor regaled them with a speech 'showing the rapid progress that Popery had made in the Legislature, and throughout the Empire at large, since . . . 1829'. In June 1840 congratulatory addresses were prepared to the Queen and the Prince on 'their late Providential deliverance from the designs of an assassin'. At a 'numerously attended' February meeting the industrialist Robert Monteith of Carstairs was thanked for his long interest and his support for a memorial to Hamilton. By June subscriptions had been collected for the reading room and contact was made with the Barrhead operative Tories.[38]

In November the troublesome library was opened. But at the meeting of February 1841 'the disorganised state of parties in Scotland, occasioned by the discussion of the Church question' was ominously noticed. Duncan Menzies and Hugh Blyth carried a resolution pledging

> continued and stedfast [sic] adherence to Conservative principles, as
> the only security, under Providence, for the maintenance of
> constitutional government . . . and for the preservation of our
> institutions in Church and State.

Reading room facilities were improved and district superintendents appointed in preparation for the summer elections. But the continuing dispute within the Kirk seriously worried the committee, which in June urged the Association to support the 7th Duke of Argyll's Bill, legalising a congregational veto of lay patrons' right to nominate Presbyterian ministers. The operatives thus followed Thomas Chalmers' Evengelical Covenant, against majority Conservative opinion.[39] The 'new prospect of a general election' led to 'a very numerous meeting' on 22 June (one day before Parliament's dissolution), when the establishment of district superintendence was completed. A 'valuable and appropriate' gift of portraits of William III and Mary from one McKechnie,

---

[37] 'Minutes', 23 May, 4, 20, 28 June, 3 Oct 1837, 30 Jan, 25 Mar, June, Oct, 30 Nov 1838, 28 Jan, Feb 1839; *Glasgow Herald*, 24 Dec 1838; J. T. Ward, *Sir James Graham* (1967), 165–7.

[38] GCOA 'Minutes', Mar, 18 Apr, 13 Aug, 6 Nov 1839, 20, 21, 25 Feb, 15, 20 June 1840.

[39] Ibid, 6 Nov 1840, 17 Feb, 10 Apr, 16, 22 June 1841; see C. S. Parker, *Life and Letters of Sir James Graham* (1907), II, 467–74; William Hanna, *Memoirs of the Life and Writings of Thomas Chalmers* (Edinburgh, 1852), IV, 91–174; Ward, *Graham*, 198–202.

a reedmaker, was rewarded by honorary membership. And support was urged for Argyll, by petitions to Lord Wharncliffe and Graham, an address to the Queen and wide publicity.

Reading room matters proved increasingly troublesome, as rows developed with the agents. But Church affairs dominated proceedings. In February 1842 thirteen committee men heard that the general membership wished to express its views; they resolved to submit resolutions, only four members 'deeming it inexpedient to move in the matter at present'. In March a long fifth annual meeting congratulated the Party on its electoral success (of 1841) and then turned to the Church. It debated a complicated motion by William Bennet and William Collins on 'Spiritual Independance [sic] and Non-intrusion', supporting the General Assembly's Evangelical majority, condemning the minority Moderate League, attacking decisions in the Court of Session and House of Lords, demanding 'the total abolition of the Law of Patronage' and stressing that

> It is from a deep and growing conviction that upon a right
> settlement of this momentuous [sic] question depends not only the
> continued existence of the Church of Scotland, but also the future
> prosperity of the other institutions of the country, that we, as
> Conservatives, feel it to be our bounden duty, at the present crisis,
> to give this no less distinct than decided expression of our sentiment.

Moderating amendments by James Brown and Robert Kelly and a delaying motion by Duncan Menzies and James Campbell followed. Menzies beat Brown by 8 votes to 2 and then lost to Bennet by 70 to 15. Obviously, the Association was predominantly 'Chalmersite', but subsequent discussion showed that members were determined to remain united, under the new president, Robert Kelly. Nevertheless, the Church argument became increasingly divisive. In April there was a heated (and almost equally divided) committee discussion on the published minutes of the new (and inferior) secretary, James Thorne, and the memorial was altered.

1842, with its industrial depression (notoriously hard among Paisley weavers), was a bad year for many operative Tories. Unlike their English colleagues, the Glasgow committee favoured 'Sir Robert Peel's Financial and commercial schemes', and the full Association next resolved that

> in seasons of great commercial depression and embarassment [sic] of
> the national finance it would be as unjust as impolitic to releive [sic]
> such general distress by and [sic] increase of the assessed taxes, or by
> any system of general indirect taxation as thereby the burdens of the
> state would be made to fall chiefly on the poor and working
> classes who always suffer most from the stagnation of trade and
> commerce.

There followed a motion favouring Peel's reintroduction of income taxation upon 'thoses [sic] who of all others were most able to pay it' and the tariff reductions; petitions were sent to Argyll and Peel.[40]

40 GCOA 'Minutes', 22 June, 5 Oct, 20 Dec 1841, 28 Feb, 1, 10 Mar, 4, 11, 14 Apr 1842.

As the Church crisis mounted there followed a long gap in Glasgow operative Tories' minutes. Graham (now Home Secretary) rejected the Assembly's 'Claim, Declaration and Protest' of 1842 and in January 1843 bluntly told the Moderator that Churchmen had 'no exemption from the duty of obedience to statute law'. The tragedy of the Disruption of 18 May was becoming inevitable.[41] But as the religious argument reached its peak, the committee was engrossed in reading-room business. By February its 'revenue . . . [had] become quite inadequate to its support', but as the factor 'refused to take the premises off the society's hands on any terms' it was decided to sub-let the rooms. Members had obviously failed to support the reading room, and only twenty-four men attended the March meeting. A 'respectable tenant' of the room soon proved unable to pay his rent (even 'a shilling in the pound') and a declining committee found that it could not meet its 'positive liability' of £2 4s 5d and other expenses arising 'from Mr McLean's insolvency'. A levy of 1s 6d per member was ordered, and in April eight committee members advertised in the Herald the lease of the room and the sale of its contents. However, the district superintendents 'declined to collect the levy', the solitary potential lessee lost interest and in May nine committeemen informed McLean of their 'inability to dispense with his payment of his rent'. McLean 'having shown no disposition to meet, in any way, the wishes of [the] sub-committee appointed to deal with him about the rent, an officer had been commissioned to wait upon him, and in the event of his still declining to come to any settlement, to secure what belonged to him on the premises'. McLean simply removed his property and sent the keys to Taig (a committee member). By 30 May the much-reduced committee resolved (by a majority of one) to offer the rooms to the Young Men's Evangelical Church of Scotland Society at a rent of £25 and to rename the building the 'Free Presbyterian Reading Room'.[42]

Thereafter the records abruptly ended. Obviously, Glasgow Tory operatives were divided over various forms of Presbyterianism. Perhaps some shared English colleagues' disappointment with Peel's policies. Interest seems to have declined, as committee membership fell from 35 in 1840 to 34 in 1841 and 31 in 1842, with actual attendances amounting to only 9 by 1843.[43] But it is impossible to determine whether the theocratic principles of the Evangelicals or simply opposition to conservatism in practice killed the Glasgow group. The repeal of the Corn Laws effectively ended most Tory workers' organisations, along with most other Tory groups. The Protectionists, under Derby, Bentinck and Disraeli, had to start afresh, without a Bonham to arrange constituency affairs.

III

Although organised Operative Conservatism largely disintegrated after 1846, its spirit survived – in particular that religious Tory-Radicalism with which

[41] The Times, 14 Jan 1843; Annual Register (1843), 463–70; Hanna, op cit, IV, 320.
[42] GCOA 'Minutes', 21, 29 Feb, 8 Mar, 28 Apr, 18, 30 May 1843.
[43] Ibid, 21 Feb 1840, 17 Feb 1841, 10 Mar 1842, 30 May 1843.

Oastler had contoured the Factory Movement. Early in the campaign he typically urged Lancashire supporters[44]

> Operatives. This cause is your own – never desert it – bend your thoughts to it – publish the Horrors of the System – subscribe what you can, by what you can – and be assured God will prosper the right. Oppression has reigned long enough. Let the nation see you have resolved your Sons and Daughters shall be free.

In areas where the Movement had been strong some societies survived. At Bradford, for instance, Oastler's old friend William Walker, a worsted manu-facturer with whom he had not always agreed, became president of the local Society in 1851 and Oastler rejoiced that such good men existed in 'the very hot-bed of political weeds'.[45] But in general the network of societies simply disappeared. Nevertheless, there was wide Protectionist activity among working-class groups. Oastler visited many trade unionists – bakers, dyers, shopworkers, mechanics, miners, iron-workers, silk-weavers, textile operatives and others – under Protectionist auspices: he was, as Lord John Manners told his brother, the Marquess of Granby, 'the one engine by which the Manufacturing Districts could be worked'; 'rosewater' was useless. Oastler bravely attempted 'to unite the working classes of London against Free Trade, &c'[46] – with some success.

Ferrand was equally active, organising opposition to the triumphant League. First he turned to the small farmers, urging them and their labourers to fight Free Trade. His panacea for agricultural ruin was an eccentric plan to weaken Leaguers by substituting home-grown wool and flax for slave-produced cotton. He revealed the scheme at Doncaster in March 1850, appealing for unity among farmers and workers; like many Protectionists, he had long given up hope of aristocratic leadership.[47] Reactions were predictable: Protectionists praised Ferrand's 'honest, uncompromising and plain-speaking' style and 'great natural ability'; Liberals condemned his 'coarseness and RUFFIANISM'; *The Times*, typically uncommitted, defended amiable eccentricities.[48] Protec-tionists were much encouraged by the formation of such bodies as the 'Scottish ProtectiveAssociation for the Defence of the Industry and Capital of the Empire' under the 4th Duke of Montrose and the 13th Earl of Eglington, Augustus Delaforce's metropolitan proletarian groups and Ferrand's 'Farmers' Wool League', with its hatred of 'bloodstained cotton'.[49] The FWL had a wide

---

[44] Oastler to Thomas Daniel, 14 Mar 1832 (collection of the late Prof Cecil Driver; I am indebted to Mrs C. M. Lyman of New Haven, Conn, for photostat copies).

[45] J. T. Ward, 'Two Pioneers of Industrial Reform', *Bradford Textile Soc J* (1964); *The Home*, passim. I am indebted to Miss L. R. Walker for information.

[46] Ward, *Factory Movement*, 368–9, 382, 391, 405–6; Charles Whibley, *Lord John Manners and his Friends* (1925), II, 26–7.

[47] cf G. L. Mosse, 'The Anti-League, 1844–46', *Economic Hist Rev*, XVII (1947); Mary Lawson-Tancred, 'The Anti-League and the Corn Law Crisis of 1846', *Historical J*, III (1960).

[48] *Doncaster Chron*, 29, *Morning Chron*, 28, *The Times*, 28, 30, *The Standard*, 30 Mar 1850.

[49] *The Standard*, 19, 26, 27, 30, *Doncaster Chron*, 26 Apr, 21 June, *Nottingham J*, 25, *Liverpool Courier*, 26 Apr, *The Constitution*, 4 May 1850; W. B. Ferrand, *The Farmers' Wool League Movement and the Cotton Trade* (1850); *The Home*, passim.

following, as Ferrand stirred Northern farmers and workers in a series of rallies. It was formally organised under the presidency of the rough, sporting 4th Marquess of Downshire – a Tory in the Ferrand mould. When it took the title of the Farmers' Wool and Flax Association *The Standard* rejoiced that 'the dishonoured name of League had been abandoned'. Ferrand carried the campaign to the South; but, despite all the bucolic dinners and angry oratory, the Association achieved nothing.[50]

In January 1853 Oastlerites welcomed the formation of a Labour League by London workers. Ferrand's prize of £10 for the best essay on the effects of Free Trade was won by a young Scotsman, Samuel Kydd, a Chartist organiser who became Oastler's secretary, an early historian of the Factory Movement and ultimately a barrister.[51] And in August Kydd greeted Ferrand's 'Labour League of Lancashire, Yorkshire and Cheshire for the Protection and Regulation of the Interests of Native Producers', which held its first rally at Manchester in September. Its 'principles and objects', Auty told Oastler,[52]

appear to me to be just what is wanted in the present times. They
mean real and substantial benefits for the working classes of this
country, in opposition to Cobden and Co's flimsy, hollow and
delusive free-trade League. But will the working-men believe in it?
The old cuckoo-cry of 'Tory trick', or some other, will, no doubt,
be raised by the enemies of the 'workies', and, I fear, will, as usual,
succeed.

He was right. But at first the League did well, as Ferrand, Kydd, Luke Swallow (an Ashton factory reformer), Le Gendre Starkie (the squire-MP for Clitheroe), the Rev Charles Whitaker of Padiham, the Rev G. H. Moore of Sabden and Robert Alexander of Liverpool addressed audiences throughout the Northern textile districts. Kydd was especially active, offering 'the Labour League [as] the Cure for Strikes'. Oastler's weekly journal, *The Home*, was adopted as the League's organ and published optimistic reports by Kydd – who thought that within weeks he had addressed 'not fewer than 12,000 people' at Clitheroe, Padiham, Burnley, Todmorden, Colne, Bacup, Haslingden, Bury, Blackburn, Bingley, Bradford, Halifax, Oldham and Stockport.[53] But the socialistic Ernest Jones, a late leader of the Chartist remnants, condemned 'a trick of Tory factory lords', a 'Tory factory lords' Protection dodge' and 'a stale protective trick': to him,

The protection of Labour is to set it free – so that it will want no
artificial protection at all. 'Free Trade, Free Land, Free Labour' –

[50] W. B. Ferrand, *The F.W.L. and the Cotton Trade* (Leeds edn, 1850); *Leeds Intelligencer*, 11, *Morning Chron*, *The Times*, 8 May, 1, 21 June, *Yorkshire Gazette*, 11, *Doncaster Chron*, 17, *Nottingham Guardian*, 23 May, 20 June, *Bell's Weekly Messenger*, 11 May, 21 June, *Hull Packet*, 7 June 1850; W. B. Ferrand, *F.W.L. . . . Speech . . . Goole* (1850); *Morning Herald*, 24, *Standard*, 21, *Bell's Weekly Messenger*, 22, *Eddowes's Shrewsbury Chron*, 22, *Doncaster Chron*, 21 June 1850.
[51] I am indebted to Dr Alex Wilson of Manchester University for information.
[52] *The Home*, 1, 8 Jan, 16 Apr, 20, 27 Aug, 3 Sept 1853; Auty to Oastler, 12 Aug 1853.
[53] *The Home*, 24 Sept, 29 Oct, 12, 19 Nov, *People's Paper*, 8 Oct, *Manchester Guardian*, 29, *Stockport Advertiser*, 28 Oct 1853; Ferrand's diaries, passim (Yorkshire Archaeological Society collection).

founded on and guarded by the FREE VOTE – these are the
securities for our future and the redeemers of our present.

Ferrand and his friends – squires, Anglican priests and operatives – were no
'factory lords'. But their Labour League gradually disappeared – and so did
socialistic Chartism; Jones became a Liberal.[54]

The ideas of Ferrand's socially-conscious Protectionism offered little to the
mid-Victorian labour aristocracy of craft unionists, but exercised considerable
attraction for the declining handworkers. In October the Spitalfields broad silk
weavers – an Oastlerite group – urged 'fellow operatives' to work for Protection. The cause was not dead –[55]

with the 'Labour Question' now agitating the whole country, and
with such men as the Cobbetts, the Bulls, the Fieldens, the Ferrands,
the Oastlers to aid them, both in and out of Parliament . . .

They were wrong. Liberal Britain, entering the boom period as the 'workshop
of the world', cared little for opponents of *laisser-faire*. Protectionism, which to
men like Oastler and Ferrand involved wide social concern, was not only dead
but damned.

IV

The original Tory working-class organisations clearly failed after a few years.
They are of interest primarily as pioneering constituency groups. But they also
established a British political tradition of working-class support for Right-wing
politics. There was some continuity between the Operative Conservative
Societies and the Working Men's Conservative Associations which rapidly
expanded after the second Reform Act; at Wigan there may have been a completely continuous existence.[56] Other forms of continuity were personal. The
Huddersfield WMCA was led by Oastler's old Radical friends, like Joshua
Hobson, the first printer of the *Northern Star*, who had a 'somewhat chequered
political career, beginning with chartism and ending with conservatism'.[57]
John Leech, a tradesman and factory reformer, also became an Oastlerite
Tory.[58] John Hanson, an Owenite operative and shopkeeper, Chartist and
atheist, ended his life as an Anglican Sunday school teacher and Disraelian
imperialist; he 'had embraced all shades of politics, from communism up to
conservatism'.[59] Samuel Glendinning, Chartist businessman and Primitive
Methodist lay-preacher,[60] the cabinet maker James Brook[61] and the socialist
manufacturer Lawrence Pitkeithley[62] never travelled such a long road. But they

[54] *People's Paper*, 8, 15 Oct 1853; John Saville, *Ernest Jones, Chartist* (1952), passim.

[55] J. Horsham and W. E. Burroughs, *Address* . . . (25 Oct); *The Home*, 26 Nov 1853.

[56] H. J. Hanham, *Elections and Party Management. Politics in the Time of Disraeli and
Gladstone* (1969), 105.

[57] *Huddersfield Weekly News*, 13, 20, *Huddersfield Chron*, 13, *Huddersfield Examiner*,
13 May 1876; *Death of Mr. Joshua Hobson* (Huddersfield, 1876).

[58] *Huddersfield Observer*, 7 Jan 1871.

[59] *Huddersfield Chron*, 19 Jan 1878; *Huddersfield Weekly News*, 20 May 1876, 5 Jan 1878.

[60] *Huddersfield Weekly News*, 14 July 1883.

[61] *Huddersfield Observer*, 23 Apr 1870.

[62] *Huddersfield Chronicle*, 5 June 1858; J. T. Ward, 'Centenary of Lawrence Pitkeithley's
Death', *Huddersfield Daily Examiner*, 2 June 1958.

had all fallen under Oastler's spell. 'Mr Oastler had not a more constant, indefatigable and affectionate friend ... than [Pitkeithley]', wrote Kydd.[63] At Glasgow William Russell told the Working Men's Conservative Association of the old Operative Association in February 1877, and the trade unionist C. Wardell recorded similar memories at Stockport, as did the ironworks foreman (and later manager) Daniel Hall at Salford.[64] In the North of England Ferrand was again active, addressing WMCAs in Bradford, Huddersfield, Leeds, Manchester, Bolton, Halifax, Leicester and other towns.[65] And many other Oastlerites survived into the age of Leonard Sedgwick's network of WMCAs, meeting in taverns, schools, church-halls and (rarely) Party offices.[66]

Some such Associations grew rapidly. The Bolton Working Men's Church and Conservative Society had 502 members by June 1867. The London and Westminster Working Men's Constitutional Association, patronised by W. H. Smith, existed to

> unite the friends of constitutional principles in resisting any attempt
> to subvert the Protestant faith or the Constitution of the Country,
> to protect the prerogative of the Crown, and to defend the rights and
> privileges of the People.

By 1874, Professor Hanham tells us, there were at least 150 such bodies.[67] But while they represented a notion of 'Tory Democracy', they were not always supported by their hero, Disraeli. 'Of all men', he declared in 1878, 'I think workingmen should be most conservative'. But (as he stated at Glasgow in 1873) Dizzy opposed 'a system which would lead Conservatives who were working men to form societies merely confined to their class'. His proletarian followers appear to have agreed with him. The new Conservatism was primarily working-class in its original organisation; working men created the National Union of Conservative and Constitutional Associations at the Freemasons' Tavern in London in November 1867, when fifty-five English societies banded together under John Gorst and Victor Raikes. This little body, presided over by the 5th Earl of Dartmouth, insisted that its leaders should be aristocrats; but it gradually became important, as (in Lord Blake's words) 'the first centralised mass organisation to be formed by a British political party', dropping its 'Working Men's title in deference to Disraeli's views.[68] The experience of the Glasgow WMCA was typical. Planned in newspaper notices by William Cadman in November 1868, it was established at a rally in the Merchants' Hall in

[63] 'Alfred' (S. M. Kydd), History of the Factory Movement (1857), II, 192.

[64] Glasgow Conservative Association, MS Reports, I (12 Feb 1877), in Scottish Conservative and Unionist Association Collection; Manchester Courier, 28 June 1867; R. L. Greenall, 'Popular Conservatism in Salford, 1868–1886', Northern History, IX (1974).

[65] Yorkshire Post, 21 Nov 1866, 24, 31 Jan, Manchester Courier, 28 June, Yorkshire Post, 1 Aug, 25 Sept 1867, Standard, 5 Oct 1867, 16 Dec 1869, Yorkshire Post, 4, 25 Feb 1868.

[66] Hanham, op cit, 106 seq.

[67] Manchester Courier, 28 June 1867; Hanham, op cit, 106–7.

[68] The Times, 13 Nov 1867, 7 Aug 1868; W. J. Wilkinson, Tory Democracy (New York, 1925), passim; M. Ostrogorski, Democracy and the Organisation of Political Parties (1902), I, 256; McKenzie and Silver, op cit, 37–40; Robert Blake, A Century of Achievement (1967), 17, 21, Conservative Party, 114–5, 145–6, 151, Disraeli (1969 edn), 536; J. T. Ward, 'Derby and Disraeli', in Donald Southgate (ed), The Conservative Leadership, 1832–1932 (1974), 98.

January 1869. It was a great success: it had branches in every ward, owned its own office from 1872, enrolled 2,800 new members in 1873–4 and helped in 1874 to return the first Conservative MP since the Reform Act. In 1876 it became Glasgow Conservative Association, and opened its doors to bourgeois members.[69]

Some old attitudes were long maintained. Religious interests (especially over Ireland) continued, particularly in Scotland, where a National Union of constituency associations was formed only in November 1882.[70] Similar beliefs certainly influenced parts of Lancashire, though it remains difficult to determine the relative importance of anti-'Popery' and social reform.[71] Both appear to have played a part. The Orangeman William Murphy[72] of the Protestant Evangelical Mission and Electoral Union undoubtedly had some riotous influence in Lancashire; but so did Scott Russell's 'new social movement' of 1871, which brought together an assortment of trade union leaders and Tories, including W. H. Wood, Secretary of the Manchester Trades Council, and his president and fellow-printer, Samuel Nicholson. Two Conservatives, Wood and Nicholson, called the first conference of the TUC in 1868.[73] Elsewhere, that extraordinary Tory Michael Maltman Barry – friend of Karl Marx, leader of the English section of the first International, journalist and, on several occasions, Conservative candidate – represented the tradition of support for industrial reform. He fought elections in both Scotland and England, his best chance of entering Parliament arriving in 1894, when the South Aberdeen Conservatives endorsed his candidature but their Liberal Unionist allies refused to support such a radical, 'mainly on the ground of unsoundness in his Unionist principles'.[74] And cotton Conservatism was upheld by James Mawdsley, the leader of the spinners' union and joint Conservative candidate with Winston Churchill at the Oldham by-election of 1899. The Webbs explained such 'backwardness' in terms of Lancashire's 'ancestral Conservatism'. They obviously thought that a trade unionist Tory candidate was extraordinary. As (although they knew Mawdsley) they dated the event in 1906, it certainly had an extraordinary aspect; Mawdsley died in 1902.[75]

[69] G. C. A. Reports (25 Jan 1870, 9 Jan 1872, 13 Jan 1874, 16 Feb 1875, 14 Jan 1876); cf Barry Henderson, Ian Lang, *The Scottish Conservatives – A Past and A Future* (Edinburgh, 1975), 4–7.

[70] National Union of Conservative Associations for Scotland Minutes, I (1882–8); J. T. Ward, *Toryism in West Renfrewshire* (Paisley, 1972), 2–5.

[71] R. L. Greenhall, 'The Rise of Popular Conservatism in Salford, 1868 to 1874', paper read to the Urban History conference, 1973; cf Greenhall, loc cit.

[72] Hanham, op cit, 304–9.

[73] W. H. Fraser, *Trade Unions and Society. The Struggle for Acceptance, 1850–1880* (1974), 163–5 et passim; A. E. Musson, *The Congress of 1868: The Origins and Establishment of the Trades Union Congress* (1955).

[74] J. T. Ward, 'Tory Socialist', *J Scottish Labour Hist Soc*, II (1970); H. Cunningham, 'M. M. Barry', ibid, V (1972); Aberdeen Conservative Association and Aberdeen Liberal Unionist Association Minutes (1894), by courtesy of Mr David Reid.

[75] Randolph S. Churchill, *Winston S. Churchill, i: Youth, 1874–1900* (1966), 444, seq; *Constitutional Year Book* (1900), 188; S. and B. Webb, op cit, 479; Beatrice Webb, *Our Partnership* (1948), 516, cf G. D. H. Cole, *British Working-Class Politics, 1832–1914* (1941), 275, *Short History of the British Working-Class Movement, 1789–1947* (1948), 298; G. D. H. Cole and R. Postgate, *The Common People, 1746–1946* (1949), 420–1.

Tory working-class support has continued to be an essential ingredient of modern Conservative electoral successes. It continues to baffle opponents, And it continues to provide a uniquely undenominational buttress for a party of the Right.[76] Yet it survives not because of some historical continuity of organisation or issues[77] but, it seems, because of a continuing admiration for the Right-wing 'flair' in British politics.

J. T. WARD

[76] See Peter Shore, *The Real Nature of Conservatism* (Labour Party, 1952), quoted in McKenzie and Silver, op cit, 14–5; Willis Roxburgh et al, *Tory Trade Unionists* (Edinburgh, Scottish Conservative Party, 1972), 6; David E. Butler and Donald Stokes, *Political Change in Britain* (1969), 108; Arnold Beichman, 'The Conservative Research Department . . .', *J British Studies*, XIII (1974).

[77] See Norman McCord, 'Some Limitations of the Age of Reform', in H. Hearder and H. R. Loyn, *British Government and Administration: Studies presented to S. B. Chrimes* (Cardiff, 1974), 187 seq.

Shipbuilding Machine Tools

Ian McNeil opens his recent book *Hydraulic Power* by commenting on the sparseness of references to his subject in modern textbooks and in historical writing on engineering. This curious gap is paralleled by the absence of any general account of the history of those iron and steel plate-working tools that were essential to the development of iron and steel shipbuilding and other branches of structural engineering, and of boilermaking, that neglected component of steam technology. A. M. Robb suggested that punching and shearing machines and bending rolls were 'probably' introduced by boilermakers, and mentioned the adoption of the hydraulic riveter in 1871, the plate-edge planer in 1874 and the general use of hydraulic power in 1879. Apart from this sketchy account and a brief supplement to *Industrial Archaeology*, nothing appears to have been written in recent years.[1]

Before discussing the development of shipbuilding machine tools, a brief indication of the function of the main types may be useful. The tasks to be performed in the construction of a riveted iron or steel ship of traditional type were, firstly, the erection of a framework made largely of bar and angle iron and forgings, consisting of a keel, with stem and stem-posts, and frames, rising vertically from the keel, but shaped in pairs to suit the form of the hull. These frames were linked laterally by stringers, and transversely by deck beams, and the deck beams were often supported vertically by pillars. The second stage consisted of covering the framework with appropriately shaped and curved iron or steel plates forming the shell, decks and bulkheads. Though changes were made in the layout and structural significance of the different members of the hull frame during the currency of riveted construction, these did not markedly influence manipulative techniques. Common to both 'framing' and 'plating' was the fastening technique of riveting which consists of piercing the pieces of metal to be joined, inserting a white-hot rivet – short piece of iron

---

[1] A. M. Robb, 'Shipbuilding', in C. Singer et al, *A History of Technology*, Vol 5, 365–7; Sir William White, 'The Connection between Mechanical Engineering and Modern Shipbuilding', address to the Institute of Mechanical Engineers, reported in *The Engineer*, 1899, 87, 454; John Butt, 'Extracts from a Catalogue of Machine Tools prepared for Craig & Donald, Engineers of Johnstone c 1900', *Industrial Archaeology*, Vol 6, No 3 (August 1969), Supplement, 1–16. In the early days of iron shipbuilding, the machine tools of shipyards were comparatively few and simple, mostly borrowed from boilershop practice.

rod, formed with a head at one end – and hammering over the projecting end, forming a second head and filling the holes in the metal.[2]

The basic manipulations were, therefore, to punch or to drill holes in plates and angles, to cut them to size and shape, to curve them appropriately and to rivet them together. To perform these functions machines were developed for punching, drilling, shearing (often combined with punching), angle-iron (section) cutting, plate-bending and straightening, flanging, angle-iron (section) bending, bevelling, and riveting. Closely linked with these were various types of mechanical handling equipment. It is these tools and their variants which form the subject of this paper.

Punching machines, like most of those mentioned above, were essential to the working of iron in shipbuilding from its effective beginnings in the 1820s and '30s. One of the leading firms of shipyard toolmakers was said in 1901 to have specialised in this branch of manufacture since its foundation in 1836[3] and the French naval architect, Guy Dupuy de Lome, commenting on the yard in Bristol used in the construction of the celebrated iron ship *Great Britain* described tools for punching, shearing and bending which are recognisably ancestors of what became the standard forms.[4] The combined punching and shearing machine, mentioned by de Lome, appears to have been well-established by the end of the 1840s. A hand-operated single-ended device of this type by Charles Walton of Leeds was illustrated in 1843,[5] and six years later a larger tool by Caird & Co of Greenock was mentioned as a typical machine. This had the driving gearing and flywheel overhead, to aid accessibility, and had the punching and shearing apparatus on opposite sides 'to obviate confusion among the men'. The same writer commented:

> The punching machine, from being confined to the tinsmith and
> ornamental metal worker's shop, has latterly become an instrument
> of no small importance to the engineer, whose ponderous
> adaptations of this tool excite the greatest wonder in the mind of a
> spectator unaccustomed to their operations. Here the punch or
> cutting tool seems to pass through an enormously thick piece of cold
> metal, as if the latter was so much pasteboard, the whole of the
> operation being conducted without producing the least noise.[6]

Once the classic form had been introduced, modifications in layout were few. Two mechanical devices for producing the up and down movement of the punch and shear blades were developed.

The cam-lever mechanism, in the simplest form of which a revolving cam exerted a positive pressure on the end of a long lever, and the eccentric were both in use in the 1840s and remained current at least until 1914. The eccentric

    [2] Elijah Baker III, *Introduction to Shipbuilding*, 2nd edn, London, 1953, passim.
    [3] A. McLean (ed), *Local Industries of Glasgow and the West of Scotland*, Glasgow, 1901, 45.
    [4] E. C. B. Corlett, 'Wood to Iron in Early 19th Century Ship Construction', paper presented to the National Maritime Museum Symposium, 9 Nov 1973.
    [5] *The Practical Mechanic and Engineer's Magazine*, 1843, 2, 376.
    [6] *The Engineer and Machinist's Assistant*, Glasgow, 1849, Vol 1, pages 32 and 33 of the description of plates; Vol 2, plate 51.

type was commoner until the 1880s but for certain purposes the cam-lever machine, in which the punch could descend slowly, and return quickly, was preferred.[7] Another mechanism, the hydraulic ram, was applied to rivet-hole punching machines by R. H. Tweddell in the 1870s, but never became popular.[8] Manhole-punching machines, where the rate of punching was not critical were, however, commonly hydraulically operated.[9]

The combined punch and shear became *the* standard shipyard tool, largely on account of the very many holes that required to be punched, and the number of plates and sections that had to be cut to size. In a medium-sized cargo liner – Denny's TSS *Southwark* of 1893 – there were about 975,000 rivets, each of which passed through at least two holes, and there were 17,000 separate plates and angles. A good rate of punching holes in frame angles was then reckoned to be 36 holes per minute.[10] During the life of the type, three important changes came about as the result of the introduction of steel. First, the size of plates increased, with a corresponding reduction in the number of rivets necessary to fasten them together. John Biles in 1901 referred to the plates of about 1880 as about 12 ft by 4 ft maximum size, weighing perhaps 0·625 tons, capable of being handled by the men who were necessary to mark and punch them. At that date plates of twice the length, one and a half times the breadth, three times the weight required power cranes, iron railways and improved plant. The saving – one quarter fewer rivets per ton of plate and a gain of 33 per cent in labour productivity – fully justified the increased expenditure on plant. This change – which was progressive rather than sudden – created a steady demand for new machines from the toolmakers, for machines with deeper gaps were necessary to punch to the centre of wider plates.[11] Plates also tended to become thicker as vessels grew larger, though the increase in thickness levelled off at $1\frac{1}{2}$–$1\frac{3}{4}$ in about 1900. Because rivet holes were normally the same diameter as the thickness of the plate, and since the power required and hence the strength of the machine frame increased as the cube of the diameter, an apparently modest increase in thickness of plate could have a marked effect on machine size. In 1881 a $1\frac{1}{2} \times 1\frac{1}{2}$ in punching and shearing machine weighed $21\frac{1}{2}$ tons as compared with $14\frac{1}{2}$ tons for a $1\frac{1}{4} \times 1\frac{1}{4}$ in machine of similar construction. The costs were £380 and £225.[12] The third change, which came too late to have a

[7] *Minutes of Proceedings of the Institute of Civil Engineers*, 1857–8, *17*, 173 referred to the cam-lever machine as the old form; *The Engineer*, 1866, *19*, 166, described an improved cam-lever machine by John Cameron of Salford, with positive return by the use of a second cam; *Mins of Proc Inst of C.E.*, 1877–8, *52*, 232, mentioned the cam-lever machine as being 'extensively used' in the United States; *The Engineer*, 1886, *62*, 443, discussing a cam-lever machine by James Bennie & Sons, referred to the type as 'now so greatly preferred by ship platers'.

[8] Hydraulic punching, shearing and angle-iron cutting machines described and illustrated in *Proceedings of the Institution of Mechanical Engineers*, 1874, plates 57, 58; ibid, 1882–3, 73, 64, 76, plate 6 fig 11.

[9] See order books of Craig & Donald, Dept of History, University of Strathclyde, passim, and of Hugh Smith (Glasgow) Ltd in the possession of the firm.

[10] Archibald Denny, 'The Design and Building of a Steamship', *The Marine Number of Cassier's Magazine*, 1897, 406.

[11] *The Engineer*, 1886, *62*, 490.

[12] Craig & Donald cost book.

EDITORIAL NOTE

The following illustrations are primarily intended to show the physical appearance of the types of tool discussed by Mr Hume in his chapter. The University of Strathclyde, on the initiative of Professor Lythe, has been a member of the Business Archives Council of Scotland since its formation. The Department, with his encouragement, has been closely associated with the work of listing and preserving technical as well as other classes of business records in the west of Scotland.

ACKNOWLEDGMENTS

The author and editors would like to express their gratitude to the Scottish Machine Tool Corporation for donating to the Department the records of Craig & Donald and James Bennie & Sons from which most of these illustrations are taken. Plate 4 is reproduced by kind permission of the Court of the University of Glasgow from the Biles Collection, University of Glasgow Archives.

PLATE I. A typical hydraulic manhole-punching machine, built by Craig & Donald, Johnstone, in 1889 for Barclay, Curle & Co, Whiteinch (works No. 1438). The oval punch, V-form in elevation to give a shearing action, is about to descend. It could cut a hole 36 by 21 in through $\frac{5}{8}$-in plate. (See pp. 160–2.)

PLATE 2. An early electrically-powered shipyard tool (Craig & Donald No 1816 of 1895), of cam-lever type, with twin one-inch punches at the ends, and a side cutter at one side for notching 10 in by 8 in gaps out of $\frac{7}{8}$-in thick plate. The open electric motor, supplied by Paterson & Cooper, of Dalston, London, with its exposed brush-gear, is obviously unsuited to service out-doors. Note that the motion of the centre punch is of the eccentric type. This machine was supplied to William Denny & Bros, Leven Shipyard, Dumbarton. (See p. 161.)

PLATE 3

A heavy set of plate-bending rolls in service, showing the stiffening girder and support rollers of the Hugh Smith patent. (See p. 163.)

PLATE 4

A hydraulic keel-plate bender in use at Clydebank Yard about 1900. Some samples of the work of the machine can be seen on the left and in the foreground. Note the use of a hand crane as an aid in manipulation. (See p. 163.)

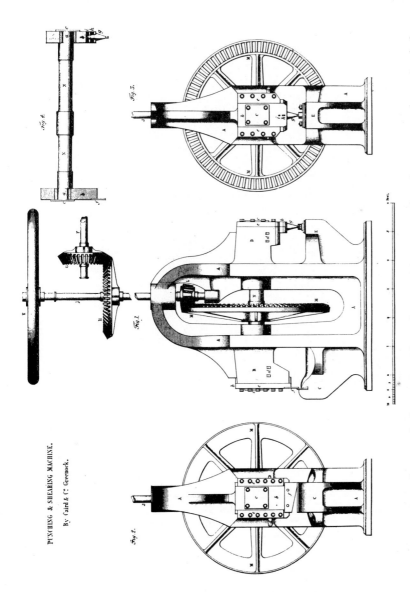

PUNCHING & SHEARING MACHINE.

By Caird & Co. Greenock.

Fig. 4.

Fig. 3.

Fig. 1.

Fig. 2.

FIG. 1. A punching and shearing machine by Caird & Co of Greenock, of the eccentric type. The eccentrics are shown in the top right-hand corner, with the punching and shearing heads in position. Note that the gear on the main shaft appears to have wooden teeth mortised in, providing a 'weak link' in the event of the machine being overloaded. (See p. 159.)

Fig. 2. A punching and shearing machine of the eccentric type, made by Craig & Donald of Johnstone, capable of punching and cutting steel plates 2-in thick for armour deck-plates. The size of the machine may be estimated from the gap at the punching end, which was 3 ft 6 in deep. (See pp. 159–60.)

FIG. 3. A cam-lever punching, shearing and angle-iron cutting machine by Craig & Donald, to punch 1½-in holes through 1½-in plate. The levers may be seen, with their pivots, on either side of the cam shaft, to the end of which the crank operating the angle-iron cutter is attached. The machine illustrated was supplied in 1896 to Scriven & Co, Leeds, probably for resale. Note the bearings for cranes at the top of the frame. (See p. 160.)

Fig. 4. An electrically-powered steel-framed punching, shearing and angle-iron cutting machine made by Henry Pels & Co, Berlin. This illustration is taken from their 1914 catalogue. Note the economy in the use of metal as compared with figures 2 and 3, where cast-iron framing was employed. (See p. 161.)

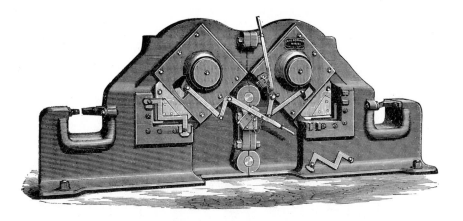

FIG. 5. A double horizontal punching and double angle-iron cutting machine, made by Craig & Donald. Note the horizontal punching action. (See p. 161.)

FIG. 6. A steam-driven plate shearing machine capable of cutting steel plates up to ¾-in thick. The blades were 8 ft long. This machine was built by Craig & Donald in 1891 for the Calderbank Steel Co, Lanarkshire. (See pp. 161–2.)

Fig. 7. A typical large plate-edge planing machine, by Craig & Donald, for planing 2-in steel plate 24 ft long at a time. The tool holder is in the centre of the bed, and is moved along by a screw inside the box bed in the foreground. (See p. 162.)

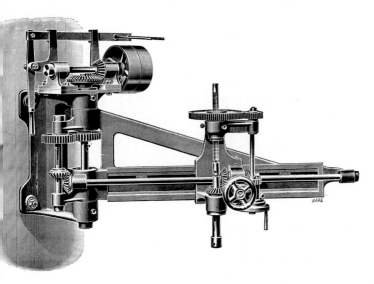

FIG. 8. A wall-mounted radial drilling machine, of the type used for countersinking, as made by Craig & Donald. (See p. 162.)

FIG. 9. A 'powerful set' of plate-bending rolls, with power screw-down. The rollers in this Craig & Donald machine were 24 ft long, the top roller being 32 in in diameter. (See p. 162.)

F<small>IG</small>. 10. A keel-plate or garboard strake bending machine, by Craig & Donald, for bending (hot) steel plates up to 20 ft long by hand power. The garboard strake was the name for the line of plates next to the keel plate on either side. (See p. 163.)

Fig. 11. A bevelling machine to Davis & Primrose's patent. The angle-iron is in the centre of the machine, with the conical rollers used to alter the angle of bevel according to the scale above. This machine was arranged for steam engine drive. The rail wheels allowed the machine to be brought up to the mouth of the furnace in which the iron was heated. (See p. 164.)

FIG. 12. A Craig & Donald patent five-roll straightening machine, for plates up to 11 ft by 1½ in thick. The machine is arranged for belt drive. (See p. 164.)

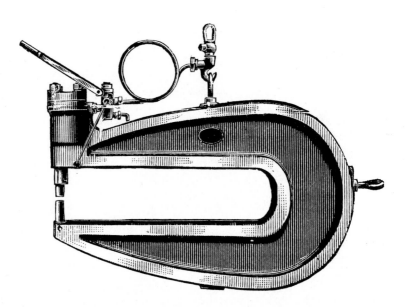

FIG. 13. A hydraulic riveting machine of the gap type, as used in shipbuilding. This illustration, from a catalogue of P. & W. MacLellan Ltd, machinery merchants, is almost certainly of a riveter made by Sir William Arrol & Co. The hydraulic cylinder is on the left. (See p. 165.)

particularly significant effect on the tool-manufacturing industry, was the introduction of the steel (sometimes high-tensile steel) plate frame to replace the heavy iron castings of the older machines. This was a German invention, adopted by American firms and studied by the West of Scotland manufacturers before its introduction about 1908.[13] The depressed state of shipbuilding between the wars, the existence of a flourishing second-hand market, and competition from American and German firms during the 1930s, the robust construction of the cast-iron framed machines, and the introduction of welding in place of riveting in ship construction all prevented the emergence of a large local market for the new design though a wide range was illustrated in Scottish Machine Tool Corporation catalogues from the foundation of the firm in 1937.[14] Much earlier, the existence of the punching machine was threatened by a controversy which developed as to the relative merits of drilling or punching holes for a riveted joint.[15] It was eventually proved that punching was, if anything, better than drilling, though drilling enjoyed a rivival when portable pneumatic and electric machines were introduced.[16] Even then the greater energy consumption and overall costs of drilling prevented it from displacing the traditional methods for general work.[17]

Though the combined punching and shearing machine was the commonest variety, the range of related tools was almost limitless. An angle-iron cutter was often incorporated in the centre of the machine, and triple or quadruple machines, with three or four operating heads, were fairly popular in the years before the First World War.[18] For angle and other iron and steel sections, specialised punching and cutting machines, usually with a horizontal action, were also developed.[19] Single-purpose punching or shearing machines were not uncommon, particularly the latter. Some very large and powerful plate shears were built by the leading makers, the same types often being supplied to rolling

[13] Johns shearing machines were described in *The Engineer*, 1904, *96*, 209, 240. These machines, which cut in small stages, were taken up by Henry Pels, who introduced punching machines and related types, ibid, 1910, *110*, 325. J. Bennie & Son's punching and shearing machine No 1693, built for stock in 1908, and sold in 1910, had a plate frame of a type new to the firm, J. Bennie & Son, Contract Book No 2, 1905–10, Dept of History, University of Strathclyde.

[14] Scottish Machine Tool Corporation catalogues, Dept of History, University of Strathclyde. The North British Locomotive Co Ltd bought the shares of Henry Pels & Co in 1950 and made Pels machines for some years, *The North British Locomotive Co Ltd*, Glasgow, 1953, 109–11.

[15] In 1864 a leader in *The Engineer*, 1864, *18*, 240, referred to punching as one-quarter the price of drilling, commenting that the 'conical hole of the punch forms a lengthened kind of countersink of much value in shipbuilding'; ibid, 1872, *34*, 362, commented on recent experiments that had shown that drilled hole joints were weaker; ibid, 1878, *45*, 407, summarised the renewed controversy over the best technique for steel plates.

[16] A. F. Yarrow was using pneumatic and electric drills for the plating of the highly-stressed hulls of torpedo-boat destroyers in 1903, with no marked increase in cost over punched holes, ibid, 1903, *95*, 644. See also John Hume and Michael Moss, *Clyde Shipbuilding from Old Photographs*, 1975, illustration 68.

[17] Carlile Wallace quoted A. W. Stewart's experience at Clydebank, where in 1894 electric punching removed 4·5 cubic inches of steel per minute per horsepower, steam punching 2·25 cubic inches and electric drilling 0·3, *Transactions of the Institute of Engineers and Shipbuilders in Scotland*, 1894–5, *38*, 182–3.

[18] Craig & Donald Order Books; J. Bennie & Son Cost Book No 2, passim.

[19] Craig & Donald Catalogue and Price List, 1881.

mills as well as to shipyards.[20] The very heaviest were used for light armour plate:[21] heavier armour had to be forged and machined to size using special planers and shapers. The preparation of plate edges was of little consequence when plates were thin, but from the 1860s the plate-edge planer and the scarfing (scarphing) machine gradually came into use.[22] Another significant tool, and in its own way the most spectacular of the class, was the manhole punch. Like a gigantic rivet punch, its function was to punch out manholes in the 'floors' – vertical transverse partitions of the double bottom of the ship – to allow the space to be used for water ballast. A typical tool of this type was able to punch an oval hole 12 by 17 in in one operation. In this application hydraulic transmission could compete with direct mechanical drive.[23] Though drilling never effectively rivalled punching in hole-forming for shipbuilding, it became normal practice to countersink punched holes using drills, and wall-mounted countersinking drills feature regularly in the output of Craig & Donald, one of the leading makers.[24] Radial drills, rare in shipyard work, were used for special purposes, and were more generally used in boiler and girder manufacture.

The forming of plates into simple curves, like punching holes, was a tin-smith's technique. The author of the *Engineer and Machinist's Assistant* commented in 1849 on a large set of rolls designed by David Elder of Robert Napier's yard for bending iron plate: 'this species of machine, originally confined to the tinsmith's shop, has become indispensable in the operations of boiler-making and iron-ship-building, in which plates are required to be bent to different degrees of curvature. The present machine being principally intended for the use of the ship building yard, where few plates are required to have a regular curve throughout, is not provided with geering [sic] for simultaneously altering the position of the ends of the front roller. The arrangement adopted allows of the setting of one of the ends of the roller at any position with regard to the other, so as to give any required twist to the plate.' Interestingly, for the relationship was later reversed, 'in the building yard plates of greater thickness come under operation than are required in boiler making'.[25] Plate-bending rolls did not alter much in principle until the early years of this century, though for the largest sets power screw-down of the central roller was introduced in the early 1880s.[26] About 1880 vertical bending rolls were introduced,

[20] Craig & Donald Order Books, passim.

[21] A 'very large' punching and shearing machine made by Bennie & Co for Sir W. G. Armstrong, Mitchell & Co could punch holes in 2 inch plate 33 inches from the edge, and, it was claimed, 'This and other machines in construction provide the Elswick Works with the most powerful plant in the world', *The Engineer*, 1886, *62*, 366.

[22] A plate-planing machine was described in *Engineering*, 1867, *4*, 423, seven years before the date of introduction quoted by A. M. Robb (see footnote 1).

[23] R. H. Tweddell's hydraulic manhole punching machine for Raylton, Dixon & Co excited comment in *The Engineer*, 1882, *53*, 107.

[24] In 1889 it was opined that steel loses ductility and tenacity through punching, which is recovered by countersinking, ibid, 1889, *68*, 87.

[25] *The Engineer and Machinist's Assistant*, Vol 1, 204, description of plates 37.

[26] Craig & Donald's large bending rolls did not have power screw-down in a catalogue of 1881, but did in a catalogue of 1886.

[27] Vertical bending rolls by Scriven & Co, Leeds Old Foundry, were in use in Jarrow, Barrow, Hull and Hartlepool in 1881, *The Engineer*, 1881, *52*, 73, 83.

though these were more commonly used in boiler-making than in ship-building.[27] The other important modification in design was strictly applicable to ship plates, and arose out of the incompatibility of small-diameter rollers, which are more efficient at bending plates, with the stiffness required in long rollers to bend large plates. This problem was overcome by 'backing' a small-diameter roller with pairs of short rollers mounted on a stiff girder frame, usually of riveted construction. This type is still in production, notable examples being made by Hugh Smith (Glasgow) Ltd, who patented the idea in 1890.[28]

Not all hull plates were curved in one direction only, and 'compound curved' plates were made by hammering heated plate over a former. Hull design generally reduced the number of these naturally expensive plates to a minimum. Another type of plate bender was designed to make a small-radius curve in a plate, the rest of which remained flat, in the construction of a plate keel or of the row of plates (garboard strake) adjacent to such a keel. Hand-operated machines of this type were in use in the late 1870s but were supplanted by hydraulic machines of massive construction and great power from the late 1890s.[29] Vertical hydraulic machines operating on a similar principle have been developed in recent years, to some extent supplanting large shell-plate bending rolls.

Flanging, that is the bending of plates at a sharp angle to obviate two riveted connections to an angle iron, was another technique borrowed by ship-builders from boilermakers, and made its appearance in the 1890s. It was not particularly common before 1914, but subsequently became a standard tech-nique, and is widely used in welded ship construction.[30]

Bending angles or other sections (Z, H, T, or bulb sections) called for other classes of tool. The commonest consisted of a reciprocating hammer which forced the section between two projections, generating the required curve in rather jerky stages. Later, vertical three-roller machines were introduced.[31] For frames, hand bending of hot sections was standard practice, sometimes assisted with hydraulic rams or 'bears'. A feature of frames was that, unless in a parallel mid-ships section, the angle or other section had to be bevelled to fit the shape of the hull. The degree of bevelling varied over the length of the frame and was individual to each frame in a particular ship. Until the 1880s

[28] Patented by Hugh Smith & Sons in 1890, patent No 12,152. Described as a 'unique feature' of a set of bending rolls at Fairfield in 1898, *Historical and Descriptive Account of the Works of The Fairfield Shipbuilding and Engineering Co Ltd*, Glasgow, 1898, 31.

[29] A manually-operated garboard-strake bending machine by J. Bennie & Son is illus-trated in *The Engineer*, 1877, *44*, 386; there was a hydraulic keel-plate bender at Gray & Co, Hartlepool in 1888, ibid, 1888, *66*, 345; a Smith keel-plate bender was 'new' at Fairfield in 1897, ibid, 1897, *84*, 75 and an example is illustrated in John Hume and Michael Moss, *Clyde Shipbuilding from Old Photographs*, 53.

[30] *The Engineer*, 1889, *68*, 87, 'already machine makers are competing with each other in the production and perfection of appliances for safely and economically shaping cold steel to the various forms required in ship construction'; there was a Hugh Smith flanging press in Harland & Wolff's Belfast Yard in 1896, ibid, 1896, *82*, 30; 'the cold working of steel plates began with garboard strakes, and spread to the flanging of floor plates, inter - costals and bulkhead stiffeners', ibid, 1896, *82*, 30.

[31] For example an electrically-powered machine by Rushworth & Co, Sowerby Bridge, illustrated in *The Engineer*, 1901, *91*, 513.

bevelling was done by hand, but it was often done badly, resulting in poor joints between the plates and the frames and sometimes seriously weakening the frames.[32] A hand-controlled bevelling machine was developed between 1879 and 1884 by a Mr Arthur, an employee of the Leith shipbuilding firm of Ramage & Ferguson. The patent was purchased by Davis & Primrose, also of Leith, and the device became very generally used.[33] Newer methods of hull construction, in particular the use of welding, have reduced the number of frames and increased their depth. Though bevelling is no longer necessary, sections must still be bent, and hydraulic cold frame-bending machines of great power are now produced.

One of the problems facing early iron shipbuilders was how to make a tight joint between the plates and the frames. If 'in and out' plating was adopted, as became standard, spacers or 'liners' had to be introduced between the 'out' plates and the frames. These were expensive to make, and contributed nothing to the strength of the hull. In the 1890s, the practice began of 'joggling' plates or frames in a zig-zag fashion, making better joints, and joggling machines, often with hydraulic mechanisms, were developed.[34] The technique became less important with the spread of the Isherwood system, in which the number of frames was reduced and longitudinal stringers introduced instead[35] – and died out completely with the introduction of welded construction.

Plates and angles received from the rolling mills were often kinked. It was possible to use bending machines, with care, to eliminate these distortions, but the skill involved in treating plates led in the 1880s, or earlier, to the construction of four, five or seven roller 'straightening' machines, in which the fourth and subsequent rollers counteracted the over-correction of the first three.[36] Similar machines were later developed for angle straightening. An interesting variant of the plate straightening rolls was a four-roller machine in which one roller could be moved out of the way, allowing the device to be used for bending.[37]

[32] Ibid, 1889, *68*, 87.

[33] By 1890 it was to be found 'in most of the large shipbuilding yards in this country and the Continent, also in the dockyards of our own and several foreign governments', ibid, 1890, *69*, 457–8. Initially hand-powered, by 1902 it was 'generally driven by electric power', ibid, 1902, *93*, 258–9. See also *Transactions of the Institution of Engineers and Shipbuilders in Scotland*, 1885–6, *89*, 105.

[34] It was an active issue in the 1890s whether to joggle plates or frames. At Denny's in 1897, the weight saving by the abolition of liners consequent on the adoption of plate joggling was 60 tons in a 3,000 ton vessel (*The Engineer*, 1897, *84*, 75). This, of course, represented a permanent addition to the carrying capacity of the ship, as well as a saving in raw material. By 1899 it could be stated that joggled plating, introduced by Doxford & Co, Sunderland, had been adopted by 'a good many' firms in the North East of England and that joggled frames were more common on the Clyde. (Ibid, 1899, *88*, 108.)

[35] David Dougan, *A History of North East Shipbuilding*, 1968, 117–8.

[36] A Craig & Donald catalogue of 1881 contains a manuscript reference to plate-flattening rolls, while the next edition, dated 1886, includes an illustration of a roller machine. The order books of Craig & Donald and James Bennie & Son contain numerous references to 4, 5 and 7 roller machines.

[37] The type was patented by Craig & Donald in 1904 (No 5868), and became a standard variant after the patent expired. The fourth roller could also be used to 'set' the edge of a plate, giving entry to a smooth curve.

The operation of 'closing' a rivet using hand hammers is an arduous and hence expensive one. Mechanical riveters were therefore developed at an early date. Fairbairn's steam riveter was not unusual in being 'invented . . . upon an emergency to supply the loss of a set of hand riveters who had left their employment on account of some business disagreement'.[38] This and subsequent steam riveters were in general use for boiler work by the 1870s, but being cumbersome were not much used in shipbuilding.[39] R. H. Tweddell's invention of the hydraulic ship riveter in 1883 was also slow to be adopted, and when it did come into use, was confined in the main to riveting the top and bottom rows of hull plating, where the greatest strength was required, and where long runs of rivets were normal.[40] The real breakthrough in mechanical riveting came with the introduction of much lighter pneumatic tools by the American shipbuilders. The excessively cold winter climate of North America made it impossible to use water-hydraulic machinery, and the high cost of manpower encouraged the substitution of capital for labour.[41] Pneumatic riveting was adopted in this country in the late 1890s and quickly became standard, though it was noisier than other methods, and hard on the riveter's hands.[42] The sound of pneumatic riveting became the 'signature tune' of shipyards in the interwar period, and its

[38] *The Engineer and Machinist's Assistant*, 1849, description of plates 33–5, plate 52.

[39] In 1867 MacFarlane Gray's steam riveter could close 1,000 rivets in a ten hour day, and riveters were willing to reduce piecework rates to a third of the hand price, that is to 1s/100 or 3s/100 with holder-up and two boys, *The Engineer*, 1867, *21*, 109, 143. In 1876 A. MacMillan & Son, the Dumbarton shipbuilders, introduced a steam riveter 'being forced some months ago, by the strike of their riveters to try the experiment'. The results were approved by Lloyd's surveyors, ibid, 1876, *41*, 472.

[40] Ibid, 1883, *56*, 428. Pressure grew in the 1880s for the development of power riveters for shell plating. The Chief Surveyor of the Underwriters' Registry for Iron Ships observed to the Institute of Naval Architects in 1884 that men could work up to $\frac{7}{8}$ in rivets, but that with larger diameter rivets the quality was uncertain. Ibid, 1884, *57*, 288–9. By 1899, in one of the most completely equipped yards, that of Harland & Wolff in Belfast, and in the greatest ship of her day, the White Star liner *Oceanic*, of 1·7 million rivets used only 72,000 were machine closed, all hydraulically. Ibid, 1899, *87*, 305.

[41] Ibid, reporting Durand's paper to the International Engineering Congress. The Chicago Shipbuilding Co (building Great Lakes steamers, which at that time could not leave that closed system, and for which there was therefore no effective foreign competition) had 'owing to unreasonable demands and frequent strikes' of riveters introduced pneumatic tools extensively. In their last ship, 250,000 out of 340,000 rivets had been pneumatically driven. Relative costs in the United States were estimated in 1899 as 3·99 cents hand piecework, 7·69 cents hand daywork and 2·96 cents air, including capital charges. By 1906 these had fallen to 3·68 cents hand piecework, 1·62 cents pneumatic. The overall saving in 1900 was estimated as 28 per cent. Ibid, 1900, *90*, 446.

[42] A demonstration outfit was sent to Glasgow by the Chicago Pneumatic Tool Co in 1899, ibid, 1899, *87*, 305. R. T. Napier in a paper to the Institution of Civil Engineers in 1899 referred to the introduction of electric and pneumatic caulking machines about 1890, when the men would not work them on account of noisiness and vibration, ibid, 1899, *87*, 321. W. I. Babcock concluded a paper on pneumatic riveting to the American Society of Naval Architects and Marine Engineers by saying, 'that the quality for the work done by portable pneumatic riveters in shipbuilding is such that the various classification societies cannot ignore it, and before very long will doubtless recommend, if not require, that all rivets in at least the principal portions of the ship be driven by power'. Ibid, 1899, *87*, 147. Despite this propaganda, and the development of manufacturing capacity for pneumatic tools in Britain (eg Consolidated Pneumatic Tools, Fraserburgh, in 1904, ibid, 1907, *104*, 154, 164), adoption of pneumatic riveting was not particularly rapid. At Fairfield in 1909 there were twenty-eight hydraulic riveting machines, air being used 'occasionally' for

loudness a barometer of trade. Electric riveting was tried, using electromagnetic
and electrohydraulic coupling, but did not become popular.[43]

The impact of the introduction of steel as a substitute for iron in ship construction has been mentioned in connection with the development of punching
and shearing machines (see p 160) but the influence of this change on shipyard
tools was general. The first experiments in steel construction began in the
1860s, when John Elder & Co and others made small vessels (probably American
Civil War blockade runners), but the Bessemer carbon steel plates available at
the time were of variable quality and were liable to failure when worked by the
current ironworking techniques.[44] Even in the late 1870s, when there was active
interest in the construction of large steel vessels, its use posed problems.[45] Once
these had been overcome, the main deterrent to its adoption was cost, and when
the construction of new plant and its technical development had reduced the
price of ship steel to a competitive level, introduction of the new material was
rapid. By 1885 virtually all the ships being built on the Clyde were of steel,[46]
and in 1886 a leading article in *The Engineer* could assume that its adoption was
permanent, commenting:

> The adoption of steel in place of wrought iron in the construction
> of ships had led to certain modifications and advantages in the
> plating which could not formerly be obtained. Shipbuilders can now
> obtain steel plates of great length and width, and are thus enabled
> to have fewer joints, rivets and butt-straps than were otherwise
> necessary. It is not long since 10 ft to 12 ft was considered a fairly
> long plate, and 4 ft was thought a great width. If these
> dimensions were exceeded, the iron manufacturer charged an
> increased price. Naturally, from motives of economy, shipbuilders
> were loth to exceed these limits. Now, however, all this has changed;
> steel plates can be obtained of considerably larger dimensions
> without increase of price in proportion to size. Perhaps the only limit
> in dimensions is the capability of the shipyard to handle and work
> the plates. Many of the shipbuilders have rolls no longer than 16 ft,
> and their planing and punching machines confine many of them
> still to certain lengths and widths. There are indications, however,
> that these old tools and plant for dealing with short iron plates will
> very soon have to be laid aside, and either broken up or applied to

riveting, though extensively for other purposes, *The Fairfield Shipbuilding and Engineering
Works*, 1909, 99. At Belfast, however, in 1912, Harland & Wolff were using pneumatic
riveting for all but the top and bottom members and stringer plates, which were still
hydraulically riveted, but Workman, Clark & Co had gone over entirely to compressed-air
riveting, *The Engineer*, 1912, *114*, 116, 147.

[43] Ibid, 1908, *106*, 272; 1910, *110*, 272.

[44] *Trans Inst of E & S in Scotland*, 1866-7, *10*, 95.

[45] *The Engineer*, 1889, *68*, 87. Before 1875 steel was variable and uncertain in its proper-
ties. Ibid, 1881, *51*, 393-4, the only thoroughly satisfactory steel plates were made by the
Siemens process.

[46] Ibid, 1885, *60*, 195, reporting a lecture by J. H. Biles to the Iron & Steel Institute.
Biles added that for a given size iron was now equal in cost to steel, but gave greater carrying
capacity, the reduction in weight being about 13-4 per cent.

other uses, to make room for machines of much larger calibre.
Already some of our enterprising shipbuilders have provided
themselves with enlarged plant. Messrs Harland and Wolff,
Belfast, have now a plate-bending machine, by Messrs. Shanks,
Johnstone, that can admit a plate 27 ft long between the standards,
and they have just put down planing and punching machines by
other makers to correspond. On the Clyde, Messrs Alexander
Stephen and Sons are taking the lead in acquiring such machinery.
They have just contracted with Messrs James Bennie & Co,
Glasgow, for a plate-bending machine with rollers 25 ft in length.
This will be the largest machine of this kind on the Clyde. The top
roller, which is to be 3 ft in diameter, will be raised and depressed
by Messrs Bennie's power gear, now so generally adopted, and which
worked successfully on the large rolls which this machine is to
supersede. Messrs Bennie & Co have also recently made several
extra-large punching and shearing machines, capable of operating on
steel plates up to 2 ins in thickness – some being of the lever type,
now so much in vogue in Northern shipyards. These have gaps
42 ins deep, allowing of a plate 7 ft broad being punched in the
centre. It is not every shipbuilder that will be able to provide
himself with machinery of such extra ordinary dimensions, but
unquestionably those who do and can advance so far will have great
advantages in respect of securing contracts, and executing them at
lowest possible cost.[47]

To gain the maximum advantage from larger plates and tools, handling
techniques had to be improved. Cranes, hand or hydraulically (later electrically)
operated, were installed in plating sheds, and handling equipment on berths
was increased in capacity and scope.[48] Alexander Stephen & Sons had a steam
crane on a gantry over the berth, in 1872, [49] but it was apparently the Americans
who were most advanced at the turn of the century, no doubt on account of
their high labour costs (see p 165). On the berths, hydraulic and electric cranes
were in 1899 being increasingly used in the United States for supporting
electric drills and hydraulic or pneumatic tools.[50] Sir William Arrol & Co Ltd,
one of Scotland's leading firms of hydraulic engineers, were by that time
supplying hydraulic handling equipment, as well as riveters, to a wide range of
customers.[51]

American techniques were to some extent copied in Britain. Swan Hunter &
Wigham Richardson built covered berths with electric cranes at Wallsend

[47] Ibid, 1888, 62, 490.
[48] R. H. Tweddell in 1882 stressed the importance of good layout and adequate cranage
for economic production, Min of Proc Inst CE, 1882–3, 73, 71. In 1899 Sir William White
claimed that most large machines were equipped with hydraulic lifts and cranes, The
Engineer, 1899, 87, 435.
[49] John L. Carvel, Stephen of Linthouse 1750–1950, Glasgow, 1950, 65–6.
[50] The Engineer, 1899, 87, 305.
[51] Strathclyde Regional Archives TD 208; Sir William Arrol & Co, Private Cost Book
1895–1901, passim.

which were copied from the American Newport News Yard,[52] and a rather similar gantry, with hydraulic equipment, was installed by Harland & Wolff at Belfast.[53] The only large structure of the type on the Clyde was Beardmore's at Dalmuir, designed specifically for warship construction.[54] Other techniques developed were a cantilever system – a gantry between ships with a travelling crane (American); wire cableways suspended from frameworks at the ends of the berths;[55] tower cranes, fixed or travelling; and lattice-masts and derricks.[56] In a paper delivered in Newcastle in 1914, T. G. John analysed the cost-effectiveness of the different systems.[57] He was dubious of the value of covered berths, pointing out that to cover one 1,000 by 100 ft ship, with 140 ft headroom cost £150,000 excluding cranes, and if this were written off over a thirty year period, allowing for 5 per cent interest, the annual cost, excluding maintenance would be £12,500. This compared with other systems as in Table 1.

John stated that the current opinion was that tower cranes were the best; certainly they were generally adopted in most shipyards after the First World War, and still predominate. Several Clyde yards invested in the lattice mast and derrick system, notably John Brown, Fairfield and Stephens.[58]

As to the reasons for adoption of these new handling methods, John was in little doubt:

> Broadly speaking it may be stated that such developments in our
> shipyards as have taken place during recent years have been chiefly
> due to two causes, viz: (1) the increase in dimensions of ships having

TABLE 1

Costs for 1,000 × 100 ft Ship, with 5 ton Capacity Cranes

	Capital cost	Cost per Annum	No of hooks available
Cantilever	£15,000	£1,500	½–1
Travelling carriage on lattice framework	95,000	9,500	15
Wire cableway	10,000	1,000	4
Tower crane	13,200	1,320	3–6
Lattice mast and derrick	24,000	2,400	16

Source: John, loc cit

[52] *The Engineer*, 1899, *87*, 305.

[53] Ibid, 1910, *110*, 38.

[54] Ibid, 1912, *113*, 618; John Hume and Michael Moss, *Clyde Shipbuilding from Old Photographs*, 1975.

[55] For example, at Jarrow, where a cableway system was installed by John M. Henderson & Co Ltd of Aberdeen, who specialised in cableways for quarries, *The Engineer*, 1906, *101*, 68.

[56] In 1906 it was claimed that the reduction in cost of plate handling due to the use of cranes in sheds was 75 per cent, on berths 9–32 per cent, ibid, 1906, *101*, 393.

[57] Paper delivered to the Institute of Naval Architects and Marine Engineers, 7 July 1914, ibid, 1914, *118*, 35.

[58] Hume and Moss, op cit, 74, 109.

to be built, with corresponding increase in the size of items of structure; and (2) the ever-persistent desire for economy, coupled with rapidity of production and good quality of work. New methods of manufacture have influenced the developments to a comparatively small extent.

He pointed out that between 1902 and 1914 the number of passenger ships built per annum exceeding 10,000 tons had doubled, and that the average launching weight of large warships had increased by more than 50 per cent. The maximum size of plates, which had been about two tons in 1901 (see p 160) had risen to 8 tons, and prefabricated frame units of up to ten tons were being built. The full potential for prefabrication of hull sections was not, however, reached until welding had displaced riveting after 1945.[59] John, interestingly, referred to the 'great need for a reliable fusion process for connecting structural material', mentioning experiments with Quazark electric welding at Vickers' Barrow yard.

One other general technical point concerning shipyard tools should be mentioned – the method of driving. The earliest iron-working tools were probably hand-driven – some certainly were[60] – but at an early date power had to be applied to the larger ones. Naturally, the standard power-transmission technique of the 1840s was used – belt drive from a lineshaft.[61] Sometime in the next thirty years individual drive by steam engine was introduced,[62] and c 1860–70 hydraulic shipyard machines were first made.[63] These innovations allowed machinery to be placed where it was most convenient for production rather than for driving, though at the expense of long runs of piping, and losses by condensation (steam) and friction (hydraulic). Nevertheless, the balance was in favour of individually powered machines (see below) and some very heavy ools were universally individually powered, for example the heaviest plate bending rolls and the largest keel-plate bending machines. Competition to established methods came in the 1880s from the electric motor, which had numerous potential advantages; among these were reliability, low maintenance costs, and instant readiness. Early electric motors were scarcely suitable for continuous heavy service out-of-doors, but the advantages of electric lighting and the use of electric power indoors were quickly realised,[64] and the installation of generating equipment for these purposes provided a basis for expansion when suitable electric motors were developed in the 1890s. Steam-driven machines continued to be built for some of the more conservative – or

59 For example, Scott Lithgow (1969) Ltd have a 400 ton crane at their Glen Yard, Port Glasgow, for assembling prefabricated sections.

60 E. C. B. Corlett, *The Iron Ship* (1974), 248 f; *The Engineer & Machinist's Assistant*, 32, 33, plate 51.

61 Ibid, description of plates, 38, plates 53–4.

62 Steam power was applied to punching by 1857–8, *Mins of Proc Inst of C.E.*, 1857–8, 17, 173. By 1877–8 the larger sizes of plate-working tools were generally steam powered, ibid, 1877–8, 52, 232.

63 *Proc Inst Mech E*, 1874, 166; *Mins of Proc Inst of C.E.*, 1882–3, 64.

64 In 1888 Withy & Co's yard was lit by gas and electricity, and Harland & Wolff's Belfast yard was illuminated by 150 arc and 1500 incandescent electric lights, *The Engineer*, 1888, 66, 345.

impecunious[65] – customers until after 1914, but electric drive was standard in the larger yards by c 1910.[66] In many cases machines were converted from steam to electric drive, and a few of these are still in existence.[67] It was, of course, quite possible to replace the steam engine driving a group of machines through belts, but by 1908 it had become apparent that 'in shipyards and engine works machine tools are only running for about 40% of their working time, and they exert their full power for only about 15% of their whole working time' and consequently group working was far less economical than independent driving.[68] Hydraulic transmission has had a longer life. For particular applications – notably the application of great force over a short distance – it has advantages over direct electric drive, and though water-hydraulic networks, with a central power station have been obsolete for some years, many modern shipyard tools rely on oil-hydraulic mechanisms.[69]

The Structure of Demand for Shipbuilding Machine Tools

Though these tools have been discussed in the context of shipbuilding, many of them were used in boilermaking, in structural engineering and in iron and steelworks. Any discussion of demand must therefore take into account these other uses. A rough indication can be had from orders placed with Craig & Donald, one of the leading manufacturing firms. In 1890, 19 of 51 tools (39 per cent) were certainly for shipbuilders, six for structural engineers and six for iron and steel works. In 1900, 49 out of 136 (36 per cent) were for shipbuilders, two for structural engineers and sixteen for iron and steel works. In addition, of 33 machines ordered by agents in 1900, an unknown but significant proportion were for foreign shipyards.[70]

It is difficult to find accurate inventories in shipyards from which to complete numbers of machines in use at particular times, but Table 2 gives an analysis of available evidence. This makes it clear that there was no obvious

[65] In 1904–5 it was claimed by an American writer, G. T. Hanchett, that the capital cost of individual electric motor drive in ordinary workshop conditions was 200 per cent greater than belt drive, *Electrical World and Engineer*, 45, 516–7.

[66] Electric power for machine driving was introduced by Stephens in 1896, Carvel, op cit, 89; by Denny in 1897 (*The Engineer*, 1897, 84, 75); by Fairfield in 1898, ibid, 1900, 90, 161, and in 1899 *The Engineer* (1899, 87, 434–5) commented that 'electrical power is being extensively used in some of the best shipyards'. The new yards laid out by Krupp in 1901 and Beardmore from 1902 were electrically driven, though in the former case belt drive was extensively used (ibid, 1910, 110, 214) and in the latter each machine tool was driven by its own electric motor (ibid, 1912, 113, 618). When Barrow was laid out in 1900, by Robert Duncan, electrification was reckoned to save two-thirds of the coal used in steam driving. In this case, most of the plate-working tools were individually powered, ibid, 1901, 92, 364. Further impetus to electrification came with the general introduction of public electricity supply for power; for example William Simons & Co electrified in 1906 with power from the Clyde Valley Company. Some of the larger shipbuilders were, however, slow to adopt electric power. Not until 1910 did John Brown & Co convert their Clydebank yard. (Craig & Donald Order Book.)

[67] As in Lamont's Castle Shipyard, Port Glasgow. The last working steam-driven tool known to the author is a Cameron punching and shearing machine in the Bristol Port Authority Workshops.

[68] *The Engineer*, 1908, 105, 607.

[69] Most of the shipyard tools made by Hugh Smith (Glasgow) Ltd, the only Scottish manufacturers, are oil-hydraulic in operation.

[70] Craig & Donald Order Book 1457–3324, 1899–1901.

balance between different types of machine, reflecting the wide differences between yards both in scale of output and in type of product. More refined hulls demanded more bent plates than tramp-steamer hulls, and the sub-division of hull space in passenger liners and naval craft called for more plate-work for a given tonnage than for bulk carriers. Tables 3a and 3b show the balance of machines by different makers in large British and German yards, illustrating the points that it was rare for a single yard to be equipped by a single manufacturer, though not unknown,[71] and that demand from even a large yard for a single type of machine was small. As regards life expectancy of tools, many heavy shipyard tools have lasted for extraordinarily long periods;[72] distribution by age of tools in Fairfield in 1926 shows that this is not a new phenomenon. The small demand from individual yards, the widely varying requirements of different customers, and the long life of many tools posed problems for the development of a specialised shipbuilding-tool industry. The expansion of world shipbuilding capacity in the late nineteenth century,

TABLE 2

	P & S machines	Other P & S machines	Rolls	Planers	Beam machines
1891 (a) Russell & Co, Port Glasgow	11	2	1	—	1
1895 (b) Thames Ironworks, London	16S+	20P	5	'some'	2
1909 (c) A. G. Weser, Gropelingen	3	5	4	5	8
1909 (d) Bremer Vulkan, Vegesack	10	1	3	1	?
1909 (e) John C. Tecklenborg, Bremerhaven	3	2	1	1	4
1909 (f) Fairfield, Govan	20	?	7	5	7
1926 (g) Fairfield, Govan	12	6 (10P heads)	6	2	7

Sources: (a) *The Engineer*, 1891, 71, p 187.
      (b) Ibid, 1895, 90, pp 567–77.
      (c) Ibid, 1909, 108, p 414.
      (d) Ibid, p 468.
      (e) Ibid, p 519.
      (f) *The Fairfield Shipbuilding and Engineering Works*, 1909, pp 95–9.
      (g) Glasgow Strathclyde Regional Archives, UCS 2/57/1. Inventory of Plant in Fairfield Yard, 1926.

[71] For example, R. H. Tweddell designed hydraulic machinery which was built by the Hydraulic Engineering Co, Chester, for the French Naval Dockyard at Toulon in 1874, *Proc Inst Mech E*, 1878, 346 ff.

[72] Even such a world-renowned yard as John Brown's at Clydebank had in 1972 ten plate and section working machines which were more than 40 years old, and two were 73 years old. In a Coatbridge engineering works, a Bennie shearing machine of 1866 is still in use.

certainly helped to maintain a high, though intermittent, demand. The growing importance of empire and foreign markets (see Tables 9 and 10) tends to reinforce the impression of saturation of local demand. The competition between shipbuilders to reduce manufacturing costs in depressions cushioned slumps during the period when ship-plates were increasing in size. Significant innovations in roll design (see pp. 162–4) and smaller improvements in the design of other machines also reduced labour costs, though the scope for improvement was limited by the amount of hand manipulation involved in plate and section working. Electric drive in its turn gave an impetus to demand from established customers. Information on prices is difficult to interpret, owing to the problem of identifying truly comparable tools. Table 5, however, suggests that where size and type of machine remained constant prices did not vary much. The large tools for dealing with bigger plates were, however, notably more expensive.

TABLE 3a

MAKERS OF PLATE AND SECTION-WORKING MACHINES IN FAIRFIELD YARD, GOVAN, IN 1926

Craig & Donald	17
Hugh Smith	8
Bennie	7
Butler	6
Shanks	3
Smith Brothers	3
Other Scottish Makers	5
Other English Makers	6

Source: Strathclyde Regional Archives, UCS 2/57/1, Inventory of Plant in Fairfield Yard, 1926

TABLE 3b

MAKERS OF PLATE AND SECTION-WORKING MACHINES IN A. G. WESER YARD, GROPELINGEN, IN 1909

Breuer & Schumacher	13
Ernst Schiess	7
Smith Brothers	3
Other German Makers	3
Unknown	4

Source: *The Engineer*, 1909, Vol 108, p 414

TABLE 4

DATE OF MANUFACTURE OF PLATE AND SECTION-WORKING MACHINES IN FAIRFIELD YARD, GOVAN, IN 1926

1881–90	1891–1900	1901–10	1911–20	1921–6
12	17	18	12	—

Source: Strathclyde Regional Archives, UCS 2/57/1

Price variation thus probably had a minimal influence on demand. The varied requirements of customers meant that scope for standardisation was small, though Craig & Donald did have standard patterns which with relatively slight modification met a range of needs.

It is clear that the number of firms having plate and section working tools as their main product was at any time small. In Scotland, Craig & Donald of Johnstone, James Bennie & Sons, Smith Brothers and Hugh Smith & Co of Glasgow were all primarily engaged in the trade, and in England it seems likely that de Bergue & Co of Manchester, John Cameron of Salford, Rushworth & Co, and F. Berry & Sons of Sowerby Bridge were similarly committed. As already mentioned, Craig & Donald had the reputation of being founded for the purpose of building such tools, but in this they were untypical. Marine engineers and firms like Caird & Co and Robert Napier made tools in the 1840s for their own use, and possibly for sale, while general engineers like Nasmyth, Gaskell & Co, and R. Roberts & Co in Lancashire, Scriven & Co of Leeds and A. & W. Smith and Crow, Harvey & Co of Glasgow at different times from c 1840 were involved to a greater or less extent in this field. The

TABLE 5

PRICES OF TYPICAL TOOLS

		£
1881 (1)	Punching and shearing machines	20–380
	Plate shears	640, 950 (including engine)
	Scrap cutters	150–500
	Plate bending rolls	45–400
	Plate flattening rolls	185
	Plate planing machines	98–250
	Beam machines, large	190–260
	Wall drills	15–35
1909 (2)	Punching and shearing machine (large)	400
	Plate shears	325
	Scrap cutter	370
	Plate bending rolls (girder type)	1,835
	Plate flattening rolls	585
	Plate planing machine	226
	Beam machine	235
	Drill	63
	Saw	230
1930 (3)	Shell plate rolls (girder type)	1,550–2,650
	Plate bending rolls	220–840
	Plate flattening rolls	540–780
	Plate planing machine	800–1,050

Sources: (1) Craig & Donald Catalogue, 1881 with manuscript prices inserted.
(2) Craig & Donald Scroll Order Book No 4, Private Order Book, typical machines.
(3) Hugh Smith & Co Price List 1930.

list in Table 6 shows how dispersed was the manufacture of these tools, and illustrates the point that specialised firms were not numerous, and that the manufacture of these machines was not at all incompatible with a general

TABLE 6

MAKERS OF PLATE AND SECTION WORKING TOOLS

Scotland
†Sir William Arrol & Co, Glasgow
*James Bennie & Sons, Glasgow
Bertrams Ltd, Sciennes, Edinburgh
Caird & Co, Greenock
Campbells & Hunter
A. F. Craig & Co, Paisley
*Craig & Donald, Johnstone
Crow, Harvey & Co, Glasgow
Crow, Hamilton & Co, Glasgow
Davis & Primrose, Leith
G. Edwards, Johnstone
Grant & Macfarlane, Johnstone
G. & A. Harvey, Glasgow
Robert Harvey & Co, Glasgow
Lamberton & Co, Coatbridge
*Littlejohn & Service, Johnstone
Loudon Bros, Johnstone
Murray & Paterson Ltd, Coatbridge
Robert Napier & Co, Glasgow
Pollok, Macnab & Highgate, Carntyne, Glasgow
A. & P. W. McOnie, Glasgow
Scottish Machine Tool Corporation, Glasgow & Johnstone
Thomas Shanks & Co, Johnstone
A. & W. Smith, Glasgow
* †Hugh Smith & Sons, Glasgow
*Smith Brothers, Glasgow
John Yule & Sons, Glasgow
England
Sir W. G. Armstrong, Whitworth & Co, Manchester
Batho & Baumer, Manchester
*F. Berry & Sons, Sowerby Bridge
†Henry Berry & Co, Leeds
*Rushworth & Co, Sowerby Bridge
Scott Bros, (Halifax) Ltd, Halifax
*Scriven & Co, Leeds
Tangye & Co, Birmingham
Charles Walton, Leeds
Bradley & Craven, Wakefield
Joshua Buckton & Co, Leeds
*John Cameron, Salford
J. Butler & Co, Halifax
*De Bergue, Manchester
Greenwood & Batley, Leeds
John Hetherington & Sons Ltd, Manchester
Hollings & Guest Ltd, Birmingham

TABLE 6 continued

England continued
†Hydraulic Engineering Co, Chester
†C. & A. Musker, Liverpool
　Nasmyth, Gaskell & Co, Patricroft
†Platt & Fielding, Manchester
　R. Roberts & Co, Manchester
Germany
　A. G. Weser, Gropelingen
　Breuer & Schumacher
　Maschinenfabrik Weingarten, Württemberg
　Henry Pels
　Ernst Schiess
　Stahlwerk Oeking A G, Düsseldorf
　John C. Tecklenborg A G
　Wagner & Co, Dortmund
America
　William Bement & Son, Philadelphia
　Buffalo Forge Co, Buffalo, N Y
　Cleveland Punching & Shearing Works Co, Cleveland, Ohio
*Hilles & Jones, Wilmington, Indiana
　Kane & Roach, Syracuse, N Y
　Lake Erie Engineering Corporation, Buffalo, N Y
　Niles Tool Works, Hamilton, Ohio
　Niles Bement Pond, Philadelphia
　Henry Pels
　The Schatz Manufacturing Co, Poughkeepsie, N Y
　William Sellers & Co, Inc, Ohio
　Wilkes Bros, Saginaw, Mich.
　William, White & Co, Moline, Ill.

* indicates specialist firms
† indicates makers of hydraulic tools

engineering business. In this it closely parallels precision machine tool manufacture in the West of Scotland before 1914.[73]

In an exploratory article such as this, detailed investigation of all manufacturing concerns would be impossible, and illustrations will be drawn from two firms with surviving records. Craig & Donald of Johnstone has already been mentioned on several occasions, and fairly complete order records, together with photographs and catalogues still exist.[74] The surviving material from James Bennie & Sons is more fragmentary, so that detailed comparison between these firms over a long period has not been possible. Craig & Donald's performance during the period 1889–99 has, however, been analysed, firstly because the earliest priced order book starts in 1889, and secondly, because this period spans a full trade cycle including 1889 'a period of phenomenal activity',[75] 1898 'the busiest year on record'[76] for Clyde machine-tool building, followed by the

[73] Michael Moss and John Hume, *Workshop of the British Empire* (in press).
[74] In the Department of History, University of Strathclyde, Glasgow.
[75] *The Engineer*, 1890, *69*.
[76] Ibid, 1899, *87*, 32.

even better year, together with the intervening depression. Table 7 shows the output of machines for this period compared with the output of shipping in the same period. Table 8 is an analysis of output by type, compared with the produc-

TABLE 7

ANNUAL OUTPUT OF MACHINES FROM CRAIG & DONALD IN THE 1890s

	1890	1891	1892	1893	1894	1895	1896	1897	1898	1899
	54	75	55	55	90	69	86	118	150	158
	£682,100	662,000	683,600	485,800	565,500	560,400	509,600	469,400	681,500	736,000

OUTPUT OF SHIPS FROM BRITISH YARDS (INCLUDING WARSHIPS, BUT EXCLUDING SHIPS UNDER 100 GROSS REGISTER TONS)

	1890	1891	1892	1893	1894	1895	1896	1897	1898	1899
	1,303,464	1,300,645	1,300,412	915,514	1,102,303	1,139,544	1,232,666	1,142,739	1,671,217	1,838,422

Sources: Craig & Donald Order Book 1457–3324, 1889–1901; The Engineer, December and January for the appropriate years

tion of Hugh Smith & Co in the same period. The latter firm specialised in hydraulic machinery, while Craig & Donald made very few machines of that type. Table 9 is a geographical breakdown of orders showing that though the home market accounted for most of the output there was a substantial involvement in export. The high proportion going to England and Wales suggests that the firm's competitive position was good.

For the period 1905–10, it is possible to make a direct comparison between Craig & Donald and James Bennie. Table 10 shows that in that period, Craig & Donald was a substantially larger firm than Bennie. Bennie, produced on average, heavier tools than their competitors. The scale of activity of these firms may be judged by comparison with, for example, Sir William Arrol & Co, a leading structural engineering firm, with an annual turnover of around £100,000 in the late 1890s, or with the Fairfield Shipbuilding & Engineering Co Ltd, whose turnover was about £1 million per annum in the period 1895–1900.[77] The figures in Table 10(c) are interesting in that Craig & Donald had a

TABLE 8

OUTPUT OF CRAIG & DONALD AND OF HUGH SMITH & CO, 1889–99 ANALYSED BY TYPE OF MACHINE

	Craig & Donald	Hugh Smith
P & S machines	244	12 (3 per cent)
Punches	133	25 (6 per cent)
Shears and cutters	119	—
Bending and flattening rolls (inc keel plate benders)	178	79 (18 per cent)
Flanging machines	17	28 (6 per cent)
Plate planers	46	44 (10 per cent)
Drills	96	12 (3 per cent)
Saws	38	—
Beam machines	81	24 (6 per cent)
Others	17	209 (48 per cent)
Total	969	433 (mainly hydraulic)

Source: Craig & Donald Order Book 1457–3324, 1889–1901;
Hugh Smith & Co Order Book No 1

TABLE 9

GEOGRAPHICAL DISTRIBUTION OF MACHINES SUPPLIED BY CRAIG & DONALD 1889–99

Scotland	England & Wales	Ireland	Europe	Rest of World	Agents
276	270	18	91	103	86
33 per cent	32 per cent	2 per cent	11 per cent	12 per cent	10 per cent

Source: Craig & Donald Order Book 1457–3324, 1889–1901

[77] Moss and Hume, op cit.

substantially larger share of the roll market: in this field the Johnstone firm had secured a number of patents which seem to have given them a superior product in the medium size range. Bennie, however, specialised in the large girder-

TABLE 10

OUTPUT OF CRAIG & DONALD AND JAMES BENNIE & SONS 1905-10

(a) Distribution of Products

	Turnover	No of machines	Average price	West of Scotland	Rest of Scotland	England, Wales & Ireland	Europe	Rest of World	Agents (unidentified)
Craig & Donald	£176,479	601	£294	183 (30%)	8 (1%)	164 (27%)	32 (5%)	89 (15%)	125 (21%)
Bennie	125,649	279	467	27 (10%)	9 (3%)	99 (35%)	113 (40%)	23 (8%)	8 (3%)

(b) European Sales

	Belgium	Denmark	France	Germany	Holland	Italy	Norway	Poland	Russia	Spain	Sweden	Finland
Craig & Donald	4	—	10	—	3	4	3	—	1	3	—	—
Bennie	1	1	9	37	8	32	9	4	—	2	8	2

(c) Distribution of Products by type

	Punching & Shearing machines	Other P & S machines	Rolls	Plate planers	Beam machines	Drills	Saws	Others
Craig & Donald	127 (21%)	127 (21%)	139 (23%)	26 (4%)	90 (15%)	37 (6%)	17 (3%)	38 (6%)
Bennie	77 (28%)	75 (27%)	48 (17%)	27 (9%)	27 (9%)	8 (3%)	8 (3%)	5 (2%)

Sources: Craig & Donald Scroll Order Book No 4, 1906-10; Private Order Book 1901-15; James Bennie & Sons, Contract Book No 2, 1905-10

frame bending rolls then in demand by the most advanced builders. The geographical distribution of products in Table 10(a) and 10(b) shows that Bennie had much stronger links with Europe, and in particular with Germany and Italy, than did Craig & Donald, and much weaker links with the rest of the world, especially as it is likely that most of the machines ordered by agents were for empire or far-eastern markets. This is another slender strand of evidence for the seldom-documented but nevertheless increasingly clear division of markets by 'rival' west of Scotland engineering firms.[78] Doubtless these interlocking interests aided the amalgamation of these two firms with Loudon Brothers (important agents for Craig & Donald), G. & A. Harvey, heavy precision tool makers, and James Allan Senior & Son, ironfounders, to form the Scottish Machine Tool Corporation in 1937. Another significant point emerging from Table 10 was the importance of the English market (Irish and Welsh demand was tiny) to both firms, particularly to Bennie. It is quite clear that these firms were experiencing little difficulty in competing with their English counterparts, and indeed a succession of Admiralty orders came to Craig & Donald.

It is difficult to assess just how significant Bennie and Craig & Donald were in a world context. Certainly there seems to have been little competition from America until after 1918, and German competition was apparently slight until the plate-steel-framed machine was generally adopted after the First World War.[79] It is quite probable that for larger tools these two firms, with Smith Brothers of Glasgow, led the world in the period 1890–1914, if not earlier. Possible rivals for this distinction were the English firms John Cameron of Salford and Rushworth & Co, Sowerby Bridge, but further detailed research, if sources exist, would be necessary to arrive at a definite conclusion.

Conclusion

Many more general questions are raised by this brief look at one branch of technology. What skills were involved in the construction of these machines, and in what proportions? How typical or atypical was the demand for these skills in comparison with other local industries? What specific skills were involved in operation of these tools in shipyards and elsewhere, and in what ways and to what extent did they change? How did skilled tradesmen react to these changes? How typical of engineering firms in general were the manufacturers of shipbuilding machine tools? Unfortunately space does not permit them to be answered, but it is hoped that this article will stimulate interest in this and in other neglected branches of technology. Underpinning the physical basis for nineteenth century civilisation were often machines or techniques that were either so simple in principle or so esoteric that they have attracted little attention. Brickmaking, quarrying and stone dressing equipment, bakery and woodworking machinery, and much of the 'average' technology of, for example,

[78] For example, sugar machinery firms divided up the sugar-growing areas into 'spheres of influence'. (Oral evidence from manufacturers.)

[79] See footnote 13, also files on competitors' products of Craig & Donald, which seem to have been started about 1920.

power transmission have failed to grip the interest of economic and technical historians. Lest anyone doubts the significance of the machines mentioned in this article, it should be pointed out that they made feasible that large-scale manufacture of iron and steel ships, locomotives and stationary steam boilers without which the enormous expansion of world trade in Victorian times would have been impossible.

J. R. HUME

[80] In the preparation of this essay, the author has incurred certain debts. He would like to thank the following firms and individuals: the Scottish Machine Tool Corporation for giving the surviving records of Craig & Donald and James Bennie & Sons to the Department of History, University of Strathclyde; Hugh Smith (Glasgow) Ltd for allowing access to the order books of the firm; Michael Moss for discussions on engineering and ship-building over a long period; Richard Dell, Strathclyde Regional Archivist, and his staff for access to records in his care; John Imrie, Keeper of the Records of Scotland, for access to the records of Upper Clyde Shipbuilders, and Robert C. Smith, Liquidator of Upper Clyde Shipbuilders, for allowing first-hand study of many of the types of tool discussed.

Index

Authors' Index

References are given to the first mention of works